A DANGEROUS ENTERPRISE

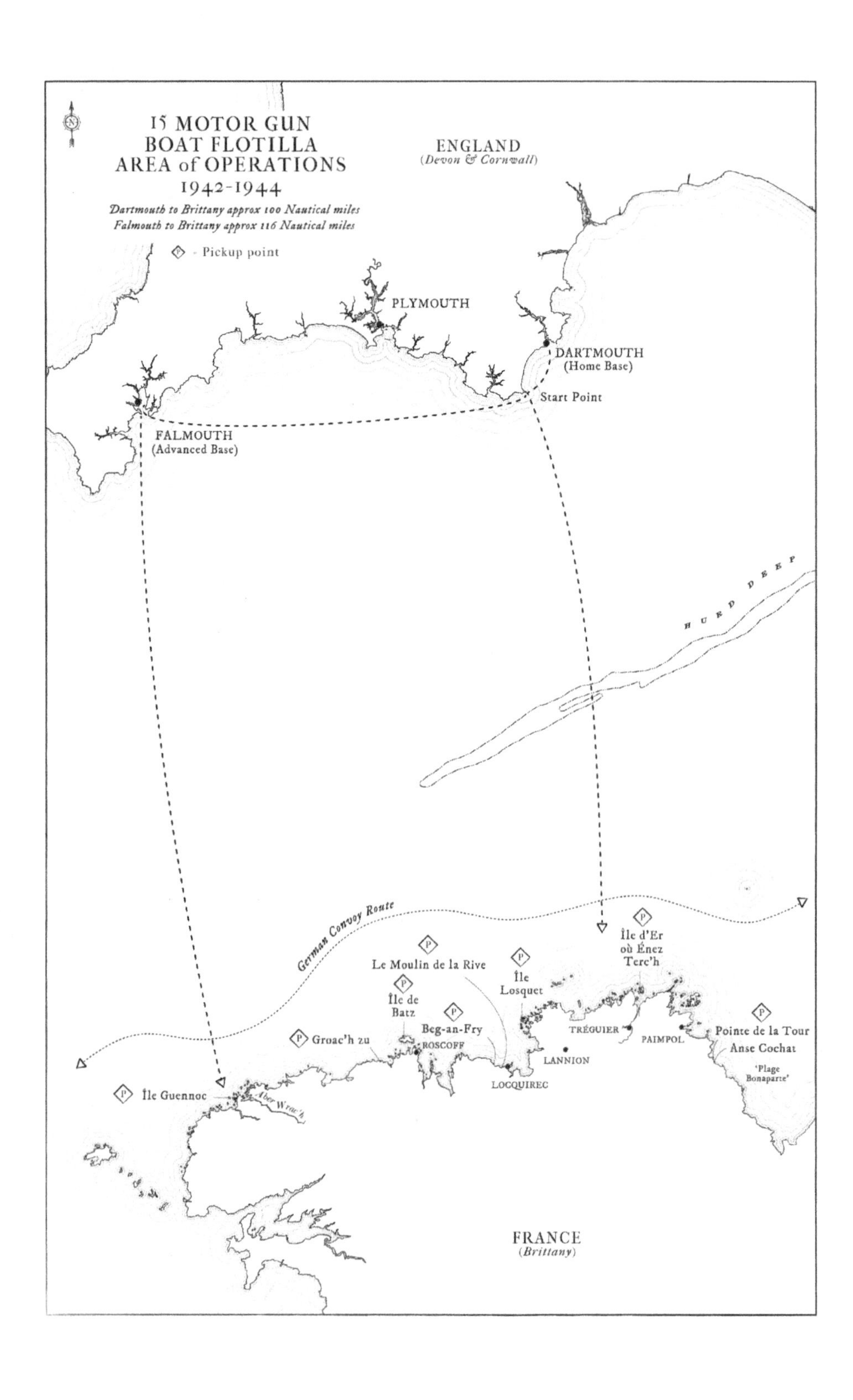
15 MOTOR GUN BOAT FLOTILLA AREA of OPERATIONS 1942-1944
Dartmouth to Brittany approx 100 Nautical miles
Falmouth to Brittany approx 116 Nautical miles
- Pickup point
ENGLAND
(Devon & Cornwall)
PLYMOUTH
DARTMOUTH
(Home Base)
Start Point
FALMOUTH
(Advanced Base)
HURD DEEP
German Convoy Route
Île d'Er où Énez Terc'h
Le Moulin de la Rive
Île Losquet
Île de Batz
Beg-an-Fry
Groac'h zu
ROSCOFF
LOCQUIREC
LANNION
TRÉGUIER
PAIMPOL
Pointe de la Tour
Anse Cochat
'Plage Bonaparte'
Île Guennoc
Aber Wrac'h
FRANCE
(Brittany)

TIM SPICER

A DANGEROUS ENTERPRISE

Secret War at Sea

BARBRECK

First published in 2021 by Barbreck Publishers

ISBN 978-1-9995891-3-4

A CIP catalogue reference for this book is available from the British Library

 Published in the United Kingdom by
Barbreck Publishers, 50 Albemarle Street, London W1S 4BD
and distributed by Penguin Random House UK,
20 Vauxhall Bridge Road, London SW1V 2SA

Typography and typesetting by Clarendon Road Studio

Printed and bound by CPI, Moravia

Dedicated to J J J P

'Four elements make up the climate of war; danger, exertion, uncertainty, and chance'

Von Clausewitz, *On War*

CONTENTS

NIGHT MISSION 1944

Alfred F. Harris
(Seaman Gunner MGB 502) 15th Motor Gun Boat Flotilla

Sombre and sleek she slipped through the water
Closing the Enemy Occupied Shore.
Poised to evade the many that sought her,
HM Motor Gun Boat was fighting her war.

Low silhouette and camouflaged paintwork.
Special her purpose and secret her plan.
Cloaked by the night and dark sea around her,
On smooth silent engines so softly she ran.

Action stations, with eyes ever watchful,
Men sought the white of an enemy wake.
Down in the waist, the boat's crews were gathered,
Stowing the gear that the small boats would take.

Reducing speed, now stop both the engines.
Starting to roll as she slowly lost way.
Charthouse and bridge both checking position,
Sure to locate the right spot in the bay.

Glasses to shoreward watch for the signal.
Green glow that briefly shines through the night.
Small boats are outboard – in go the seamen,
Setting their course for the faint distant light.

Clear the ship's side with a pull on the sweep oar.
Give way together, start in on the run.
Muffled and greased – the oars in their crutches,
Bowman and stroke oar dipping as one.

Feel the surf catch her and race for the shoreline.
Out boat the oarsman, feet grip the sand.
Turn her bows seaward, hold fast to gunwales.
Senses alert to the danger at hand.

Whisper of voices, forms in the darkness,
Quickly the cargo is moved up the beach.
Crunch of feet running, American airmen,
Head for the small boats, packed tightly in each.

Into the surf with the boats overladen,
Heavy the pull with the oars digging deep.
Seeing the mothership loom from the blackness,
Up ropes and scrambling nets hanging so steep.

Lash up the small boats, set course for England.
Feel the wind's bite through soaking wet clothes.
Welcome the dawn and first sight of Dartmouth,
Rig ship for Port Side to, All Engines Slow.

ACKNOWLEDGEMENTS

This book could never have been written without the considerable help, support and advice given to me by many people. First, David Lingard, Chairman of the Dartmouth Museum, who introduced me to the Flotilla. Stanley and Lisa Weiss for introducing me to David Campbell, who not only encouraged me to write this story but, as good as his word, he has published it. His advice and counsel have been invaluable.

Early attempts at writing were well critiqued by Brian Morton, and the almost finished article knocked into proper shape by my excellent editor Tom Bromley. Typing the manuscript was done in the midst of a national lockdown by Emma Sandford, and the final stages of detailed preparation by my outstanding Personal Assistant Lauren Smith. Phil Tomaselli spent long hours carrying out research for me at the National Archives, ferreting out important material against the odds. Ella Carr at Barbreck for her meticulous editorial attention to detail. Peter Willberg for his skilful typography and design. Hannah Davies at Four Communications for her PR savvy.

I am totally indebted to the families of members of the Flotilla for access to private papers, photos and artefacts. The book could not have been written without the help of Jane and Andrew Birkin. Andrew has created a meticulous archive of his father's and mother's papers, film, photographs and paintings. He has given me complete access, and has been helpful in reviewing an early version of the book. David Birkin documented his wartime exploits in considerable detail, and much of this book is based on his accounts. Jane Birkin has been invaluable towards helping me find the relations of the JADE FITZROY network in Brittany, and arranging for me to meet them. Among these were Edouard Tanguy, son of Claude Tanguy, and the last living member of JADE FITZROY.

Cécile le Roux, Mayor of Lannilis, who opened the town archive for me (at very short notice) and arranged for me to meet the granddaughters of Amédée Rolland – Colette Pronost and Sylvie Carette – who provided me with photographs and their grandfather's papers.

A key figure in this adventure was Frank Slocum, and I am indebted to the Slocum family for providing excellent photographs and material from the DDOD(I) scrapbooks, and to Nick for his enthusiastic support.

A chance email to the Pierre Hentic website led me to his daughter, Anne Alexandre, who lives in London. She has been incredibly helpful with providing photographs, as well as reading over the parts of the book relating to her father, and helping me to sort out the more complicated aspects of Resistance work in Brittany in 1943/4.

Rodney Seddon, son of Ronnie Seddon (the skipper of 718), provided outstanding support in the form of photographs and access to his father's papers. Other family members I am indebted to include Donal McQuoid Mason, son of Lt Commander Jan McQuoid Mason (the skipper of 318), James Luard, Anthony Agar and Andrew Pollard.

In addition I have had invaluable help from the following: Geoffrey Pidgeon (SIS), Noreen Riols (SOE), Peter Hore – the eminent naval historian, Kevin Costello from the Coastal Forces Veterans Association, Paul McCue and his excellent SOE archive, John Andrews (Special Forces Club), David Anderson (Secretary of White's), Jill Millard Shapiro (Windmill Theatre archive), Sabine Stein (Buchenwald archive), David Hewson, Aurélien Coquil (Musée Mémoires, Plougonvelin), Daniel Dagorn (Le Télégramme), Jane Harold, Rachel Glen for her outstanding maps, Michel Fournier (photos), Captain Roger Readwin RN (HMS BRITANNIA), Charles Cassells, Claude Bénech, Alex Younger, Robin and Roki Schiffner.

I have had great encouragement from friends who are established writers, Jon Swain, Charles Glass and Justin Marozzi, as well as motivational support from Jamie Lowther-Pinkerton, Mike Scott, John Cummins, Sarah and Jack Smith, James Ellery, Don and Catherine McCullin, Philip and Catherine Mould, and my dear friend Jeremy Phipps, who very sadly is not here to read the finished article.

Last, but certainly by no means least, my dearest wife Pauline and my son Sam. Sam who, when not dealing with the rigours of military life in Covid times, or on overseas deployment, provided pithy criticism and bags of enthusiasm. Pauline Amos, artist, photographer, musician and herself an accomplished author, kept me up to the mark during the year of lockdown it took to write, with lots of love, constant encouragement, motivation, support and friendly competition, as she was writing two books at the same time. Thank you both, and thank you to all for helping get this enterprise across the start line.

Tim Spicer

SECRET INTELLIGENCE SERVICE 1940

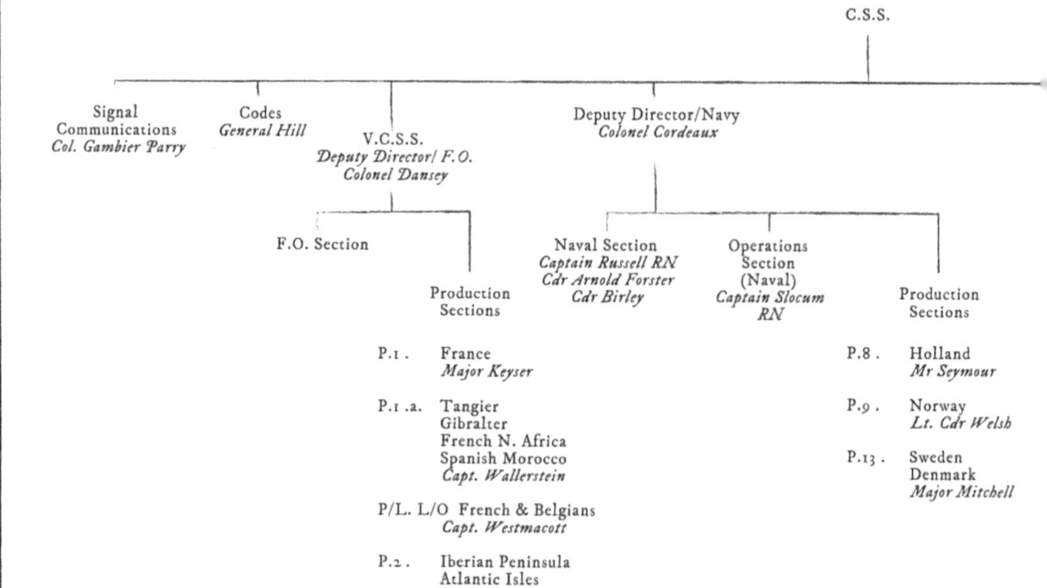

P.1. France *Major Keyser*

P.1.a. Tangier, Gibralter, French N. Africa, Spanish Morocco *Capt. Wallerstein*

P/L. L/O French & Belgians *Capt. Westmacott*

P.2. Iberian Peninsula, Atlantic Isles *Mr Fenwick*

P.3. Switzerland *Capt. Arnold Baker*

P.7. Belgium *Major Jempson*

P.8. Holland *Mr Seymour*

P.9. Norway *Lt. Cdr Welsh*

P.13. Sweden, Denmark *Major Mitchell*

MOST SECRET. COPY NO ....

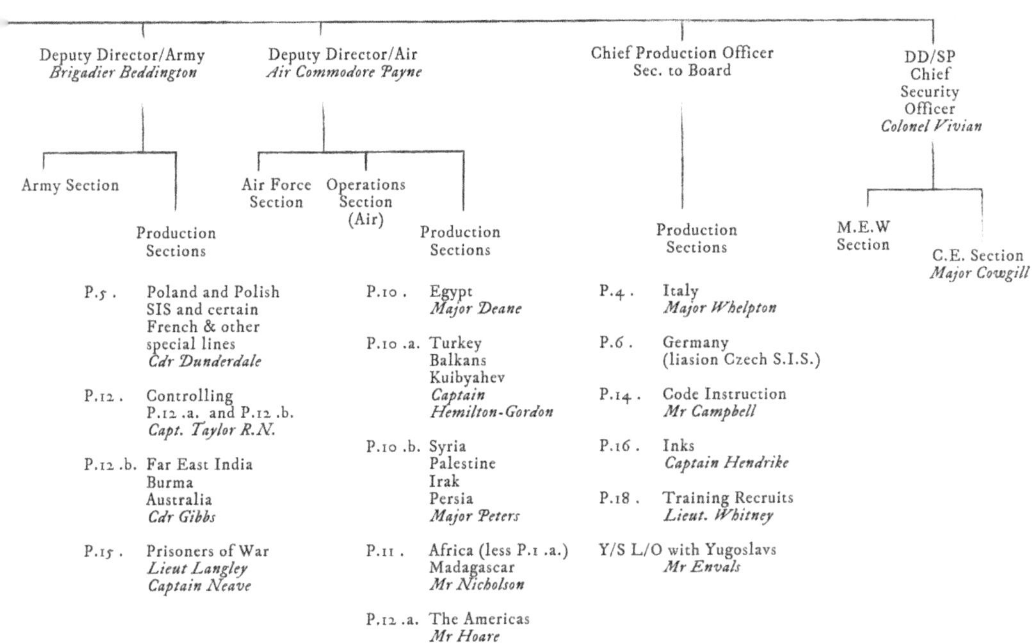

Captain Frank Slocum

INTRODUCTION

Between 1942 and 1944 a very small, very secret, very successful clandestine unit of the Royal Navy operated between Dartmouth[1] in Devon, and the Brittany coast in France. It was a crossing of about 100 miles, every yard of it dangerous. The unit was called the 15th Motor Gun Boat Flotilla. At the height of its operation in 1944 it consisted of four boats, MGB: 318, 502, 503 and 718, crewed by 125 officers and men. It was the most highly decorated Royal Naval unit of the Second World War. The Flotilla was commanded directly by the Secret Intelligence Service (SIS).

Their home was a converted paddle steamer, the *Westward Ho*, and a luxury yacht, the *Kiloran*, and their headquarters spread between the Royal Dart Hotel – renamed HMS CICALA – and HMS BRITANNIA, the Royal Naval College.[2] Their job, to ferry agents of SIS and Special Operations Executive (SOE) to pinpoint landing sites on the Brittany coast in occupied France. Once they had landed their agents, and stores for the Resistance, they picked up evaders, escaped POWs who had had the good fortune to be collected by escape lines run by MI9, as well as returning SIS and SOE agents.

This is a story of clandestine warfare at its best. The 15th MGBF was an extraordinary group of men thrown together in a secret adventure. Very few were regular Royal Naval officers. They were mostly Royal Naval Volunteer (RNVR) Officers, called up for the duration. Some had considerable maritime experience. Others learnt very quickly. Likewise, the crew were made up of 'duration only' sailors with a few seasoned regular Royal Navy Petty Officers.

1 The Flotilla was spread between Kingswear, the River Dart and Dartmouth. For ease of description 'Dartmouth' will be used throughout.

2 In Royal Naval parlance shore establishments are named like ships, with the prefix 'HMS'.

Their story is inextricably entwined with that of the agents of SIS and SOE – Pierre Hentic, Yves Le Tac, Virginia Hall, André Hué, Jeannie Rousseau, Suzanne Warengham, François Mitterrand and the infamous Mathilde Carré, as well as many others.

And it is the story of SIS's intelligence gathering networks, JADE FITZROY and ALLIANCE; the SOE's VAR Line and MI9's SHELBURNE Escape Line; and the men and women who ran them. How they collected escaped POWs and airmen evading capture in France, gathered them in Paris, took them by train to Brittany, hid them in safe houses, often in plain sight of the Germans, and moved them at night on foot, through minefields, between German bunkers, to a precisely pinpointed rendezvous with a Motor Gun Boat from Dartmouth.

The methodology used by the 15th MGB Flotilla was an extraordinary feat of courage, fortitude, military skill and seamanship. Although their presence in Dartmouth was visible, very tight security surrounded all their activities. Their cover story was that they were engaged in normal coastal operations in the Channel. The reality could not have been more different.

*

This book came about as a result of two chance encounters. The first was with a retired Naval Officer, David Lingard, who runs the excellent Dartmouth Museum. He showed me the material held by the museum about the wartime operations of the 15th Motor Gun Boat Flotilla. These included the personal accounts of Lloyd Bott and Michael Pollard, as well as a 16mm film shot in 1944 by David Birkin. Having read these accounts and watched the film, I was hooked, and wanted to know more. This led me to the only two published books I could find, *The Secret Navies* by Cecil Hampshire and *Secret Flotillas* by Brooks Richards, the latter being an official government history. Brooks Richards had taken part in early operations to the Brittany coast and subsequently worked with SOE in the Mediterranean. Both books were fascinating, Richards' being the more comprehensive, as the author had access to government papers. However, although a detailed account, I felt there was more to this story, both from the perspective of the Flotilla operations and 'the end product' in France, and so I began to research it in detail. I had always been interested in clandestine warfare and stories of brave leaders and lonely fighters – to quote T. E. Lawrence, 'Irregular war was far more intellectual than a bayonet charge…'

I began my research in the obvious place, the National Archives, with the help of my invaluable researcher Phil Tomaselli, who almost immediately came up with a very interesting organisation chart of the SIS at the outbreak of war. What caught my attention was the person of Captain Frank Slocum – in command of Air and Naval clandestine operations. From here, it became apparent that the 15th Motor Gun Boat Flotilla was in fact not 'owned' by the Royal Navy but commanded directly by SIS.

In turn this led to questions as to how the Flotilla operations, which included work for SOE and MI9 as well as SIS, actually worked, given the friction between SIS and SOE. It had all the beginnings of an intriguing adventure.

The second chance encounter was at a dinner party in London given by my friends Stanley and Lisa Weiss. They host what used to be called a 'Salon', putting together evenings with many interesting people. It was here that I met David Campbell who, as a very eminent publisher, encouraged me to pursue the story – 'if you write a book, call me'. I did both. Between then and now, I began a detailed investigation into both parts of the story – Dartmouth and Brittany. My research led me to many interesting, helpful people – mostly children and grandchildren of those who took part. They are all mentioned in my acknowledgements. The driving force, and the emergence of David Birkin as the key player in the story, was due to the help given to me by his children, Jane and Andrew Birkin. Andrew has meticulously ordered and documented his father's extensive private archive and Jane has been most helpful with contacts in Brittany. I also received considerable help and encouragement from Rodney Seddon, the son of Ronnie Seddon who commanded MGB 718; Anne Alexandre, Pierre Hentic's daughter; and the Slocum family.

The book's title reflects exactly what this was – a dangerous enterprise, for the men of the Flotilla, the agents of SIS and SOE and the

French men and women who worked in the intelligence gathering networks, the sabotage and offensive action 'réseau' and the all-important escape lines. It is a story that had its antecedents in SIS operations in the Baltic in 1919, and continued after 1945, also along the shores of the Baltic, involving the delivery of agents behind the Iron Curtain, planned and overseen by some who had worked in this dangerous enterprise during the Second World War. It is a story of a small band of men whose contribution to the war effort and ultimate victory was out of all proportion to their size.

I hope what follows will engage the reader as much as it has the author.

CHAPTER 1 – PRECEDENT

> 'Knowledge of the enemy's condition has to be derived from men'
>
> Sun Tzu, *The Art of War*

Petrograd, Russia, 1919. The dark line of rushes that fringed the shoreline shushed and whispered in the shore breeze. A quarter of a mile away, in his Coastal Motor Boat (CMB), Lieutenant Augustus 'Gus' Agar scanned the coastline in hope of seeing the pre-arranged signal of three short flashes. Nothing. He looked again and checked his watch. They were bang on time, but there was no sign of the courier. He breathed out. There was nothing to do but wait, even though he knew that every second there increased their risk of being caught.

The CMB was anchored in the mouth of the River Neva, off the Russian island of Krestovsky. Beyond was the Russian city of Petrograd, formerly St Petersburg and about to be renamed as Leningrad. Russia, as Churchill was later to remark, was a riddle wrapped in a mystery inside an enigma for the British. That was certainly true at the time of Agar's mission: all normal communication with Russia had ceased, the British missions and consulates had left, and the Moscow embassy had been closed for over a year. The only credible and reliable intelligence coming out of the country was via a solitary agent, Paul Dukes, known as ST25. Dukes had remained in Russia working as a pianist and assistant conductor at the Petrograd Conservatoire. Fluent in Russian, his skill for disguise led to his nickname of 'The Man of a Hundred Faces'. Dukes had somehow managed to infiltrate most levels of Soviet politics and the Secret Services.

Gus Agar had been to Russia before, serving with the Royal Navy at Murmansk during the Allied interventions following the Russian Revolution. Honourable, exceptionally brave and dedicated to King and Country, Agar epitomised the tough sea dog of British Naval tradition. When the offer of Special Service came up, he jumped at the chance. Agar was taken by Commander Goff of the Naval

Intelligence Division to meet Captain Sir Mansfield George Smith-Cummings, KCMG, CB, Head of the Secret Intelligence Service (SIS) and more commonly known through Whitehall as simply 'C'.

Cummings explained that there had been a secret courier service from the newly independent Finland and Estonia to Dukes in Petrograd, but the couriers had been captured and executed, and Dukes was now isolated and vulnerable. Cummings needed Agar to re-establish these courier links, getting these individuals into Petrograd, deliver messages to Dukes, bring back his reports and, ultimately, bring Dukes out. As far as the British government were concerned, Cummings told Agar, he wouldn't exist. He was to go in plain clothes, which meant that he could be shot as a spy if caught. The alternative, going in uniform, would confirm British intervention in a sovereign state's internal conflict.

Agar's unit consisted of two CMBs, three Sub-Lieutenants of the Royal Naval Reserve and two Chief Motor Mechanics: his own boat being crewed by Sub-Lieutenant John Hampshier and Chief Motor Mechanic Hugh Beeley. The CMBs were very fast, light, three-man boats. Designed by Thorney Croft Motor Boat Company, they were 55ft long and usually equipped with two torpedoes and Lewis machine guns (though for this mission, they were unarmed). The CMBs were forerunners of the World War Two Motor Torpedo Boats and Motor Gun Boats. However, they had an Achilles heel: in order to make

Gus Agar's CMB

them as light as possible, they were constructed with a skin of thin plywood. One shot, even just landing close to a CMB, could blow the entire boat to smithereens.

Getting couriers in and out of Russia required speed, daring, determination and outstanding navigation and seamanship. The Gulf of Finland is almost 250 miles long but only thirty miles wide, narrowing gradually as it approaches Petrograd. Square in the middle of the last few miles of the approach is the Russian island of Kotlin. Every inch of its surrounding water was swept by the gun batteries of the eight fortresses which lined its shore, the largest of all being one of the most formidable in the world – Kronstadt. If that wasn't enough, these defences were supplemented by minefields, breakwaters and a chain of sea fortresses, nine to the north, six to the south, which formed an almost impenetrable barrier for any who might be tempted to slip past. The minefields were less of an issue for a CMB: with mines at a depth of six feet, the boat could skim over without getting hit. But the breakwaters were only three feet below the waterline. At full speed a CMB drew two feet, nine inches, leaving a clearance of just three inches. There was a route through the breakwaters to the south of Kotlin Island by going through the main shipping channel, but that was so closely guarded and heavily patrolled that there was little chance of slipping through undetected.

It is hard to overestimate the skill and bravery of Agar and his team in navigating their way through all of this to drop off the courier, Pyotr Sokolov, whom they'd left forty-eight hours earlier in a small rowing boat to make his way ashore. Now they'd cheated death for a second time to pick him up and as Agar searched the shoreline for a signal, he was unsure whether the courier would return.

Then, finally, Agar spotted a faint flickering of light. Was that the flash of an electric torch? Was that Sokolov? Agar was certain it was, and gave the reply signal back in the same direction. A few minutes later and there, in front of the rustle of the rushes, was a new sound: the gentle splash of a pair of oars on the water. Next was a shout – someone was calling Agar's name.

'Khorosho,' Agar replied. *All right.*

Sokolov pulled up alongside, and Agar helped him aboard. He

Agar's crew: Hampshier, Agar, Beeley

Paul Dukes

was exhausted, all but collapsing from the stress of the previous forty-eight hours. Hampshier gave him some sustenance in the form of biscuits and rum and Sokolov fell asleep, oblivious to the CMG going full speed back to Finland, navigating its way back among the minefields, the breakwaters, the sea fortresses and the Russian guns to the small, disused yacht club at Terrioki in Finland which was their operating base.

*

The original inspiration for the 15th Motor Gun Boat Flotilla can be found in Gus Agar's adventures in the Gulf of Finland. Agar's exploits (for which he was awarded the Victoria Cross and Distinguished Service Order) were well known in both naval and intelligence circles, and when Captain Frank Slocum RN[3] found himself tasked with setting up clandestine route links into occupied Europe during the Second World War, Agar was firmly in his mind. Slocum both knew of Agar's achievements and, as a fellow officer, knew Agar himself (Agar continued to serve in the Royal Navy until 1945). He sent for the files on Agar's mission, but as with many reports from the early years of SIS, they were nowhere to be found.[4]

Frank Slocum's career had parallels to Agar's, beginning in the

3 Initially a Commander, later promoted to Captain.
4 After numerous attempts by Agar to exfiltrate ST25 (Dukes) failed, the agent eventually managed to escape via Latvia, meeting Agar back in London outside C's office. Dukes was knighted for his operations in Russia.

Navy and moving over to Intelligence. Slocum came from a family rich in seafaring tradition: he was related to the seaman and adventurer Joshua Slocum, who in 1904 had become the first man to sail single-handedly around the world. Frank Slocum served with the Grand Fleet in the First World War, going on to qualify as a navigation specialist. During the inter-war years, he served in the Persian Gulf Squadron, Home and Mediterranean Fleets, passed through the Staff College and taught in the Tactical School. In the early 1930s he became victim to the ongoing knock-on effect of the 'Geddes Axe', the cuts made to government expenditure in the years after the First World War. Having been transferred to the Royal Navy Reserve, Slocum was then recruited into SIS in 1937 by Admiral Hugh 'Quex' Sinclair,[5] then Chief of SIS, to take charge of the Naval Section.

Slocum was a shrewd appointment. A small dapper man with a deceptively mild manner, he was in fact a hard taskmaster who demanded a high standard from those working for him. He had a passion for accuracy of detail which he drummed into his staff, and it was this, together with his unrelenting persistence and determination, which was to be the driver for the success of his department. Slocum inspired the greatest respect and affection among the officers and men under his command, who knew that their success was as much due to his leadership as to their own abilities. He was intensely loyal to his staff, always taking responsibility for their actions and backing them up, while taking miscreants aside for a severe private dressing down. David Birkin, who will emerge as one of the key figures in this story, described him as 'one of the nicest men I have ever had the good fortune to meet'.

Certainly, SIS were sorely in need of figures like Slocum in the 1930s. By the outbreak of the Second World War, the British Secret Intelligence Service was in poor shape. Since the end of the First World War and Agar's generously funded expedition to the Baltic, its budget had been continually cut and it was not properly prepared to fight a major war. The voices in the organisation who, like Churchill, could foresee what was coming, were few and far between.

5 Sinclair is often considered to be the model for Fleming's 'M'. In reality, M, rather like Bond, was probably an amalgam of different people Fleming met during the war.

One such example of disarray was in the Netherlands. By the time the German attack on France and the Low Countries had begun on 10 May 1940, Anglo-Dutch intelligence coordination had reached a particular low. This was because of the Venlo Incident, a German covert operation carried out on 9 November 1939, in which two British SIS officers were abducted five metres from the German border on the outskirts of Venlo. The incident was later used by the Germans as a pretext for the invasion of Holland.

On top of this, the invasion was one whose element of surprise could have been avoided and countered. Colonel Hans Oster of the Abwehr – German Military Intelligence – was both a member of the German Resistance and an anti-Nazi. In March 1939 he had begun to pass detailed intelligence to his friend, the Dutch Military Attaché in Berlin, Major Gijsbertus Sas. This included the details and attack date for FALLGELB, the plan to attack France and the Low Countries. This information was passed on by the Dutch to other Allied Military Attachés but after a series of German postponements was forgotten about. It was only when Oster phoned Sas on 4 May to say that attack was imminent that Dutch troops were put on alert. On 10 May, those at Broadway, the headquarters of SIS, were as bewildered as anyone at the turn of events.

What followed next from a military perspective is well documented. The British and French responded by pushing their best forces, including the British Expeditionary Force (BEF) into Belgium. Although the initial stages went reasonably well, a French force advancing towards Breda in Holland was pushed back, exposing the British flank. By advancing into the Low Countries the Allies had over-extended themselves. On 13 May the first German forces emerged from the Ardennes near Sedan, on the River Meuse, cutting the Allied lines of communication. In a two-day battle, they crossed the river. Under the dynamic command of General Heinz Guderian, a pioneer of armoured warfare, the German Panzers broke out of the bridgehead. They began to race towards the Channel coast, aided by the German aircraft that provided close air support and maintained air superiority.

Lacking a centrally placed strategic reserve, the Allies tried to pull their armies out of Belgium to respond to the new threat emerging in their rear. At Arras in Northern France on 21 May, a composite force of British tanks and infantry mounted a well-planned counterattack and gave a rough reception to Erwin Rommel's 7th Panzer Division. But it was too little, too late. With German forces pushing through Belgium and the Panzers looping up from the south and west, the Allies were encircled. On 23 May, General Lord Gort, Commander of the BEF, took the morally courageous decision to abandon his role in a projected Anglo-French counterattack, and fell back on the Channel ports. Between 26 May and 4 June, a hastily organised evacuation by sea, code-named Operation Dynamo, lifted 338,000 Allied troops from Dunkirk. That the German forces failed to press home their attack on Dunkirk was largely thanks to the grim defence of the Dunkirk perimeter by British and French troops, and the efforts of the much-depleted RAF.

France was next to fall. On 5 June, the Germans struck southwards from the River Somme. Despite the fact that the French in many areas fought well, the Germans destroyed the French forces in short order. The Germans launched a major offensive on Paris on 9 June, and on the 13th Paris was declared an open city, as the French government fled to Bordeaux. The first German troops entered the French capital on 14 June, little more than a month after the campaign began. France surrendered on 22 June. The French collapse was as sudden as it was unexpected. Overnight it left the strategic assumptions on which Britain had planned to fight the war in tatters. With France out of the equation, Britain was on its own.

On Tuesday, 18 June, at 3:49 PM, Churchill got up in the House of Commons to deliver one of his most important speeches and one of his greatest moments of oratory. Churchill described the use of parachute troops, airborne landings and of bombing attacks 'which will certainly be made very soon upon us. Germany has more bombers, but Britain has bombers too, and would deploy them, without intermission, to attack military targets in Germany.' He reminded the nation that Britain had a strong navy but made no attempt to underplay the gravity of the French collapse. 'The Battle of France is over, and I expect that the Battle of Britain is about to begin. The whole fury and might of the enemy must very soon be turned on us. Hitler knows that he will have to break us in this island or lose the war. If we can stand up to him, all Europe may be free, and the life of the world may move forward into broad, sunlit uplands; but if we fail then the whole world, including the United States, and all that we have known and cared for, will sink into the abyss of a new dark age made more sinister, and perhaps more prolonged, by the lights of a perverted science. Let us therefore brace ourselves to our duty and so bear ourselves that if the British Commonwealth and empire lasts for a thousand years, men will still say, "This was their finest hour."'

After Dunkirk and the fall of France, in London, the secret world was in turmoil and trying hard to pick up the pieces. SIS had no immediately available assets in France, where it had had a gentleman's agreement with its French counterpart, the Service de Renseignements, not to conduct espionage. Whatever coverage it had had in the Low Countries had been severely disrupted by the Germans. It had to therefore start from scratch by recruiting, training and briefing agents; developing clandestine radio W/T communications for agents' use, and training operators to use them; and devising means of transport to get them into, and out of, German-occupied territory.

Which was where Frank Slocum and the 15th Motor Gun Boat Flotilla would play their part.

*

Battling alongside Slocum were a key group of individuals, whose knowledge and experience would prove crucial in leading the intelligence fightback. No one here was more vital than Claude Dansey, the new Deputy Chief of SIS. Dansey was a complex character. He was a very experienced intelligence officer, with a tough and hard exterior that concealed a surprising sensitivity. He hated the incompetence and complacency that he saw in the pre-war SIS and was determined to do something about it.

Dansey had served as an Intelligence Officer during the First World War and left the Service in 1918. He began a series of enjoyable occupations and associations with the rich and famous, which both

Claude Dansey

paid the bills and gave him cover for his ongoing freelance intelligence activities. In 1929, Admiral Sinclair asked Dansey to rejoin the Service and take over the running of the Rome station. The newly appointed Foreign Secretary Robert Vansittart had identified Germany as an ongoing enemy and Hitler as a specific threat, long before others did. Sinclair needed accurate information and Dansey had created his own network of bankers, businessmen, industrialists, politicians, journalists and those with unusual access – particularly those who visited Germany.

In 1930 Dansey's 'unofficial' organisation became 'official', a parallel organisation outside SIS known as 'Z', which he ran from Switzerland under several 'covers'. As well as being partially funded by SIS, the Z Organisation also included the Rothschilds, Oppenheimers and the film director Alex Korda among its patrons. By the start of the 1930s, SIS had become very run down and not particularly effective: Z's steady flow of high-grade intelligence was therefore all the more important. Many of Dansey's recruits were rich and famous men and women. He also recruited as many Germans as he could and targeted British nationals, 'young people interested in living or travelling abroad'. One of his officers in Switzerland was Frederick Langley, father of Jimmy Langley who became Dansey's man inside the newly formed escape organisation MI9.

In 1940, with SIS in turmoil, Dansey was asked to return to London. Not only had most of its European networks been rolled up, but Sinclair was dying. Dansey was best placed to replace him but instead chose to let Sinclair's deputy, Stewart Menzies, have the job. Dansey believed he would be able to control much more by serving as deputy himself. The Z organisation was now fully absorbed into SIS, with Dansey's personal mission to emulate its success by turning SIS into a thoroughly professional and effective organisation, gathering strategic intelligence across Europe.

Two figures who were particularly important here were Wilfred 'Biffy' Dunderdale, the SIS Head of Station in France, and Kenneth Cohen, another SIS officer who had been part of Dansey's Z Organisation. Born in Odessa in 1899, Biffy Dunderdale had been in Petrograd, studying naval architecture, when the Russian Revolution broke out in October 1917. Speaking fluent Russian, German and French, Dunderdale was so useful to Naval Intelligence as an undercover agent during operations in the Black Sea and the Sea of Marmora that, by the age of 21, he held the honorary rank of Lieutenant RNVR, had been mentioned in dispatches twice and awarded an MBE. Dunderdale joined SIS in 1921 and was posted to Paris in 1926 as Head of Station. He adopted the role of the quintessential Englishman abroad, driving his Rolls-Royce around France and commuting between the elegant office of SIS in the rue Charles Floquet and his country home, the Château de Chêne in the Loire Valley – more 'Bond' than 'Smiley'. He built up a good working relationship with the French Service de Renseignements under Colonel Rivet, with the French Counter-Intelligence Service under Captain Paillole and with Colonel Gustave Bertrand, the chief French cryptanalyst. Dunderdale had also established a good relationship with the Polish Intelligence Service and in January 1940 had arranged for Alan Turing to meet his Polish counterparts, who gave him insights which led to the design of the first British cryptanalytic machine and ENIGMA.[6]

6 Dunderdale's chauffeur in Paris was Paul Kilesso. Born in the Ukraine, Kilesso went to France in 1916 as part of the Russian Expeditionary Force, and fought at Verdun. After the war he did not want to return to a Communist Russia, and moved to Constantinople, where he met Dunderdale, who recruited him. They returned to Paris in 1926. In 1939 Kilesso wanted to join up but Dunderdale, who had been quietly 'putting things in place', persuaded him to remain in Paris and take over the running of the Hotel du Harve at 37 Boulevard Montparnasse. The Hotel had been bought by SIS as a 'safe house' and cover for the transit of agents, money and equipment. Kilesso was one of the earliest members of the JADE FITZROY network (see Chapters 7/8). He was eventually arrested on 24 January 1944 and deported to Mauthausen death camp. He survived.

Colonel Bertrand had also obtained two Polish copies of an Enigma machine, and gave one to Dunderdale to send to London. The machine was put in a diplomatic bag and, accompanied by his Chief of Staff, 'Uncle' Tom Green, Dunderdale and Bertrand boarded the Golden Arrow boat train for London. Also on the train was the French playwright Sacha Guitry with his wife Yvonne Printemps, who were neighbours of the Dunderdales in Paris. Dunderdale arranged for the bulky diplomatic bag to be hidden amongst the Guitrys' vast amount of luggage, which Dunderdale then arranged to have waved through the customs hall at Dover – much to the delight of the Guitrys, as it contained a large amount of dutiable Chanel No. 5 and Cognac.

As Paris fell under German hands, Dunderdale was one of the last members of staff to leave the British Embassy. He made his way south through the chaos of the French collapse keeping such contact as was possible with his French colleagues, as they retreated from one château to another. With the armistice looming, he took his leave of Rivet and was flown out from Bordeaux by an RAF Hudson, which SIS had sent to ensure he could get home.

Kenneth Cohen was a qualified barrister, joining the Royal Navy in 1918 and transferring to SIS in 1935. He spoke fluent French and Russian and was known for his intelligence, sharp mind, sensitivity and tact. Soon after joining SIS, he was posted to work with Dansey's Z Organisation in Switzerland, working under commercial cover as Kenneth Crane through a front company, Menoline Limited in London. His job was to recruit sources including several distinguished Foreign Correspondents of British newspapers in France, Holland, Switzerland, Czechoslovakia and Italy.

In the chaos of summer 1940, many of Dunderdale and Cohen's contacts turned to Switzerland as the best route for re-establishing communications with the British. Soon, there was a steady flow of information from France into Geneva, Berne and Basel. Major Frederick (Fanny) van den Heuvel was appointed Head of Station in Geneva. Victor Farrell was given the cover of Press Attaché at the Embassy in Berne, where the station consisted of Freddie West VC, MC and Colonel Cartwright MC. Lancelot de Gaston worked out of Lugano and Ted Franken out of Basle.

Wilfred Dunderdale

Kenneth Cohen

Back in London, Menzies established two new staff sections to produce intelligence on French targets: one under Dunderdale; the other under Cohen. Dunderdale's brief was to operate independently of the Free French as far as possible (though he found it necessary, particularly in the early days, to borrow personnel from them). Cohen's role was to cooperate with the Free French and their newly formed Bureau Central de Renseignements (BCRA).

Dunderdale and Cohen sought help wherever they could in France, not only from de Gaulle's Deuxième Bureau (later BCRA) but also from intelligence professionals who had remained in France and though working for the Vichy government were in reality sympathetic to the Allied cause. They also communicated with the Intelligence Service of the exiled Polish government. There was continuous friction to begin with, with the Free French, but between them, Dunderdale and Cohen were able to work effectively together.

Re-establishing networks was a difficult enough job for SIS in the circumstances. But Menzies and Dansey had further problems closer to home with the creation of two new rival organisations. As well as an urgent need to re-establish intelligence networks in France, Churchill demanded offensive action to 'set Europe ablaze'. This led to the setting up of the Special Operations Executive or SOE, an organisation with a diametrically opposed philosophy and approach to SIS. SIS traditionally conducted espionage for which it needed 'peace and quiet' in enemy territory. By means of sabotage and offensive action, SOE was aiming to do precisely the opposite.

Claude Maurice Buckmaster

In SOE, there were two French sections. In September 1941 Colonel Maurice Buckmaster, who had been Head of the French Division of the Ford Motor Company, was appointed Head of F Section of SOE, the section responsible for SOE operations in France. Buckmaster was working at a newspaper, *Le Matin*, in Paris when he was commissioned into the Intelligence Corps: left behind at Dunkirk, he made a spectacular escape by dressing as a nun and smuggling himself into a convent. Over the next three years he would send over 500 agents to France. In parallel with F Section, a second department, RF Section, was linked to General de Gaulle's Free French Intelligence Service. Whilst Buckmaster headed F Section throughout the war, RF leadership kept changing: Eric Piquet-Wicks, James Hutchinson, Bickham Sweet-Escott and L. H. Dismore ran it sequentially.

The potential for friction between SIS and SOE was clear from the start, and combined with the prickly relations with the Free French made the set-up difficult to handle. To complicate matters still further, it was decided that there was also a pressing need to assist evaders and escaped POWs to get out of Europe. Rather than assigning this to SIS, a new escape and evasion organisation was created in December 1939 called MI9. With the foundation of both SOE and MI9 combined, SIS had lost its monopoly on clandestine activity, and the ability to decide when to quietly gather intelligence or conduct sabotage and other offensive action.

Dansey was sharp enough to realise that SIS needed to try and control all of this. He rapidly took control of MI9 by installing his

Jimmy Langley

own man, Jimmy Langley, the son of one his former officers, as its Chief of Operations. He was not so successful with SOE, although its first director, Head of SOE from 1940–42, Sir Frank Nelson had been part of the Z Organisation. He also succeeded in infiltrating his own man into F Section of SOE, Nicolas Boddington, who had worked for Dansey before the war when he was the Paris correspondent of Reuters.

Jimmy Langley was commissioned in the Coldstream Guards as a reservist in 1936 and was mobilised in August 1939 to serve in the 2nd Battalion Coldstream Guards in the British Expeditionary Force. In June 1940 he was seriously wounded in the head and arms at Dunkirk. Unable to walk, he was left behind at a Casualty Clearing Station where he was captured, and later had his left arm amputated by a German army doctor. On 10 October he escaped from a hospital in Lille and made his way to Marseille. While in Marseille, Langley worked as a courier for the Pat O'Leary escape line run by the Scottish officer Ian Garrow and Minister Donald Caskie. In February 1941, Langley was declared 'unfit for further military service' by a medical board headed by Doctor George Rodocanachi, and was repatriated in March.[7] On his return to England Langley was recruited by Claude

7 George Rodocanachi was an extraordinarily brave man. From 1941, until the betrayal of the line in 1943, over 600 Allied soldiers, sailors, airmen and secret agents were either hidden at or processed through Rodocanachi's large Marseille apartment. Rodocanachi was also responsible for saving the lives of over 2,000 Jews by procuring false medical certificates justifying their escape to the USA.

Dansey into the Secret Intelligence Service to serve as Liaison Officer between SIS and MI9.

'Theoretically, you will be on loan to MI9, which is commanded by Colonel Crockatt,'[8] Dansey told him. 'In practice you will be on my staff and under my orders in MI6.' For the next four hectic years, Langley worked under the code name IVZ, running a section designated P15. He managed successfully to serve his two masters: representing Dansey to MI9 and MI9 to Dansey. It was not always easy. 'Dansey was one of those powerful men who prefer to keep their power hidden,' Langely recorded, 'an eminence grise rather than a ruling monarch. What Dansey wanted done was done and what he wanted undone was undone.'

*

Twenty-one years after Gus Agar's adventures in the Gulf of Finland, Frank Slocum was tackling the same type of conundrum: how to set up clandestine links to occupied Europe with very few resources and manage the conflicting interests of his three customers – SIS, SOE and MI9. Slocum was very firmly on the staff of SIS and this rankled with SOE who believed – with some justice – that they were being deliberately marginalised. This caused SOE to attempt to set up a parallel clandestine sea route to France based in the Helford River in Cornwall, under the very forceful Commander Gerry Holdsworth. Slocum and Holdsworth did not get on at all. The parallel operation was to create great friction and waste resources until common sense prevailed and it was brought under Slocum's command. Holdsworth was posted to North Africa. He was replaced by Lieutenant Commander Bevil Warington-Smyth. In future they were to 'work in the closest cooperation'.

Initially Slocum was based in the SIS Headquarters at 54 Broadway. Given the internecine strife between SIS and SOE, that MI9 was effectively 'owned' by SIS, and that the Admiralty was in the SIS camp, Slocum sought to create a satisfactory cover for his organisation to manage everyone's expectations. In May 1941 it was agreed that he

8 Colonel Norman Crockatt DSO, MC, Head of MI9.

SIS HQ, Broadway Buildings

59 Palace Street, DODD(I) HQ

could redesignate his department Naval Intelligence Department (Clandestine) – NID(C) and move it to an office at Prince's House, 59 Palace Street, just around the corner from Broadway. Later, in June 1943, in order to control all clandestine sea operations from Norway to the Adriatic, Slocum was redesignated Deputy Director Operations Division (Irregular) – DDOD(I)[9] and known as 'O'. This enabled him to not only command his own assets but call on commands of all services to provide support. While this made operational sense, it was seen by SOE as a sleight of hand between SIS and the Admiralty, something that Slocum was never really able to shake off.

The ongoing friction between SIS and SOE was to continue until the end of the war.

9 For ease of reference DDOD(I) will be used throughout.

CHAPTER 2 – 'YOU ARE IN'

'His activity and zeal are eminently conspicuous, even amongst the Band of Brothers'

Horatio Nelson

The air raid siren sounded so frequently across the Naval Hospital at HMS HASLAR in Gosport, Hampshire, that the staff and patients could be forgiven for treating the latest alarm with a resigned shrug. With its key naval links, Gosport was heavily targeted during the Second World War: over the duration of the war, there were almost 1,600 alerts and over sixty raids. It is estimated that 11,000 out of the town's 13,000 buildings were damaged, with almost a thousand badly so, and 453 completely destroyed.

The Naval Hospital was one of the town's most iconic buildings. Opened in 1753, it was described by one of its first physicians as 'an immense pile of a building, and when complete it will certainly be the biggest hospital in Europe'. According to another account, it was also, when built, the largest brick building in both England and the continent. It should have been larger still: its famous three-sided U-shaped layout came about after the fourth side was cancelled due to over-spending. Over the years, the Naval Hospital had treated casualties from Trafalgar, Corunna and Waterloo, as well as the Crimean and First World War. By the Second World War, however, its distinctive appearance, combined with its 120-foot water tower, made it an easy spot for German bombers.

As the air raid sirens sounded, one of its patients, David Birkin, dreamed of being able to take the fight to the opposition. But his war was turning out to be a continuation of a childhood of bad luck and ill health. Born in November 1914, Birkin had been brought up in Nottingham where his father, Major Henry Birkin, a retired First World War veteran, ran the family lace business, Birkin & Co. Thanks to what he described as a 'bungled sinus operation' when he was seventeen, Birkin had been in and out of hospital for years.

Haslar Hospital

Having 'fallen victim to a charming but unscrupulous ENT surgeon', Birkin had endured thirty-four operations on his lungs and eyes by the time war broke out: one of the operations left him with double vision and a weak and bleeding lung. He was reduced to living the life of a semi-invalid, at home, passing the time painting and playing tennis.

Both Birkin's brothers joined up, leaving David behind, increasingly frustrated by home life and his father considering him an invalid. He resolved to prove himself, paying to train as a wireless telegraphist at the North Eastern School of Wireless Telegraphy at Bridlington in Yorkshire. Having gained his Merchant Navy Telegraphist Certificate, he decided to try and join the Royal Navy. With a bit of cunning and the connivance of the medical board he was passed 'fit' to join as a telegraphist. He went to the Navy's Wireless School at Portsmouth in November 1941 as a Naval Rating, having no intention of applying for a commission.

Portsmouth did not go well. Although the medical board had passed him 'fit', Birkin spent considerable time in and out of hospital, plagued with double vision, bleeding lungs and chronic sinus headaches. Worst of all, for a member of the Royal Navy, Birkin had a guarantee of violent seasickness whenever setting foot on a boat. By the time the air raid warning sounded, he was back in the Naval Hospital suffering from a bout of measles.

This time, however, his luck had started to turn. With an almighty thud and a low, vibrating rumble, the hospital was hit by a stick of German bombs. But it was the next-door ward that suffered the full force of the blast. In one of those 'there but for the grace of God' moments, Birkin had survived. And then, whether it was due to the effects of this air raid or by 'some other means', Birkin's medical records were mysteriously lost. Alive and recovered, he left hospital with a clean bill of health, ready to play his part in the war.

On 12 January 1942, after two years as a Rating Telegraphist, Birkin was ordered to report to the Admiralty in London for an interview. Given everything he had been through, the request came as something of a surprise. Nervous and uncertain as to why he had been called in, Birkin reported to Room 516, an office of the Royal Marines in the main Admiralty building. Having arrived on time at 11.00 AM, he then proceeded to wait, rather uneasily, for an hour and a half before Frank Slocum walked in. Birkin later described his first impression of Slocum as 'a slightly built ball of fire in Naval uniform'.

Slocum explained to Birkin in the broadest terms precisely what his organisation did and warned him of the extreme secrecy under which he would work if he joined. *If I joined*, Birkin thought,

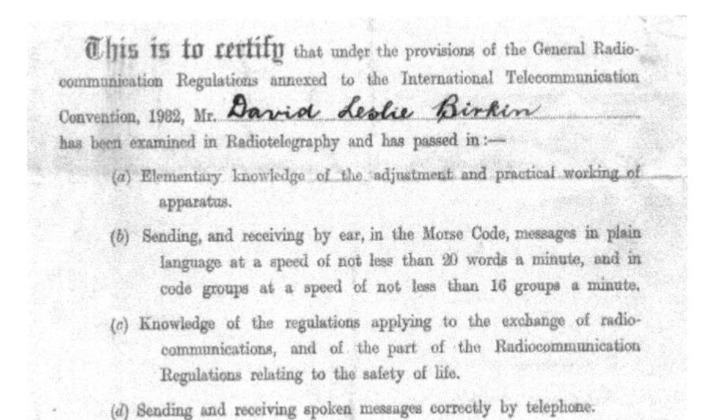

This is to certify that under the provisions of the General Radio-communication Regulations annexed to the International Telecommunication Convention, 1932, Mr. David Leslie Birkin has been examined in Radiotelegraphy and has passed in:—

(a) Elementary knowledge of the adjustment and practical working of apparatus.

(b) Sending, and receiving by ear, in the Morse Code, messages in plain language at a speed of not less than 20 words a minute, and in code groups at a speed of not less than 16 groups a minute.

(c) Knowledge of the regulations applying to the exchange of radio-communications, and of the part of the Radiocommunication Regulations relating to the safety of life.

(d) Sending and receiving spoken messages correctly by telephone.

David Birkin's Telegraphist Certificate

Height 6 feet 1 inches
Colour of Eyes Brown
Colour of Hair Brown
Complexion Fresh
Any special peculiarities scar on eyebrow

David Birkin's first ID card

bemused. He remembered the meeting as being 'cloak and dagger in the extreme. I left realising that I was under a pledge of secrecy never, for the duration of the war, to discuss, divulge, or hint at the nature of DDOD(I)'s activities.' Slocum explained how the relationship between the Navy and SIS worked. 'Based on what you have heard so far,' Slocum asked, 'do you want to join as a Staff Officer?'

For Birkin, it was an offer too good to refuse. In order to join, he needed to pass an SIS selection board, which was arranged for the next day. A room was booked by SIS for Birkin at the St Ermines Hotel, around the corner from 54 Broadway, SIS Headquarters. That evening Birkin amused himself by taking in the Phyllis Dixey Striptease Revue at the Whitehall Theatre, and had an early night. The following morning he reported to Broadway at 10.00 AM. After the interview he was told to go to Room 402 on the fourth floor, which was where Slocum's office was situated. Slocum told him to sit down. As Birkin did so, the phone rang. Slocum picked up and listened.

'Right sir.' Slocum put the phone down and looked up at Birkin. 'That was "C",' he smiled. 'You are in.'[10]

*

Starting on his own in June 1940, and with no visible assets other than a lively imagination and great strength of character, Frank Slocum had been tasked with building up a system of clandestine transport which was to successfully carry many hundreds of agents to occupied Europe in the next four years, ranging from Norway to the Mediterranean. At the outset, and indeed until 1941, he was responsible for operations by air as well as by sea, and all the early parachute landings and pick-ups by Lysander aircraft were carried out under his control.

In 1941 the RAF took over the air side, leaving Slocum to concentrate on the sea routes. In the early days, any kind of craft, naval

10 There is more than a hint that Birkin's friendship with Minister of Information (and later, the Founder of the *Financial Times*) Brendan Braken, and Louis Mountbatten, Chief of Combined Operations, and a friend of Birkin's cousin Angela Laycock, may have helped with this unusual turn of events.

W. B. 'Bill' Luard

or civilian, which Slocum could get his hands on, was requisitioned and pressed into service. Among the varied vessels Slocum acquired were a former French trawler, an air/sea rescue boat, and two French fast patrol boats. When possible, he borrowed small, fast craft from Coastal Forces for staging specific operations to Holland and Belgium, before increased enemy control of the Channel coast areas forced his clandestine operations to be shifted further west.

All the while, Slocum was gathering around him a staff of officers, both Royal Navy and Reservists, all volunteers for special service, to act as navigators and escorting officers on the clandestine trips made by surface craft, and for various duties concerned with planning, communications, engineering and small boat work. Because the risk of enemy air interception was high, adequate air cover had to be ensured to prevent the enemy from investigating and attacking his vessels on their hazardous trips across the Channel. Slocum therefore established a close liaison with RAF Coastal Command, and was able to instal his own operational liaison officer in the headquarters of No 19 Group at St Eval, in Cornwall, whose commander, Air Vice-Marshal Geoffrey Bromet, had begun his flying career in the Royal Navy Air Service (RNAS) before transferring to the RAF.

Slocum's Liaison Officer was Commander W. B. 'Bill' Luard, a remarkable character, who as a young sub-lieutenant had been invalided from the Navy in 1917 with a tubercular hip. This left him with a bad limp but did not prevent him from becoming a professional ocean racing yachtsman. He had also gone to sea with east coast trawlers

Steven Mackenzie

and drifters and with Breton tunny men, purely for the experience, and thus became something of an expert on English and French fishing fleets. His specialist knowledge was to prove very useful.

At the beginning of World War II Luard renewed his commission in the Royal Naval Volunteer Reserve (RNVR). While serving in a minesweeper in 1940, Luard saw his vessel blown up by one of the first German acoustic mines, and he suffered further injuries. Once out of hospital his services were acquired by Slocum, who took him on as an (almost) unpaid volunteer. He received a flat fee of £100 a year from the Admiralty, although he was allowed to wear the uniform of a lieutenant. Subsequently he was given a more appropriate rank and placed on full pay and went on to render outstanding service.

When not arranging for the provision of intelligence and air cover for the vessels of Slocum's flotillas, Luard dreamed up a number of useful inventions, which included a submersible target for improving the accuracy of depth charge attacks on U-boats by Coastal Command aircraft; a set of special sailing gear for the RAF's one-man dinghy; and a power-driven catamaran canoe for offensive warfare in the Far East. To aid in aircrew survival, he also drew up tidal stream vector diagrams of the English Channel, and compiled drift curves for aircraft dinghies, essential information for clandestine small craft activities and for finding downed airmen. His duties included many hours of operational flying in combat areas, and in the early days he himself conducted the navigation of search and rescue aircraft.

Another early member of DDOD(I)'s staff was Steven Mackenzie, a peace-time yachtsman. He joined the RNVR in March 1939 and, after basic training, was posted to the British Naval Liaison staff at Maintenon, near Chartres, the HQ of Admiral Darlan. Ian Fleming, who was attached to the Director of Naval Intelligence, was a frequent visitor, and they became close friends. Fleming was charged with assessing what the French would do in the event of surrender. The second part of the mission was to assist the evacuation to Britain of anyone or anything of strategic value – gold, industrial diamonds, codes and ciphers, and above all 'heavy water' (deuterium oxide), as well as scientists and other technicians. Fleming, Mackenzie and others had some considerable success with this, including Charles Howard, the rather eccentric 20th Earl of Sussex, who brought out French nuclear scientists,[11] and twenty-six containers of deuterium oxide – essential for the production of a nuclear weapon. After the fall of France, Mackenzie spent several days in Bordeaux and Saint Jean de Luz helping to evacuate refugees. Among them was King Zog of Albania with his wife and baby. The King had some £10 million in gold bars which were piled up on the jetty and guarded by his sisters, who were in battledress and armed with submachine guns. Mackenzie helped them get it all on to a British destroyer.

On 25 June 1940 Mackenzie himself got away on a Canadian destroyer. That night, in the Bay of Biscay, while he was asleep, he was thrown on to the cabin floor. The vessel had collided with a cruiser and been sliced in half. Somehow Mackenzie managed to jump on to the deck of another destroyer as she came alongside: many others on the destroyer were not so lucky and there were a number of fatalities. Mackenzie took over an MGB and, in August, landed two agents at the mouth of the River Orne in Normandy. When the boat was sunk during a bombing raid on Portsmouth, he became a full-time staff officer in Slocum's London office.

The role of Fleming and Admiral Godfrey here is well worth mentioning. In 1939 Admiral John Godfrey had been appointed Director of Naval Intelligence. An intellectual, who acted 'ruthlessly, relentlessly and remorselessly', his insistence on the independence and integrity

11 One of these was Jules Guéron, who after the war pioneered the French atomic energy programme.

of Intelligence and his dislike of 'wishful thinking' and 'Very Senior Officer Veneration' incurred the displeasure of Churchill and the Chiefs of Staff and provoked hostility among his Army and Air Force colleagues. Although dismissed by Admiral Sir Dudley Pound at the end of 1942, he had by then saved the reputation of British Naval Intelligence by his exertions, and Allied Intelligence by his example.

Commander Ian Fleming was recruited by Admiral Godfrey to become his Personal Assistant. He had been commissioned into the RNVR, initially as a Lieutenant, becoming a Commander a few months later. Fleming was invaluable to Godfrey, not least because he was often able to smooth over ripples caused by Godfrey's arrogant and irascible behaviour and his ability to make enemies throughout other government departments. Godfrey used Fleming as liaison with SIS, SOE, the Joint Intelligence Committee and Churchill's staff.

In this role Fleming worked extensively with Frank Slocum. He often used his club, White's, as an 'offsite, off the record' meeting place to sort out problems – not all of them caused by his boss's abrasiveness, but just as often by inter-agency rivalry. He became adept at back-channel discussion and agreements in highly confidential matters. It was Fleming who remembered Steven Mackenzie from France and recommended him to Slocum to become his Principal Staff Officer.

Mackenzie's job was to meet the sections concerned; select feasible dates for missions; pinpoint the target beaches; provide

Slocum in his office

Steven Mackenzie and
Angela Sykes Wright

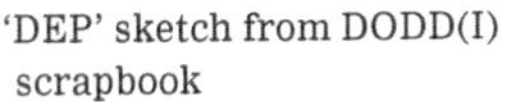

'DEP' sketch from DODD(I) scrapbook

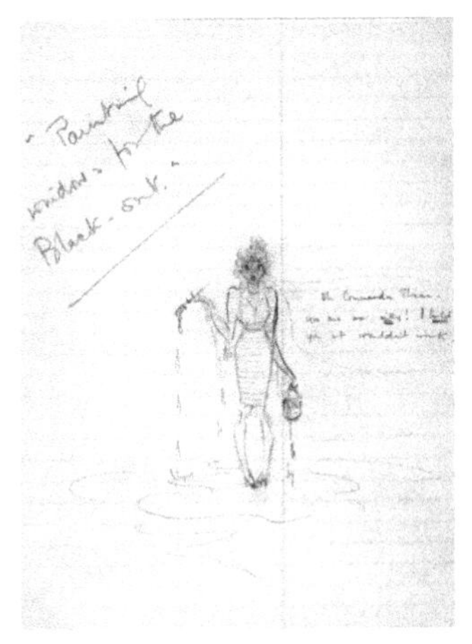

'Blackout' sketch from DODD(I) scrapbook

information on the string of German coastal radar stations and other enemy defences; and brief the commander of the motor gunboats at Dartmouth.

He was joined on Slocum's staff by Pat Whinney and together with Angela Sykes Wright – Slocum's Personal Assistant – they formed the nucleus of what was to become DDOD(I). Slocum was affectionately nicknamed DEP, by his staff – the Damned Elusive Pimpernel. It was this group that were joined by David Birkin, who they quickly learned was a highly intelligent and capable man, a very competent artist and had a head for mathematics. Birkin was to become one of the key players in clandestine naval operations because of his exceptional navigational skills. This led to Slocum nicknaming him 'The Pigeon' – due to his ability to always find his way home.

*

As early as 1940 the imperative to re-establish links within France was both clear and urgent. However, like most things in 1940, both thinking and action were chaotic. On the one hand Britain was fighting for its very existence, on the other it needed to demonstrate the confidence and resolve to get back on the offensive. Resources to conduct clandestine operations were scarce, and there was constant, debilitating conflict of aims and methods between intelligence gathering and offensive action, best represented by the friction between SIS and the fledgling SOE.

The truth was that SIS needed to make use of the Breton beaches, both for its own purposes and for the escape service MI9, to which it acted as carrier. These two services alike were absolutely unprepared to discuss with any other agency, where or when they would operate; and were both keen to keep the Brittany coast as quiet as possible. SOE's work was bound to run counter to this; so, in pursuit of their own interests, SIS did their best to check it. The Admiralty held a high opinion of SIS and imposed for a time a complete ban on activities by SOE between the Channel Islands and St Nazaire. This ban undoubtedly had an effect, different in each case, on British and German strategy, for it made unavailable the part of the continent most suited to raiding and other offensive action, while on the other hand it gave the Germans a false sense of security.

The Admiralty was a very powerful department of state and had been the instrument of survival of Great Britain throughout history, with a great tradition stretching back through Nelson to Drake. The Royal Navy has a long tradition of working closely with SIS and its predecessors, stretching back to Walsingham.

The Admiralty maintained that no operations could take place by sea without its approval. It eventually decreed in the spring of 1943 that all clandestine cross-channel operations would come under a newly appointed coordinator, to be entitled Deputy Director Operations Division (Irregular); adding that 'in home waters clandestine operations are controlled by the Admiralty'. Hardly anything evaded this virtual ban on SOE operations on the Breton coast. Slocum's chain of command was slightly obscure. At the outbreak of war, he was an SIS officer seconded from the Navy and made responsible for clandestine Naval operations. Then, in 1941, his section was designated NID(C), supposedly working for the Director of Naval Intelligence. In fact, he remained directly part of SIS with the full knowledge and approval of the Admiralty.

It was precisely because SOE was anxious to stir up trouble for the enemy that DDOD(I) had a sound point to make. As far back as

Commander Bevil Warrington-Smyth

16 December 1940, at a meeting held to coordinate the activities of SOE, the Director of Combined Operations, and the Secret Intelligence Service (SIS), 'expressed the attitude ... that [they] were against raiding parties as they might interfere with their organisation for getting agents into enemy-occupied territory'. Active SOE coastal operations could imperil other work of different and perhaps greater strategic importance; and in any case, Combined Operations Headquarters had been set up specifically to undertake coastal raids, so that there was no need for SOE to duplicate its work.

Moving agents in and out of France by sea was an entirely different project from landing a party of saboteurs, or commandos, to conduct raiding operations on the coast; and it would seem as if the sound excuse for preventing raiding – that raids would stir up the Germans – was extended, beyond what it would reasonably cover, to prevent the infiltration of agents from a rival firm. Lieutenant Commander Bevil Warrington-Smyth[12] who commanded SOE's Naval Outstation on the Helford River (together with his brother Nigel), saw the importance of DDOD(I) taking command of all maritime clandestine operations:

12 Bevil and Nigel were the sons of Herbert Warrington-Smyth, a World War I veteran who was still in the Navy in 1940, serving as the Resident Naval Officer Helford River. His sons took over the clandestine operations there, making them work effectively with DDOD(I).

'It enabled everyone to get to know each other, and it came as a source of great surprise to more than one Officer (and to some of the more intelligent Ratings) to discover that – contrary to what they had been educated to believe – the principal enemy was Hitler and not their opposite number in the sister organisation. Nothing but good came of this amalgamation at the same Base, and the personnel of the two Organisations worked thereafter in the closest co-operation, with the discomfiture of the Hun as their sole objective.'

Yet all the right was not on SOE's side in this prolonged and often heated controversy. If SOE had only wanted agent delivery they could probably have got there without much trouble; but both the SOE sections F and RF wanted to deliver weapons, explosives, and wireless sets as well. This requirement for stowage capacity was a constant problem for DDOD(I) staff.

Common sense prevailed, however. A system was put in place by DDOD(I) that took into account the requirement of all three of its client agencies in furtherance of the collective war effort. After initial experience of each agency calling for its own requirements, it soon became clear that it was necessary to organise this traffic, set priorities and, if only for security purposes, to establish the criteria for operational efficiency. The purpose of these operations fell into four, separate, parts:

Those involving the landing, support and recovery of intelligence agents and secret mail;

Those providing arms and equipment for Resistance groups and fighters;

Those providing the final link for escape networks (the latter involved escaping aircrew, POWs and resistance workers at risk of capture, sometimes along with their families);

Those ferrying small raiding or reconnaissance parties to and from France.

Frank Slocum and his staff became experts at deconfliction, setting operational priorities, and the detailed coordination of operations.

Clandestine naval missions to France were run from two bases in the West Country – Dartmouth and Falmouth. Dartmouth was the base for the 15th MGBF, supporting all three agencies. Falmouth was primarily an SOE operation. Although this story focuses on Dartmouth, the Dartmouth gunboats would, on occasion, launch or recover to Falmouth either due to weather, the nature and location of the operation, or enemy activity in the Channel.

*

Frank Slocum's orders to re-establish links back into France had begun almost immediately. His first operation had been on 2 August 1940 using the submarine HMS TALISMAN. The 15th MGBF was originally formed at Great Yarmouth in Norfolk to conduct a mix of traditional coastal forces offensive action, and early agent landing operations in Holland. Slocum's early operations were initially to Holland where strong coastal defence had yet to be established. There were also several 'ad-hoc' operations to France using any transport Slocum could get his hands on, including motor launches, fishing boats and converted shipping.[13]

In 1941 Slocum made the arrangements to set up a permanent base at Dartmouth in order to carry out clandestine operations to North Brittany a hundred miles away across the Channel. Dartmouth sits at the mouth of the River Dart, which rises on Dartmoor and flows for 47 miles to the sea. It is one of two communities at the mouth of the river, with Kingswear on the opposite side. The railway came to Kingswear in 1864 with a single line from Paddington that terminates at Pierhead station. Next to the station lies the Royal Dart Hotel, both of which will feature prominently in this story.

The lower section of the river forms Dartmouth Harbour, a deep-water natural harbour with a long history of maritime and Royal Naval usage. Dartmouth has had a strategic importance for centuries. It was a jumping-off point for the Crusades of 1147 and 1190 and Warfleet Creek near Dartmouth Castle is named after the

13 These early operations are not within the scope of this story. They are covered in great detail in *Secret Flotillas* by Brooks Richards.

E. A. G. 'Ted' Davis

large number of fighting ships that gathered there for offensive action. The town played its part in the defeat of the Spanish Armada sending three ships, the *Roebuck*, *Crescent* and *Hart* to join Francis Drake's fleet.

Dartmouth has had a close association with the Royal Navy since the reign of Edward III. In both medieval times and again in the Napoleonic Wars it was home to an effective fleet of privateers operating in support of the Royal Navy. At the end of the nineteenth century Naval Officer Cadet training was carried out on two warships anchored in the harbour: BRITANNIA and HINDUSTAN. In 1905 Naval Cadet training came ashore with the opening of the Royal Naval College, HMS BRITANNIA, which sits in a dominating position to the north west of the town, overlooking the harbour.

Dartmouth has also had a long historical link with intelligence gathering. For centuries it has provided a secluded, sheltered and quiet jumping-off point for intelligence operations along the French coast. During the Napoleonic Wars the speedy and highly manoeuvrable sloop *Netley*, under the command of Francis Bond, was charged with the delivery of agents from Dartmouth and Falmouth to the French coast. 'We had some French men going backwards and forwards as spies', Bond noted in his log.

These were French Royalists who were part of a network set up by Sir Sidney Smith, the brilliant and aggressive Naval officer. Smith, who had been captured and spent two years in prison in Paris, was helped to escape by a French Royalist officer, Colonel Louis-Edmond le Picard de Phélippeaux. On his return to Britain in 1798 he visited the *Netley* in Portsmouth to set up these infiltration operations. Smith's operations worked in concert with what was known as the 'Channel Islands Correspondence' set up by the Jersey-born Royal Naval officer named Philippe d'Auvergne who had strong Royalist connections in Brittany and Normandy. He ran a flotilla of fast sailing boats manned by British and French crews carrying agents and classified mail in and out of France.

As a base for Slocum's clandestine operations, then, Dartmouth seemed the perfect choice. To set up and take charge of the Dartmouth operation he appointed Commander E. A. G. 'Ted' Davis who had joined DDOD(I) in early 1941. Ted Davis was a perfectionist of great drive and ability, highly efficient, with a pleasant and friendly character, and a lifetime of experience in the Merchant Navy. He had been navigating officer on the Cunard liner QUEEN MARY on a pre-war round-the-world cruise. There was very little he did not know about ships and the sea. Davis became Slocum's representative and was appointed, for cover purposes, to the staff of the local Naval Officer-in-Charge in Dartmouth, but he was in fact directly responsible to Slocum in London. Davis was joined by Lt Angus Letty, RNVR, who was also from the Merchant Navy. He had taken part in all the Dutch operations as Navigating and Conducting

HMS BRITANNIA, the Royal Naval College

Officer. Together they set up the Dartmouth operation from offices in HMS BRITANNIA, the Royal Naval College.

*

Having accepted the job on Slocum's staff, David Birkin signed the Official Secrets Act and was fully briefed on DDOD(I)'s clandestine operations to occupied Europe and to the Brittany coast in particular. From the outset the work appealed to him. He liked the Scarlet Pimpernel flavour of it: it was exciting, dangerous, secret and completely different to normal naval routine. He also liked the idea that offensive action was forbidden except in extremis, as he was by nature a pacifist.

For his first three months Birkin worked in the DDOD(I) Headquarters with Steven Mackenzie and Pat Whinney, planning operations and occasionally delivering operation orders to Ted Davis at Dartmouth: these orders were both real and dummy, the latter to be carried on operations in case of capture. These trips, Birkin recalled 'made me increasingly dissatisfied with my staff appointment'. He wanted to get away from the office in London and take part in operations, so he asked Frank Slocum if he could go.

Despite Birkin's poor health record – 'a medical board having pronounced me unfit for any form of military service' – Slocum was sympathetic and agreed. Having spotted some hidden talents, he offered him the post of a Navigating Officer, but on the condition that he would first have to learn something about navigation. Birkin had only ever done a correspondence course on navigation, and he had not been a pre-war yachtsman as many of his colleagues had been. His was to be a steep learning curve. He was given leave to go to Captain O. M. Watts's school at Bursledon for a three-week course. Birkin recalled that he didn't really learn much about navigation, the course being more about general seamanship. His three weeks with Oswald Watts finished on 15 May 1942 and he reported back to DDOD(I). He was then sent on an Escape and Evasion Course run by Squadron Leader Evans, a well-known World War I escaper. As well as a Navigating Officer, Birkin was to be the Flotilla's Escape and Evasion Instructor.

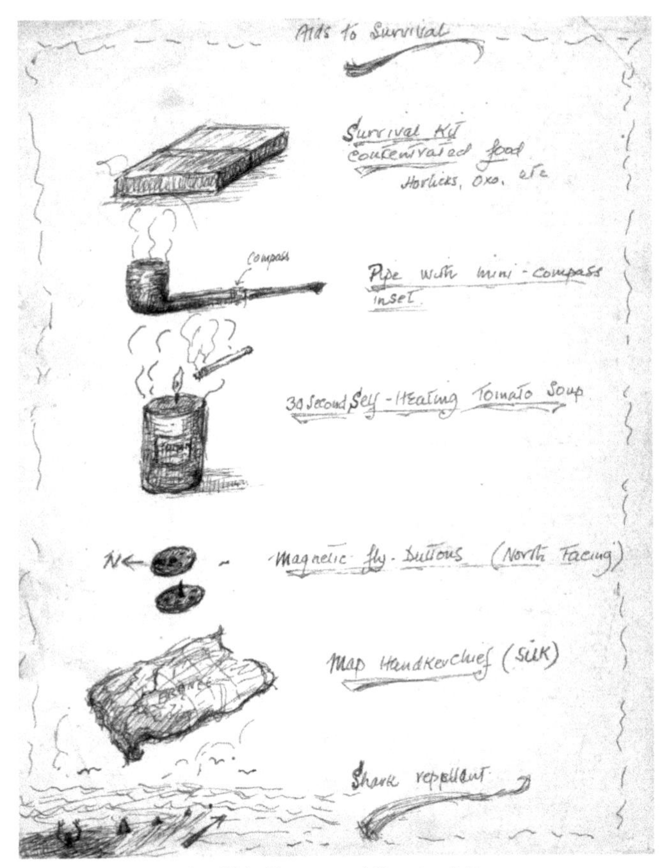

David Birkin sketch of his Escape and Evasion kit

A few weeks later Birkin arrived at Kingswear station – a route that many tourists still enjoy today, the last leg taking passengers on the Dartmouth Steam Railway from Paignton, the final miles into Kingswear running along the side of the River Dart. Birkin made his way to the depot ship, where he saw an officer dozing in the sun and politely said 'Good afternoon sir.' 'Fuck you,' was the helpful response from Charles Martin, who was to be his commander on MGB 318.

This wasn't the last time that Birkin found himself sworn at in those early weeks: '"O" had also overlooked the fact that I had not done the usual officer training course before promotion,' Birkin remembered. 'Consequently I had no sea-going experience, and

Crew of MGB 318

distinguished myself first time on board by treading on the commanding officer's fingers as he was coming up a companion way and I was eagerly hurrying down. I feared my career at sea would end before it had begun, but was let off with a volley of four-lettered abuse.'

It was Ted Davis who took Birkin under his wing, explaining that the success of every operation was dependent on precise navigation, and proceeded to teach him everything he knew about navigation. Birkin said of his tutelage that '... no one could have had better tuition, or a more patient instructor'. Being very keen, he learnt quickly. Davis's instruction lasted for three weeks, by which point Birkin was deemed competent enough to go it alone.

His tuition finished at just the right time. After a slow start the 15th MGBF were about to be thrust into a flurry of action.

CHAPTER 3 – THUS FATE KNOCKS AT THE DOOR

'... audacity often achieves what ordinary means fail to achieve'

Niccoló Machiavelli

On the dot of seven-thirty each evening, the BBC European Service would broadcast the same familiar piece of music: the opening bars of Beethoven's Fifth Symphony. This was no coincidence: phonetically the 'dit-dit-dit-dah' equates to the Morse Code for 'V' (technically, the Morse Code equates to the music, Beethoven composing his piece over a century earlier). The 'V for Victory' motif had its origins in a French newspaper headline from 1939, and was picked up by Victor de Laveleye, director of the BBC's Belgian-French-language broadcasts. It was used as a calling sign for programmes broadcast to occupied Europe. And for any German listeners with a knowledge of classical music, there was the added frisson of Beethoven's original description of the motif: 'Thus Fate knocks at the door'.

'Ici Londres,' the announcer intoned. 'Les Français parlent aux Français.' The news was then read out by Bruce Belfage, an actor turned newsreader, whose buoyant tone was reassuringly familiar to listeners everywhere. Belfage exuded calm in real life as well as on the airwaves. In October 1940, BBC Broadcasting House was famously hit by a delayed-action 225kg German bomb which exploded while Belfrage was reading the nine o'clock news. Wiping the plaster and soot off his script, Belfrage carried on reading the bulletin.

Following the end of the news, Belfrage concluded by saying, 'voici quelques messages personnels...' One of those listening carefully to the stream of seemingly nonsensical messages was Joanna Townsend, Private Secretary to the Balkan Editor of the BBC. Townsend had been handling these personal messages for some time without giving them much thought, when she received a message asking if she would like to work for, and be paid by, another organisation while formally

'ICI Londres'

retaining her status as a full-time BBC official. Townsend agreed to attend an interview in Room 238, Hotel Victoria, Whitehall, SW1, by the end of which she had agreed to become a member of the staff of SOE. She was conducted to Baker Street, the SOE Headquarters, and the various Heads of Sections were introduced.

Townsend was given an office and a telephone at Baker Street. Collecting the daily crop of personal messages and collating them, she would make her way to Bush House, home of the BBC European Service after bombs had damaged Broadcasting House during the Blitz. In her now secondary role of BBC official, she presented the various announcers with their relevant transmission. At 1930, and again at 2115 when the broadcast was repeated, she'd listen carefully to each message, checking for accuracy and volume.

Also listening carefully were those in France for whom the *messages personnels* were anything but nonsensical. In December 1940, when they heard the message 'Alfred de Musset est un Grand Poète', this wasn't the start of literary discussion over a great French writer, but the signal that OVERCLOUD II, one of the first missions that the 15th MGBF was involved in, was on.

*

The first phase of an operation involved the DDOD(I) Headquarters in Palace Street, in conjunction with whichever of the clandestine services was involved and, via their radio link, with the réseau in

Joël Le Tac

Brittany. Together they would decide that sea-transport was needed to infiltrate or collect agents or mail or pick up escapers. There might also be a requirement to land weapons, ammunition and explosives, radio sets or money. At this point, the proposed operation would be given a code name.

OVERCLOUD II was the second operation as part of setting up the OVERCLOUD network in France. Instrumental to this were the Le Tac brothers, Yves and Joël, who were early resisters. They had escaped to Britain after the fall of France in 1940 and were quickly recruited into SOE RF Section. They took part in two early operations for SOE: SAVANNAH, an attempt to kill the pilots of Kampfgeschwader 100, a German pathfinder squadron leading night raids on Britain; and JOSEPHINE B, a successful attack on an electrical transformer station near Bordeaux which disrupted U-boat operations.

Joël Le Tac volunteered to go back to France to build up an organisation through which people could covertly be passed into and out of the country – which would become the OVERCLOUD network. Le Tac's parents were both teachers and had a holiday villa at Sant-Pabu, a village on the north-western tip of the Breton peninsula. Consequently, the family knew the area well. The Le Tac family were enthusiastic resisters, though unbeknownst to the British, they had already come to the attention of the Germans. Madame Le Tac and her future daughter-in-law Andrée had been briefly detained for trying to help a British pilot who had come down in the sea. Clearly, this was not an ideal start for a clandestine intelligence network.

On 14 October 1941 Joël Le Tac had been put ashore in Operation OVERCLOUD I. This mission had been conducted by Gerry Holdsworth of SOE, not the 15th MGBF, with radio operator Comte de Kergorlay. The pair had come ashore on a pair of canoes lashed together as an improvised catamaran. This gave the stability needed to carry the heavy, precious radio set and allowed Le Tac to concentrate on navigation while de Kergorlay, who had no natural skill with boats, simply paddled. Together with his brother Yves (and with some help from their mother) they set up the OVERCLOUD network around the north west of Brittany. On 30 December 1941, OVERCLOUD II was to drop an agent for the Free French Intelligence Service (BCRA), Pierre Movreaux. The drop-off would be by dinghy at Île Guénnoc, in the Aber-Wrac'h channel – an area with which the Flotilla would become very familiar.

*

For missions involving SOE agents, those involved were called to Flat 6, Orchard Court, on the Baker Street side of Portman Square, for a final briefing. It was the last place the agents would see before departing for the field, and in intelligence circles was famous for what at the time was seen as a very louche black marble bathroom with a bidet. Arthur Park, gatekeeper at Orchard Court, was described by Buckmaster as an 'amiable Cerberus' and by Noreen Riols as 'one of nature's gentlemen'.[14] Park had worked in the Paris branch of the Westminster bank in the 1930s. He had left France in 1940, leaving behind his French wife. Too old to enlist, he was recruited by SOE.

According to Buckmaster, Park 'knew every agent by his training pseudonym and made each one personally welcome when they arrived at the flat for briefing. His cheerful countenance was beloved by all the members of the French section and his tact was responsible for avoiding many awkward meetings between men who were not supposed to know each other's appearance. We wanted to discourage our men from meeting each other in the field and the best way to do that was to see that they did not meet each other in England more

14 Conversation between the author and Noreen Riols. Noreen Riols joined SOE in 1943 and was a lifelong friend of Arthur Park.

Orchard Court

Vera Atkins

than we could help. Park would spirit people from room to room in the nick of time.'

Park's people skills were crucial in maintaining mission secrecy: 'There was one thing which was absolutely against orders, that was to tell anyone where one was going. There was a particular danger of this happening when two agents met in the flat and knew that they were due to be sent at the same time. Park tried his best to stop them knowing this. In general, he succeeded admirably, his tact and popularity enabling him to move people from briefing room to briefing room (and into the bathroom) with the agility of the characters of French farce.'

As the agents waited in Orchard Court they went over the details of their cover story, the person named on the identity cards and ration books they carried. It was crucial that the names of fictitious family members, schools attended, birth dates and anniversaries, professional identity and job history would automatically be produced instead of their real ones when they were questioned.

Vera Atkins, Buckmaster's Personal Assistant and central to the running of F Section, saw all of the agents who left for France. She made arrangements for letters to be sent to relatives while they were out of touch, taking charge of the wills they drew up and of personal possessions left behind. She would brief the agents on what to expect once they landed. Atkins continually collected scraps of detailed information about changes in the necessary documents and the conditions of daily life, such as regulations about curfew, travel, the workplace. This information came first from refugees and later from agents returning from the field and were crucial details that could keep an agent alive. It took an enormous amount of research to prepare someone to be unobtrusive – particularly when that someone was not a native of the country or had not lived there for long periods of time. Something as simple as looking the wrong way before crossing the street or the way you used your knife and fork, how you held a cigarette, all could arouse suspicion. F Section collected all sorts of ephemera to add to the supposed French citizen's wallet: reassuring photos of putative relatives, postmarked letters from old friends in other cities, Métro tickets, sales slips from French shops.

Appearance also played a vital role and SOE went to considerable effort to ensure that agents were not given away by their clothing. They established a clothing depot – Station XVA at 56 Queens Gate, SW7 – where former property buyers from the film world, under the command of Captain Kim More,[15] were recruited as buyers. A tailor's shop was established at 24/30 Great Titchfield Street just behind Oxford Circus, and another in Whitechapel was presided over by a Jewish refugee from Vienna named Haar, staffed by refugees to start providing exact replicas of European clothing. Later, when demand exceeded the capacity of their tailoring shops, several firms were vetted and recruited to help, notably Lejb Minc, a Polish tailor of 4 Savile Row.

Continental and English styles of clothing were unmistakably different, and the tiniest details – the way buttons were stitched, or a shirt collar was set – could betray you on inspection. The Security Service MI5 helped by donating the personal effects of suspects, spies and internees. The buying team, too, made the rounds of foreign communities, persuading refugees to part with used suits or dresses from which the labels could be removed and copied for an added touch of authenticity.

'I wore them regularly on trips to London,' recalled Richard Heslop (XAVIER), 'so that they would not look too new when I arrived in France. The labels of a well-known French tailor were sewn in, and I memorised the name of the tailor and the place where I was supposed

15 Believed to be an alias for another Jewish refugee who was made an honorary Captain in SOE.

to have bought them. My French wardrobe was complete down to pants, vests, socks, shoes, ties, razor blades, pocketknife, fountain pen, and pencil. I was given French matches and lighter, cigarettes, and cigarette papers – in France at that time you never threw away a dog-end. They were all stored away in a little box and re-rolled later.'

George Langelaan (LANGDON) also described how 'an expert spectacle-maker made up for me a pair of spectacles with real French hinges, and the glasses of which really corrected a slight defect of my sight. My hair had not been cut for weeks and a few days before the date fixed, a French hairdresser had given me a special haircut.'

The other critical factor in an agent's preparation was documentation. '[They] bent the corners of my identity card and ration card and chewed them for a while to soften them a little,' Langelaan recalled on preparation of his papers. 'Another man was ironing various other documents, letters and photos that are generally to be found in a man's wallet; this helped to make them yellow with age. Others in the room continually folded and unfolded documents to replicate years of use.'

To make sure that false identities couldn't be checked against real records, name and identities were borrowed from towns where it was known that the municipal archives had been destroyed in the early months of the war. But there was still a great deal to absorb and learn and make second nature before a new identity became natural: 'For several weeks now,' Langelaan remembered, 'I had been learning all about my new person and personality, the various members of my family, and of course my family history… I had a photo of myself in a French uniform and standing arm in arm with a postman, my sister's brother who had been killed in a dive-bombing attack near Lille. The picture had been taken shortly before and, of course, no one could tell that the be-whiskered French postman with his oblong box was in truth an Englishman who could not speak a word of French.'

*

At the same time as agents were being prepared for operations in London, so planning was moving through the gears for the sea transfer. As the night of the operation approached, operation orders were prepared by DDOD(I)'s office. Ship-to-shore recognition signals and their replies were agreed with the customer service and, through them, signalled to the field. From the shore these were usually by a dimmed flashlight of agreed colours, but various forms of secure walkie-talkie radio-telephone link were used increasingly as the equipment became available to both parties. Dummy operation orders were also prepared to be carried on the MGB so that, in case of capture, there would be a cover story to explain her presence and safeguard the network. Real and dummy orders would be taken (sealed) by a Staff Officer from London and delivered to Ted Davis in Dartmouth a day before the sailing date, or one of the Navigating Officers might travel to London to collect them.

On one occasion a junior staff officer was entrusted with this most secret delivery assignment to Dartmouth. He found his reserved seat on the train at Paddington, placed his locked briefcase on it and reckoned he had just enough time to grab a sandwich and a cup of coffee at the station waiting room. Unfortunately, there was a queue, the guard's whistle blew and, before he could reach it, the train was pulling out on its way to Kingswear. Thankfully, the Special Branch intercepted the train at Exeter and the briefcase was duly delivered to Dartmouth the same evening. But the officer concerned was found alternative employment.

While this was going on, an MGB, a landing party, a Conducting Officer and a Navigating Officer would all be allocated, and preparation continued apace. The MGB was readied for the operation. All compasses were corrected for deviation errors, engines and communications systems were tested and retested, guns, echo-sounder and radio were checked. Although luck played a big part in the success or otherwise of a mission, as little as possible was left to chance. There is a very true military adage – the Seven Ps – 'Prior Planning and Preparation Prevents Piss Poor Performance.'

The officer in charge of the landing party would make sure that his surf-boats and equipment were in perfect condition and that his boats' crews were ready for all eventualities, including shipwreck. The Navigating Officer consulted his charts and navigational tables.

He'd check details such as sunrise and sunset, moonrise and moonset, and tidal information: the bible here was Captain O. M. Watts's Almanac, the indispensable guide for sailors preparing a voyage anywhere in British and Atlantic waters from the Northern Isles to Gibraltar and the Azores. Long- and short-range weather forecasts were studied, and air photograph coverage of the pinpoint area was given detailed examination.

On the day of departure, agents were driven to Orchard Court in the afternoon prior to leaving to change into their operational clothing. (In 1943, when things began to 'hot up' for SOE, the facilities at Orchard Court became rather strained, and the overflow of agents was taken to another SOE flat, at 32 Wimpole Street.) When they got to the flat, their new outfits would be waiting for them. After changing, their uniform and personal effects were packed into a suitcase and placed in a locker to await their return – or, should they not return, to be sent to their next of kin. The agents' Conducting Officer would go through their pockets to make sure there were no overlooked English coins, matchbooks or bus tickets (later in Dartmouth they were checked again like soldiers going on patrol that 'they neither rattled nor shone'). This whirlwind of preparation helped to keep the fears and concerns of the departing agents at bay. Brian Stonehouse (CELESTIN) a young man in his early twenties at the time, remembers thinking before leaving for occupied France, 'My God, what the hell am I doing here? How did I get myself into this?' He still went.[16]

Towards the end of the afternoon, Buckmaster or Vera Atkins would arrive at Orchard Court to see the departing agents, now dressed in their field clothes. Buckmaster always gave each agent a present: gold pen, cigarette case or cufflinks for the men and a gold pen or powder compact for the women, 'Just to let you know we shall be thinking of you. You can always hock it if you get yourself into a tight hole and need money in a hurry.' They were given a sum of counterfeit French money and a small suitcase crammed with tins of food, cigarettes and chocolate, which could be used for bargaining, since such luxuries were almost unobtainable in France.

16 Stonehouse was a friend of the author. Personal conversation.

Palm Court Hotel Torquay

Kinsgwear Station

Some agents took a pistol and a Fairbairn-Sykes fighting knife. Some refused to take them as they felt that carrying a weapon of any sort would compromise them immediately.

Procedure complete, the agents were sent on their way to a holding area at the Palm Court Hotel in Torquay or direct from Paddington to Kingswear Station. A station wagon would arrive to collect the agent – rather irreverently called 'The Hearse'.[17] It was time to say 'Au revoir' and add the well-known word of Cambronne at his surrender at Waterloo: 'Merde'. This had somehow come to mean – 'pour porter bonheur' – to bring good luck (the equivalent of actors saying 'break a leg').

*

The main railway line from London to Kingswear was opened in 1864. The Dartmouth and Torbay Railway owned the station and opened what was then the Yacht Club Hotel at the immediate southern end of the station in 1866. The Dartmouth and Torbay Railway was amalgamated into the Great Western Railway on 1 February 1876, with the hotel later renamed the Royal Dart Yacht Club and Family Hotel. The Yacht Club has its club room in the hotel.

By the time of the war, the hotel had taken a secondary role to housing holidaymakers. As recorded in the Naval Officer in Charge's fortnightly report of events to CINC Plymouth, dated 4 June 1941, 'The Royal Dart Hotel Kingswear was requisitioned for the new site of HMS BRITANNIA III Coastal Forces Base Dartmouth.' Almost immediately it became HMS CICALA, the headquarters of the 15th

17 One of the regular 'Hearse' drivers was Mary Rogers who came from Torcross, near Dartmouth.

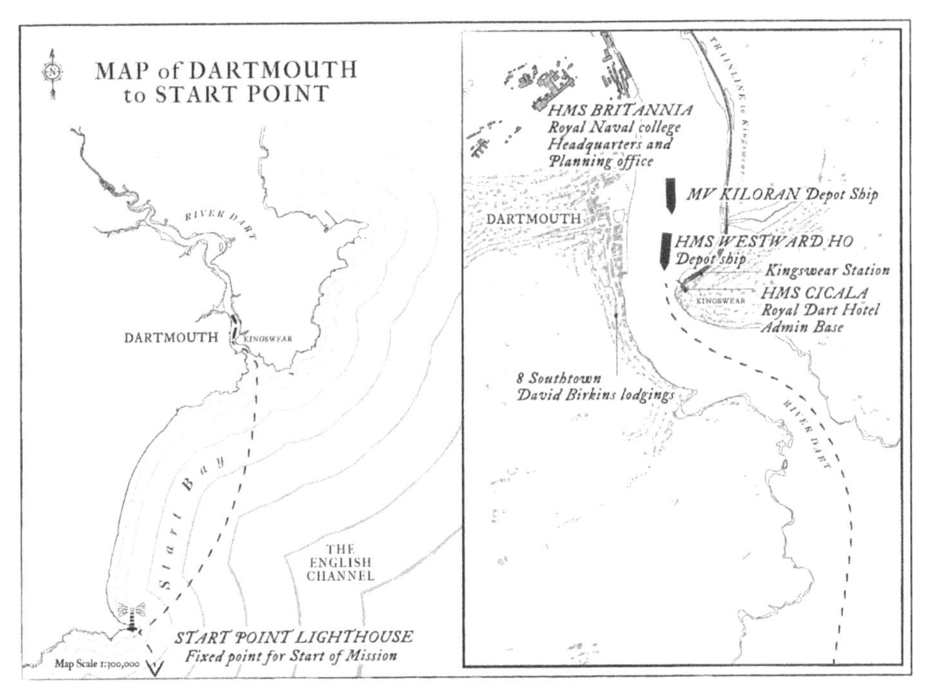

Map of Dartmouth

MGBF.[18] The building was closed to the public with an unusual exception: the downstairs bar was still open to the public. According to Reg Little, who was a teenage Civil Defence first aider in Kingswear at the time, 'We knew about the Free French Flotilla, but nothing about the 15th Flotilla and what it got up to because we thought it was all part and parcel of the same thing. The 15th operated from the old paddle steamer, *Westward Ho*, which was their depot ship. We used to hear the boats going in and out at night when they started up their engines, but we thought they were just doing normal patrols.' Little's father-in-law, Ted Willing, used to keep the bar at the Royal Dart Hotel: 'I only found out recently that one of the chaps from the Flotilla used to be given a cider bottle with gin in it which he sipped before going out on a mission. But everything about the Flotilla was kept very hush-hush, even long after the war.'

18 At some point in 1943, during one of William Joyce's (Lord Haw-Haw) propaganda broadcasts, he announced that 'HMS CICALA' had been sunk by a German U-boat, causing much mirth in the Flotilla.

HMS CICALA – the Royal Dart Hotel

While the Flotilla headquarters and offices were in HMS CICALA and Ted Davis's planning office at HMS BRITANNIA – the Naval College – there was need for a depot ship and accommodation. Some officers like Ted Davis, Jan McQuoid Mason and latterly David Birkin lived ashore with their wives. Initially, a very luxurious converted motor yacht, which belonged to Lord Strathcona, the *Kiloran*, was used but as the Flotilla grew, there was a need for a larger depot ship that could be moored mid-stream in the Dart, to enhance security. It could also be used as a floating jetty for the gunboats to moor alongside, and a secure place to bring agents prior to departure, where they could be briefed on the operation and then step straight on to the gunboat just before leaving.

The *Westward Ho* was a civilian paddle steamer built in 1894 by Samuel McKnight and Co. on the Clyde. She was requisitioned as an auxiliary minesweeper in 1914 and released back to her owners, Paul A. Campbell and Co. Cardiff, in 1919. She was requisitioned again in 1939 and resumed her role as a minesweeper and took part in the Dunkirk evacuation. She then served as an anti-aircraft ship until being handed over to DDOD(I). She was commissioned as the 15 MGBF depot ship on 1 January 1944. There was an attempt by the Admiralty Director of Personnel Services to use civilians as crew, but this was refused by DDOD(I) on security grounds. The crew of *Westward Ho* consisted of four officers under the command of Lieutenant Ferbrache, four Petty Officers and thirty-three other ranks. The Flotilla also had an additional one officer, seven Petty

Kiloran, first depot ship

Westward Ho, depot ship

Officers and four other ranks as base support staff, based in HMS CICALA.

The crews used to spend most of their time in the gunboats as they were moored alongside the paddle steamer, but they did go into local pubs to let their hair down – with strict orders not to discuss their secret activities. Frank Jones, a Petty Officer mechanic who carried out seven missions on MGB 502, said: 'We slept on the boat with four of us sleeping to a cabin. The boats had crews of just over thirty men. The agents looked like ordinary people and they would stay at local hotels and come on board about an hour before we set off. We were never allowed to talk to them.'

The proximity of the station and the pontoon proved to be very useful in the transfer of agents or returning POWs, and the maintenance of the security of the operation. Once at Kingswear they would walk the short distance to the jetty with their Conducting Officer. They were then ferried to *Westward Ho* by small launches crewed by WRNS and taken below. Here they were searched yet again to make sure they had not left something compromising in a pocket. Every possible precaution was taken to make absolutely sure that during the journey down from London they had not inadvertently slipped something into a pocket that would give them away.

David Birkin lived ashore in a boarding house at 8 Southtown overlooking the harbour and mouth of the River Dart, run by a Mrs Radcliffe. Before leaving his lodgings for a night at sea, he would tell his landlady that he was 'out for the night fire-watching on the roof of the Naval College'. Once when he came back from an operation looking very much worse for wear, she remarked 'yew bin doin tew much o'that fire watchin ...' Birkin was sure that Mrs Radcliffe thought that 'fire-watching' was a code for an orgy of WRNS and rum.

WRNS crewing transfer boats

David Birkin and Judy Campbell's wedding, 9 November 1943

Mrs Radcliffe was clearly quite tricky and did not like married couples for some reason. Which became a problem when David Birkin married Judy Campbell on 9 November 1943. Judy Campbell was a well-known and popular actress who, in addition to her acting, and being Noël Coward's leading lady, became famous for the first performance of 'A Nightingale Sang in Berkeley Square'.[19] At first, Judy Campbell knew nothing of David's night-time activities on the Brittany coast. She had bought the cover story about normal coastal defence work in the Channel. However, a fellow actor let slip that the sailors at Dartmouth were up to skulduggery on the French coast. The penny dropped. She rang David, who was furious, exclaiming 'what bloody fool told you that'.

Judy Campbell was able to come down from London between her shows as she had a special pass to visit Dartmouth. They were better off than some as David was paid a marriage allowance, and danger money. Early in 1944, they moved from Mrs Radcliffe's to the Riversea Hotel on the Kingswear side of the Dart, and had a marvellous balconied double room overlooking the mouth of the river. This afforded David a chance to recuperate between gruelling missions.

When not in Dartmouth, Judy wrote to him or sent a telegram nearly every day, in spite of her hectic schedule. Letters were sent from all over England, from the Savoy Hotel, the White Hart in Salisbury, Ye

19 Written in Le Lavandou in the South of France by Eric Maschwitz with music by Manning Sherwin, and performed in a local bar. It was published in 1940 and performed by Judy Campbell in the London revue *New Faces* at the Comedy Theatre.

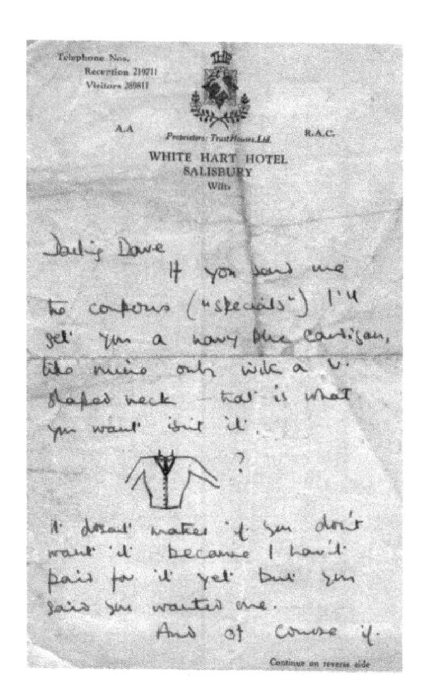
Telephone Nos.
Reception 219711
Visitors 289811

A.A. R.A.C.

Proprietors: Trust Houses Ltd.

WHITE HART HOTEL
SALISBURY
Wilts

Darling Dave

If you send me two coupons ("specials") I'll get you a navy blue cardigan, like mine only with a V. shaped neck – that is what you want isn't it.

?

It doesn't matter if you don't want it because I haven't paid for it yet but you said you wanted one.

And of course if.

Continue on reverse side

Judy Campbell

Olde Woolpack in Warwick, her dressing room in Southsea and the Duchess Theatre in London.

Theirs was an intense affair. After a year they married at Bray, in the church where they had first met, and went on to have a lasting marriage, unlike many wartime romances. They were an exotic couple. David often wore an eye patch and some of her letters to him begin 'Darling Pirate', and she once threatened to address the envelopes to 'Lieutenant Blood'. She also kept him supplied with some of the essentials of life, sending him pipe cleaners and stylish jumpers.

Judy Campbell wasn't the only link between the Flotilla and the theatre. 718's Skipper, Ronnie Seddon, had been an actor at the Liverpool Rep, and had good connections in the theatre world. When operations and training allowed, he and Guy Hamilton would regularly travel to London for parties and to see their girlfriends who were Windmill Girls. Since the early 1930s, the Windmill Theatre in Great Windmill Street, London, had been famous for its nude tableaux vivants, but also for the wartime boast 'we never closed', which wits inevitably rewrote as 'we never clothed'.

Seddon persuaded the Windmill to 'adopt' 718. The Windmill Girls

took their adoption of 718 seriously. They raised money to buy presents for the boat and crew and if any of the crew called at the stage door in London they were well looked after. John Townend described them as 'super people'. The Windmill Girls gave 718 a battery-operated radio – then very hard to come by. As 718 was coming back into Dartmouth on 6 June they heard the news of D-Day on this radio which was playing on the bridge.

On one eventful occasion Seddon and Hamilton had persuaded the Windmill Girls to take their next break in Torquay and come to Dartmouth to visit the boat. Townend remembers, 'one lovely Saturday it was announced at 1100 we would be invaded by some of the ravishing beauties from the latest production. Everything was polished and everyone was looking his best when the boat came alongside. The girls in their summer dresses looked delicious and, as I led them down the ladder to the ward-room, their scent filled the air. They had never been aboard such a small craft before and were amazed how civilised we were! Naval size gin and tonics were poured and as soon as the Coxswain had issued the men with their rum ration the whole party moved forward on to the mess deck. I had volunteered to act as Officer of the Day and having seen everyone "looked after" went on deck to smoke a cigarette.

'The party was a huge success, and, after lunch, it was suggested that I might like to row a few of them up the river. Naturally I was pleased to do so, until I found that the only takers were the two male dancers! Too late to back down, I had a rather awkward hour's rowing. It seemed to me that my passengers were rather more interested in my own "lovely shoulders and strong arms" than they were in the scenery! I cut short the exploratory row by an hour. When I entered the ward-room earlier than expected, Guy was quite upset!' Two of those ladies on board were Joan Rock and Charmian Innes who became big stars after the war.

*

By operation day, the Navigating Officer would have spent considerable time preparing the route to the pinpoint. To quote David Birkin, 'I always had a disturbed and almost sleepless night before the fateful day. When sleep did come, it took the form of nightmares involving navigational errors of every description. For days before, one had pored over Channel and local charts so intensely that every island, bay or rock in the vicinity of the pinpoint was imprinted on one's over-sensitive brain, so that when sleep came rocks assumed sinister shapes of enormous proportions. Even their names conjured up horrible visions – Le Crapaud, Le Mouton Noir, Les Boeufs, Méan Névez – all sent shivers down my unconscious spine.'

That final morning was spent in the office checking and rechecking calculations. An hour-and-a-half before departure, which in autumn and winter was usually between 1600 and 1800 (GMT +2), to ensure that the gunboat would not be more than half-way to France before darkness fell, the Navigating Officer and mission Conducting Officer would be ferried across the harbour to *Westward Ho*. All the officers taking part would attend a final briefing in the wardroom, at which the latest intelligence reports relating to the operation area would be discussed in detail, photographic reconnaissance coverage and likely enemy shipping movements would be studied, while ill-timed jokes from those not actually going on the operation would fail to raise smiles from those who were. Ted Davis was particularly well known for his jarring schoolboy humour.

Ten minutes before sailing any agents due to be landed went discreetly on board the MGB with their Conducting Officer and containers of stores would be stowed on deck. The Navigating Officer would have a brief talk with the ratings on the mess deck, indicating in fairly general terms the area of the operation in case of disaster and their being left ashore in enemy-held territory.

David Birkin sketch

At exactly the appointed time, mooring lines would be cast off, the engines would bark into action and slowly the ships – usually alone, but sometimes in company with a second gunboat from the Flotilla – would move off downstream into the gathering darkness of a winter evening. The crew stood to attention along the ship's rail. Until silence became a necessity, their progress would be accompanied by the strains of the ship's radio. On one occasion when leaving on a Sunday, David Birkin recalls clearly hearing the congregation of St Saviour's Church in Dartmouth singing the hymn 'For those in peril on the sea ...' But the crew's usual accompaniment on pulling out was the voice of Vera Lynn. As the boat made its way to the departure position off Start Point, the ship's guns would be tested. Then the radio was switched off and the crew and agents were left with their own thoughts and trepidations, above the rumble of the engine and the silence of the sea.

318 leaving Dartmouth

CHAPTER 4 – DEAD RECKONING

'Subtle, so subtle! To the point of being invisible.
Sublime, so sublime to the point of being silent'

Sun Tzu

By the time the French coast began to loom, everyone involved in OVERCLOUD II was silent. The constant chat and discussion on board 314 had dribbled to a halt. The only people speaking now were those issuing necessary commands. All operational chat was conducted in whispers.

Ten miles to land. The speed of the MGB was reduced, dropping from eighteen knots to ten. Hearts were in mouths. This band of water was the German convoy coastal route. Horizons were scanned for signs of ships. Ears were pinned back for any engine noise. Keen noses, as they'd done throughout the trip, were sniffing the air for any hint of oil, a tell-tale sign of a German submarine on the surface.

For the navigator and crew, there was an added challenge: a fierce tidal stream that swept parallel to the coastline and reached over six knots at spring tides. To counter this, the MGB had to manoeuvre itself inwards crab-wise to maintain position. Getting dragged on the tidal stream could leave the boat up to six miles off target. For the navigator, with nothing but an unfamiliar coastline and the pitch black of the night to go on, and with limited navigational aids to work with, this was a tall order to ensure the boat was still on target.

Somehow, the 314 found its way. The Aber-Benoît estuary at the north-western tip of the Breton peninsula is studded with rocks and very exposed to westerly and north-westerly winds. However, it possessed natural advantages for clandestine operations by sea in the shape of three rocky islets – Guénnoc, Tariec and Rosservor – none of which was permanently occupied by the Germans. Tariec and Rosservor were accessible from the mainland on foot at low tide. All three were used for landing pick-up operations at various times during the German occupation, though boat work was often difficult because of the exposed conditions and strong tidal streams.

The Petite-Fourche marker buoy was spotted and passed. One mile to the pinpoint and rendezvous. Now all eyes were scanning the headland. The crew and navigator had done their job. On board, the ship's 'cargo', Free French Intelligence Service (BCRA) agent, Pierre Movreaux, was wearing his waterproof cape, to ensure that his clothes weren't damaged by spray stains. The short, final leg of the journey to France would be by surf-boat.

Lieutenant Dunstan Curtis, the ship's commander, watched and waited. He was looking for a signal, a flash from the blue torch. But the looming shadows of the French coastline stayed silent. He checked the time. They were on schedule. The navigator checked the location. Yes, they were at the pinpoint. Right place, right time. No response. As the minutes ticked on, the unease for the crew began to creep up. The longer they sat there, the longer they were exposed. They could only wait so long – the boat had to be heading back, putting at least thirty miles between itself and the coastline, before dawn came up.

Curtis exhaled deeply. No one likes coming so far, getting so close. What had gone wrong? The coded message had been read out on the BBC to say that tonight was the night. But it was no good. That flash of blue light he was desperate to see was not forthcoming. With a shrug of the shoulders and a shake of the head to Pierre Movreaux, the agent to be landed, he made the only decision he could. To return back to Dartmouth, mission unaccomplished. They'd have to rerun the German gauntlet the following night and hope that this time, the hazardous 100-mile journey was more successful.

*

'Never put any faith in Navigational Aids,' David Birkin wrote in his navigational notebook as a reminder. 'Invariably they fail when most needed. Dead Reckoning is the only sure means of position finding and a meticulously kept log book should be the navigator's bible for with it he is never lost. Courses to be steered are calculated using the following factors: The compass course(s), distance travelled over the sea bed (from the ship's speed), and allowances for the tidal streams affecting the vessel (and the wind).'

Lieutenant Dunstan Curtis

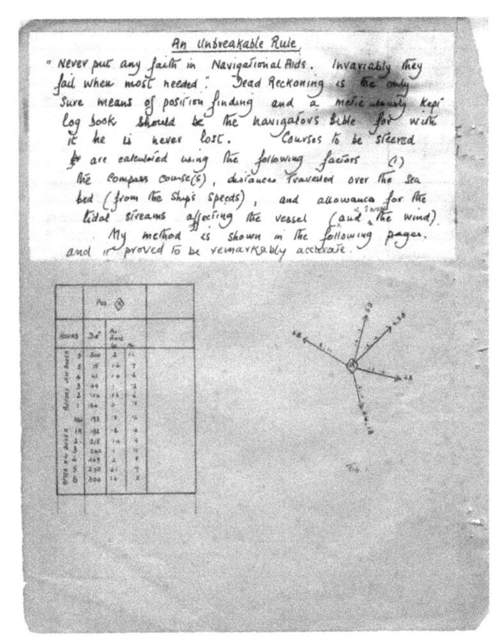

An Unbreakable Rule

" Never put any faith in Navigational Aids. Invariably they fail when most needed." Dead Reckoning is the only sure means of position finding and a meticulously kept log book should be the navigators bible for with it he is never lost. Courses to be steered are calculated using the following factors (1) the compass course(s), distance travelled over the sea bed (from the ship's speeds), and allowance for the tidal streams affecting the vessel (and the wind).
My method is shown in the following pages and it proved to be remarkably accurate.

David Birkin's golden rule

The run from Dartmouth to the Brittany coast was about 100 miles. But 'as sailed' – given tide, current, wind – the actual distance would be greater. The ideal weather conditions were a slightly choppy sea and overcast sky, but they seldom prevailed. Usually it was either too smooth and starlit or too rough for personal comfort and for boat work, and there was the occasional unexpected south-westerly gale for good measure.

Beginning at Start Point, a course would be set to the selected fixed object, and from there on to the pinpoint. An accurate compass fix of the departure position was vital and by no means easy when the weather was poor and visibility bad. A compass error of 2 degrees could set them 5 miles off course and a miscalculation of the tides put them on the rocks. In winter, mist and spray often obscured Start Point. On those occasions, the boats got as close to the headland as possible and prayed for a quick sighting. Usually, the dim gaunt shape of the lighthouse was visible for long enough to get a quick bearing and to judge its distance. Then, they would turn on to the pre-calculated course.

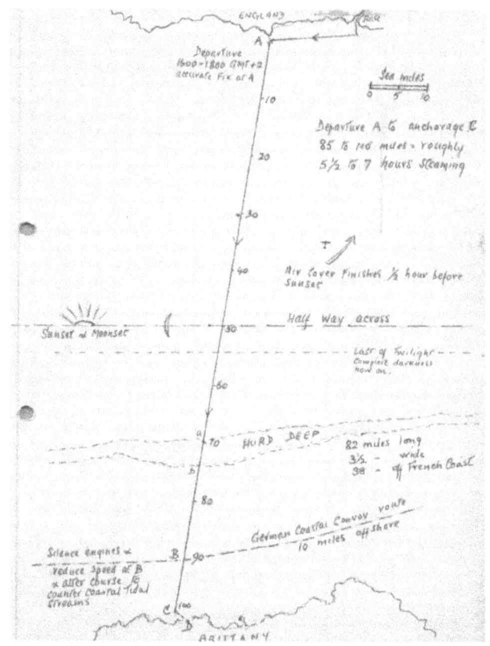

David Birkin's cross-Channel navigation schematic

Start Point Lighthouse looking south towards Brittany

'Directly an operation was "on",' Birkin wrote, 'I would settle down with charts of different scales covering the pinpoint area chosen for the cross-Channel journey and work out the allowance to be made for the tidal stream affecting our course to the pinpoint. Actually I worked on two courses (i) From the departure position off the English coast – i.e. a fix on either Start Point Lighthouse or the Lizard Head – to a position 10 miles off the Breton coast, where the MGB had to reduce speed and silence engines to cross the German convoy route; and (ii) 10 miles off the coast to the anchorage. For the final 10-mile approach a far greater allowance had to be made for the much stronger tidal stream which, at spring tides, sweeps along the French coast at up to 5 or 6 knots. Extra allowance had to be made for excessive wind etc. As mentioned before, the course from England was to some identifiable rock near the pinpoint or, in the case of Île Guénnoc, La Petite Fourche buoy.'

The Flotilla was forbidden from using radar as its active electronic signal could be picked up by German ships or monitoring stations.

However, they could use the QH positioning system, otherwise known as the Decca Navigating System.[20] The system was invented in the US, but development was carried out by Decca in the UK. It was first deployed by the Royal Navy during World War II when the Allied forces needed a system which could be used to achieve accurate landings and was not known to the Germans and thus free of jamming. The system involved the use of fixed radio beacons transmitting a continuous leave signal from which a ship could fix its position. They were based at Chichester, Swanage and Beachy Head. The Flotilla used the system with varying success, but the system eventually proved its worth in supporting mine clearance activity for the D-Day landings.

After a six-hour passage during which the QH position-finding system might or might not be working, an approximate position check could also be derived from the echo-sounder when crossing the Hurd Deep, a depression 138km (86 miles) long stretching from off Alderney to a point 51km (32 miles north) of the Île-de-Batz. At their usual point of crossing from Dartmouth, it was about 2½ miles wide and gave a dramatic increase of soundings on entering and an equally sudden decrease on leaving. One could also make an inspired guess at one's position from the time it took to cross. David Birkin wrote that, 'The main factor which had to be taken into account on our "night return" journeys to occupied Brittany was the tidal streams which ran at right angles to our cross-Channel courses and which became progressively fiercer as the French coast got closer – especially this was the case in the approach to L'Aber-Wrac'h where the influence of the Ushant Race made itself felt.'

The skill of the navigator in getting the boats to the correct position should not be underestimated. Due to the clandestine nature of the operations they all took place on moonless nights, usually in very poor weather. No star fixes were possible. Birkin was one of the best: his mathematical talent, artistic nature and ability to draw clearly and accurately helped him to design his own methodology. Birkin's system was based on 'dead reckoning'. He would gather information

20 Extensively developed after the war for aircraft and shipping. Decca led the field against stiff competition from the LORAN-C developed in 1976. Both systems were replaced by GPS in the 1980s.

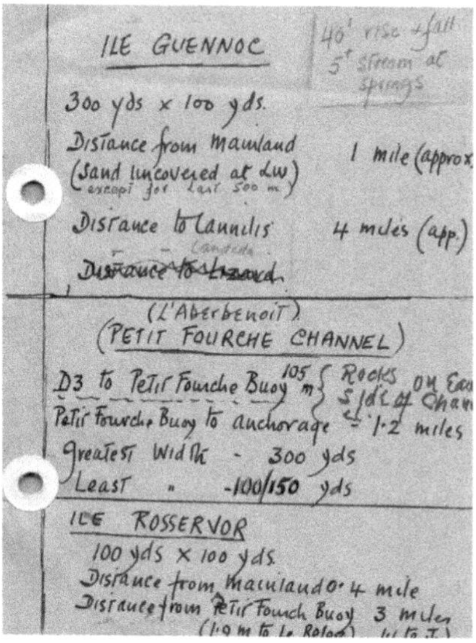

ILE GUENNOC

40' rise + fall
5' stream at springs

300 yds x 100 yds.
Distance from mainland 1 mile (approx
(Sand uncovered at LW)
(except for last 500 m)
Distance to Lannilis 4 miles (app.)
~~Distance to Lanvand.~~

(L'Aberbenoit)
(PETIT FOURCHE CHANNEL)

D3 to Petit Fourche Buoy 105 m } Rocks on Ea[st] side of Chan[nel]
Petit Fourche Buoy to anchorage } 1·2 miles
Greatest Width - 300 yds
Least " -100/150 yds

ILE ROSSERVOR
100 yds x 100 yds.
Distance from mainland 0·4 mile
Distance from Petit Fourch Buoy 3 miles

David Birkin navigating notes

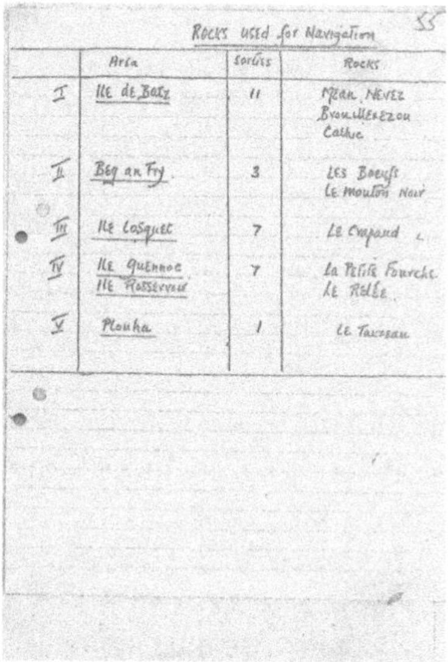

Rocks used for Navigation 55

	Area	Sorties	Rocks
I	Ile de Batz	11	Méan Névez Brouillerezou Cathie
II	Beg an Fry	3	Les Boeufs Le Mouton Noir
III	Ile Losquet	7	Le Crapaud
IV	Ile Guennoc Ile Rosservor	7	La Petite Fourche Le Relée
V	Plouha	1	Le Taureau

David Birkin rock markers

from charts and air photographs, tide tables in the Channel and along the Brittany coast. He would then select a fixed object, normally a very prominent rock or buoy. He would calculate the height of water on or above the rock at the time that the MGB intended to get there. From this fixed or known point he would then lay off a course to the pinpoint. These rocks became very important as they were about the only way one could identify exactly where you were on a coastline in the pitch dark and usually in very poor weather. Each pinpoint had its seaward marker: L'Aber W'rach estuary, La Petite Fourche Buoy and Le Relée, Île de Bas/Grac'h Zu Beach – Méan Névez 1 mile to seaward; Beg-an-Fry, Les Boeufs three-quarters of a mile to seaward; Île Losquet, Le Crapaud, and the Anse-Cochat, Le Toreau.

The conditions that the Navigating Officer had to work in were vile. The gunboats, particularly 318 in which Birkin did many operations, were extremely uncomfortable thanks to their shallow drafts. The bridge was ten foot by six foot and had to accommodate five people. At the back of the bridge and down a short flight of steps was the chart room, which was even smaller, approximately six foot by six foot. It was connected to the bridge by a voice pipe. The Navigating Officer had to constantly go backwards and forwards between the

David Birkin

chart room and the bridge. At the top of the ladder was a bullet-proof steel door.

With under six feet of headroom in the chart room and with Birkin well over average height, this represented a grim place to work: 'a model of idiotic planning' as he described it. Two paces back from the chart-table, which was designed to be collapsible, and in rough weather invariably did just that, was an open, man-sized hole from which a ten-rung ladder led down to the mess deck: Birkin described it as 'a vicious mantrap sprung for action'. Up through the same hole came the smell of stale cabbage and engine oil, guaranteed to bring on seasickness.

The chart room felt more cramped by the amount of equipment it contained. 'Over the chart-table a feeble lamp – the bulb painted red for black-out reasons – just illuminated half a chart of standard size,' Birkin recalled. 'Other fixed objects included an echo-sounder, a magnetic compass, a radar set – never used – a maze of switches and wires, and voice-pipe over the chart-table, connecting with the bridge, down which a Bovril-like mixture of salt water and rust would pour, on to carefully prepared charts and notebooks, reducing them to a pulpy mess.' The moveable features of the chart room were more numerous: dividers, rulers, notebooks and the navigator himself, all of which were constantly thrown around. In a rough sea everything was much worse, and Birkin's seasickness was exacerbated. He described a cycle of 'sick, suck pipe, sick, suck pipe'.

Conditions in the engine room were hellish. The boats were plagued with notoriously unreliable engines which could break down at any stage, especially when required to run at unhealthily low revs for long periods. If malfunctions did occur, engine room crews, well aware of the vital importance of their mission, were obliged to carry out running repairs if the operation was to reach a successful conclusion. Petty Officer Frank Jones, a mechanic who served on 502, recalls that 'the mechanic on 503 was Tommy Barker who was awarded the DSM. You always had to carry a spare cylinder head because they had a habit of going and you needed to replace it straight away. This Tommy did on the way back from a mission when the sea was really rough. He did it without the gun boat stopping – it operated on two of its three engines while he was doing the repairs.'

There were no spittoons or buckets, so crew members were sick on the deck. The smell was often indescribable. Somehow, the look-outs on the bridge also had to keep 'their noses open' as the smell of diesel indicated a submarine on the surface. How they could smell anything over the sick, stale cabbage, and pipe smoke is anyone's guess. Most people were sick on the outbound journey, but very few on the way back so pre-operational nerves may have played a part.

'It was always frightening going to sea,' Birkin admitted, 'but we all rather enjoyed it.'

*

Initially the 15th Motor Gun Boat Flotilla consisted of just two boats: MASB 36 (a small, fast, 63-foot motor anti-submarine boat) and MGB 314 (a 'c' class 110-foot motor gunboat). Each of the boats had a standard crew of three officers, three Petty Officers and twenty-one crew. They were augmented by additional personnel for specific operations as necessary, such as Navigating Officers, Surf-Boat Officers and Conducting Officers.

MASB 36, the first boat to be permanently allocated to the Flotilla, was quickly realised to be unsuitable for cross-Channel clandestine work, not having the speed and seaworthiness. The first operation carried out from Dartmouth took place in December 1941 code named 'CELERY'. It was carried out for Kenneth Cohen of SIS and the Free

French Intelligence Service BCRA with the purpose of clearing a dead letter box of classified mail and dropping an agent, Bernard Paringaux, by kayak. It was carried out by MASB 36. It did not go well. Poor weather, exacerbated by the unsuitability of the boat and a crew lacking in training and discipline, contributed to an inability to find the dead drop. Thereafter, MASB 36 was never used again on cross-Channel ops. Instead, now commanded by Lieutenant John Motherwell from the Canadian Navy, MASB 36 was given liaison duties and more suitable work in Cornwall and the Scilly Isles. She was only to go to France when there were no other large boats available.

Just prior to D-Day, 36 was ordered to Portsmouth. Of the new tasking, Motherwell explained, ‘We were given an important job to do during the invasion of Normandy. On 5 June in Portsmouth the Senior British Intelligence Officer, Colonel Guy Westmacott DSO Grenadier Guards, boarded us. We were ordered to France on 7 June, but a severe storm blew up and we were unable to land the Colonel until June 8th. We spent a most hazardous night on 7 and 8 June when our anchor would not hold, and we were continuously dodging out of control landing craft. We carried him from England to France and back again several times during the beachhead period. We also carried prisoners for interrogation and captured enemy secret material. As soon as Dieppe was cleared of the Germans, we started to run from there to Shoreham, a daily ferry service for secret material and secret people destined for the War Office.’

MASB 36’s service came to an end a few months later: ‘In October 1944 I was granted leave to return to Canada and we were ordered to deliver MASB 36 to Poole for paying off. This we did with considerable sadness, as she served us well, and I was proud of the fact that her hull was as sound as she was when she left the British Power Boats Yard.’

MGB 314, the boat used for OVERCLOUD II, was commanded by Lieutenant Dunstan Curtis. He had been a solicitor before the war and joined the RNVR in 1939. The boat was on loan from Combined Operations, who had agreed to give 314 to DDOD(I) permanently but not until the spring of 1942. MGB was a step up from MASB 36, but was generally regarded as too slow, too small and too unseaworthy.

MGB 314

As the operations continued, DDOD(I) managed to acquire more boats which were suited to this sort of operation.

MGB 318 was allocated to the Flotilla as a replacement for 314, lost on the St Nazaire raid, and she was commanded by Lieutenant Jan McQuoid-Mason with Michael Pollard as First Lieutenant. 318 was to become the workhorse of the Flotilla.

Steven Mackenzie remembered taking Ted Davis to Southampton to see MGB 501, which was being built there. 'She was the first of a flotilla of six MGBs being built by Camper and Nicholson for the Turkish Navy, and the Admiralty had finally decided to requisition them and allocate them to Captain Slocum. MGB 501 was being fitted with petrol engines, but the remaining five boats were to have newly developed high-speed Paxman diesel engines. We were delighted at the prospect of at last having properly equipped MGBs of our own, but things did not turn out so easily.'

Jan McQuoid-Mason

MGB 318

MGB 501 was completed in April 1942 and was based at Dartmouth with Lieutenant Dunstan Curtis in command. But then, on a training run from Dartmouth to the Scilly Isles, with Frank Slocum, Steven Mackenzie and Ted Davis all on board, a sudden explosion blew her in half. The explosion was probably caused by a build-up of petrol vapour in the bilges, although the official report referred to an ammunitions explosion in the magazine. Luckily there were no casualties and the passengers and crew were all rescued. They had been lucky: the entire command structure of DDOD(I) could have been lost at a stroke.

Slocum had to wait until 1943 for MGBs 502 and 503 to join the Flotilla. These MGBs were small but serious vessels of war; their armament amounted to one six- and one two-pounder guns, a twin 20mm anti-aircraft cannon, two twin 5-inch and two 303 machine guns; they had three silenced 1,000hp diesel engines, could cruise

MGB 502

MGB 503

at 21 knots for nearly a thousand miles, could go 6 knots faster for 10-minute spells, and carried a mass of radar and other navigational equipment. They needed it: for even these craft were barely a match for the German 35-knot E-boats that frequently patrolled the Channel coast of France.

MGB 502 was commanded by Lieutenant Commander Peter Williams RNVR, Flotilla Senior Officer, and Lloyd Bott as First Lieutenant. Peter Williams, son of a captain of the Union Castle Line, qualified as a solicitor and joined the RNVR in 1935. He first came to Frank Slocum's attention in October 1941 when he was commanding MGB 325 on temporary loan to DDOD(I). He had great skill and a natural aptitude for clandestine missions. He carried out six successful missions to the French coast. When a vacancy arose at Dartmouth in April 1942, Peter Williams was given command of MGB 502 and became Senior Officer of the Flotilla. He carried out a further ten operations and became an expert at clandestine operations in difficult pilotage waters surrounded by enemy ships and shore defences. Slocum felt that Williams 'wrote the book on how it should be done'. David Birkin wrote, 'He was a quite exceptional character and marvellous company. An exceedingly good Commanding Officer, it took a lot to rattle him.'

Lieutenant Lloyd Bott was Peter Williams's First Lieutenant. Bott, an Australian, joined the 15th MGBF in February 1944. He went on twelve operations, on four of which he was in charge of the surf-boats and the landing party. On two occasions 502 was in a very difficult situation with shoals on three sides and enemy forces blocking the only escape to seaward. 502 used its speed and a smokescreen to escape direct engagement with the German boats. Bott was commended by his commanding officer for his coolness in action. In 1945 he was awarded the DSC.

MGB 503 was commanded by Lieutenant Mike Marshall RNVR, with Andrew Smith RNVR as First Lieutenant. Mike Marshall was born in Pontefract, West Yorkshire. He'd been a successful sportsman who had won five caps playing rugby for England before the war. He was appointed to command MGB 503 in November 1943, after a distinguished career in a regular operational flotilla, culminating in

Lieutenant Commander Peter Williams and First Lieutenant Lloyd Bott

Lieutenant Mike Marshall

the award of the DSC. He was described by Lloyd Bott as 'big, tough, quick-witted, decisive and very competent'. At six foot six with a broken nose he looked every inch the rugby pro. His first task was to get his ship into reliable running order. Being the first of her class she had suffered a series of mechanical breakdowns, which had undermined the morale of her crew and their faith in their craft. Under Marshall's direction the ship rapidly became operational. Initially he went on two operations with 318 as an observer, and then became an expert on pinpoint insertions. He was awarded a Bar to his DSC in 1945.

MGB 718 (a D Class boat built by Fairmile) was the last boat to join the Flotilla, in January 1944. It was commanded by Lieutenant Ronnie Seddon RNVR with Guy Hamilton as First Lieutenant. Ronnie Seddon had been an actor with the Liverpool Repertory Company and on first joining the Navy he had trained as a wireless telegraphist. To achieve his ambition of holding a commission, he remustered as an Ordinary Seaman and in due course was successful, becoming first a Sub Lieutenant and then Lieutenant RNVR. After a spell as First Lieutenant of an HDML (Harbour Defence Motor Launch), he became Commanding Officer of ML 145 and together with ML 150 rammed and sank German E-boat S96 on 24 September 1943, and for his action Ronnie Seddon was Mentioned in Dispatches. Seddon was appointed to command MGB 718 and took up his post on 20 January 1944, remaining in command during the full period of the commission. He was awarded the DSC in 1945.

Lieutenant Ronnie Seddon

Guy Hamilton was 718's First Lieutenant. He had spent much of his boyhood in France, a factor which was to prove particularly useful in June/July 1944 (see Chapter 11). He interrupted his career in the film industry to join the Navy, and after initial training spent ten months as an Ordinary Seaman aboard the Tribal-class destroyer HMS ESKIMO on Russian and Malta convoys escort duty. After being selected for officer training, and passing out at the new naval college KING ALFRED that opened shortly before the war, he took up appointment as Navigating Officer of MGB 673 based at Dartmouth. After six months with 673 he was appointed as First Lieutenant of MGB 718, with effect from 20 January 1944. He was awarded the DSC in 1945.

The MGBs each carried a newly designed 14-foot surf-boat, 'almost invisible at a very short distance' in special paint, which agents learned to get in and out of promptly and silently during their courses at their Special Training School on the west coast of Scotland. Gunboats were painted in unusual camouflage – Mountbatten Pink with Dark Navy towards the waterline. Once painted the ship was washed down with sodium sulphide solution to further reduce the ship's visibility. This was known as the Chameleon Camouflage Process.

Mountbatten Pink was named after Lord Louis Mountbatten who, when escorting a convoy in 1940, noticed that one ship in the group vanished from view much earlier than the remainder. The ship, a Union Castle liner, was painted lavender mauve grey. Mountbatten

Officers of the Flotilla

became convinced of the colour's effectiveness as a camouflage during dawn and dusk, often dangerous times for ships, and had all of the destroyers of his flotilla painted with a similar pigment, which he created by mixing a medium grey with a small amount of Venetian Red. A later refinement of the basic Mountbatten Pink camouflage was the use of a slightly lighter tone of the same colour for the upper structures of the ship. The primary problem with Mountbatten Pink was that it stood out around midday, when the sky was no longer pink, and the traditional battleship grey was much less visible. However, this was not a problem for the gunboats as they operated only at night.

*

The Brittany coast, while spectacular, is well known for its navigational difficulties requiring expert seamanship. It is described perfectly in *The Michelin Guide to Brittany*:

> The Breton coast is extraordinarily indented. The jaggedness of this coastline with its islands, islets and reefs, which is due only in part to the action of the sea, is one of the characteristics of Brittany ... sombre cliffs, rugged capes ... islands, rocks and reefs give the coastline a grimness which is reflected in local names with a sinister ring; the Channel of Great Fear (Fromveur), the Bay of the Dead (Baie des Trépassés), the Hell of Plogoff (Enfer de Plogoff) ... On the north coast, the tide

> sweeps in, in exceptional cases to a height of 13.50m – 43ft in the Bay of St- Malo ... When the wind blows, the battering-ram effect of the sea is tremendous. Sometimes the shocks given to the rocks of Penmarc'h are felt as far off as Quimper, 30km – 18 miles away ...

For a navigator, such terrain represented a huge challenge. 'Our area of operations stretched between Cap Fréhel on the east, westwards to Île Vierge and L'Aber-Wrac'h,' remembered David Birkin: 'a distance of a hundred miles in a straight line, but well over double following the indentations of the coastline. It presents a most formidable approach from seaward with its rugged headlands, its complexes of islands and islets, some flat and covered with rough grass, others rocky and barren – and with its offshore reefs and rocks just breaking the surface, or rising singly and dramatically from the depths towering like icebergs above the surface of the sea, sometimes four miles or more from the mainland.'

As Birkin described it, it is as though the elements were against them: 'The coast is guarded not only by its rocky embroidery, but also by a fierce tidal stream which, at spring tides, reaches five knots or more, and runs parallel with the coast (inconveniently at right angles to an approach course). The sea is never still and even in the finest weather, a long low Atlantic groundswell pounds relentlessly against cliffs and beaches. With autumn comes the south-westerly

winds blowing in from the Atlantic, which reach gale force in a surprisingly short time: great waves smash shore-wards, like white express trains, breaking far out to sea, gathering pace as they race towards the shore transforming the white jagged coastline into a cauldron of boiling surf, which fills the air with salt-tasting spray, penetrating miles inland: an awe-inspiring sight, especially if one happens to be in the middle of it as we, unfortunately, often were.'

The mid-Channel tidal streams are difficult enough. But close in shore they become exceptionally strong and, as Birkin noted, running at 90 degrees to the approach course. Even in good weather the Atlantic swell pounds the cliffs and beaches. Huge and powerful Atlantic waves create very dangerous surf conditions. It left much of the length of this coast impenetrable to anything but very skilfully handled small boats.

It is not for nothing that navigation manuals recommend that approaches are made only in daylight (a luxury that the 15th MGBF could not afford). There are a multitude of rocky outcrops, sharp reefs hidden below the surface only marked by breaking water. Some of these extend several miles out to sea. In addition to the natural hazards, the Germans had created a forbidden zone twenty-five kilometres deep where movement was strictly controlled. Much of the coastline was defended by minefields, barbed wire and machine gun and artillery emplacements.

However, as well as presenting deadly obstacles, these defences also presented opportunities. If there was a suitable pinpoint close to a German defensive position they were considered 'possibles', the theory being that the Germans would never believe this sort of operation would take place so close to them and would therefore be less vigilant. 'My best landing beach was within 400 feet of an occupied German pill box,' Peter Harratt, the Sea Landing Officer of RF Section of SOE, remembered. Lloyd Bott, First Lieutenant on 502, commented that when anchored off Bonaparte Beach they could see the German sentries' glowing cigarettes on Île Pointe de la Tour.

The operational requirements for a pinpoint included freedom from offshore reefs, total darkness, fairly calm waters and a landmark visible from sea level – a headland, a building or a distinctive rock. The steeper the beach, the simpler and safer it would be to use at any stage of the tide. The more sheltered, the less likelihood of difficult surf. Lighthouses on the Breton coast were usually extinguished, but occasionally might be working at about half or quarter strength. This provided a useful compass bearing, but it meant that a German coastal convoy was moving along the convoy route c. 15km (10 miles) offshore and parallel to it. At about 24km (15 miles) off the coast engines were silenced and all eyes strained for signs of ships moving across their approach course.

At 10 miles from the coast they would alter course to counter the fierce tidal stream, which at spring tide reaches over 5 knots, and all available binoculars would be trained on the darkness ahead for that first indication of the denser darkness that represented the Breton coast, or for surf breaking on outlying rocks. All the while the echo-sounder would be at work to indicate any dramatic changes of depth.

Anchorage positions might be anything between 140 and 800 metres (half a mile) from the pinpoint. Then the long wait began; sometimes it was as little as an hour and a half; the absolute maximum was four hours. Walkie-talkie contact was maintained between ship and surf-boat at infrequent intervals, as the danger of transmissions being picked up by the Germans was always present. Minutes could seem like hours and hours could seem like days. There was a strange sensation of being unprotected and exposed, and knowing that within a few hundred metres, certainly within earshot, the enemy were on the look-out from their gun emplacements, searchlight and radar positions. The pinpoint and anchorage were almost always in the field of fire of German artillery or machine guns. It was difficult to believe that a 110-foot ship so close to a hostile shore could not be seen, especially on a starry, still night when every splash or ripple glowed with phosphorescence. They could occasionally see the enemy lighting cigarettes on the cliff top and their vehicles with dimmed headlights crawling along the coast roads.

Silence was demanded on board the anchored MGB. The slightest noise jarred heavily on the nerves. Occasionally, there were horrid shocks, such as the short-circuits that switched on the MGB's navigation lights or set the gun-buzzer blaring.

When the surf-boats returned, an engine had to be started up: even though silenced, it sounded to their over-sensitive ears like a lion's roar. It was considered wise to be at least thirty miles offshore on the way back to England before dawn. Occasionally, the boats were seen by the Germans and fired on; several times they were spotted by French lighthouse keepers, but on the whole, they were remarkably lucky. Or rather, over the duration of the war the 15th MGBF had become highly professional. The skippers of the boats had trained their crews hard; considerable effort was required to perfect the skills needed so that they could perform with such precision. They had to continuously practise surf landing, anchor and weigh anchor securely, move the surf-boats from various parts of the MGB to get them noiselessly into and out of the water, and get the passengers on board in a quick and disciplined manner. All this in the pitch dark, in bad weather and in total silence.

The techniques involved in providing this secret transport network were highly specialised and had to be learnt, through constant training and practice, by every crew member in every vessel. Loaded on top of the everyday job of operating a small sea-going warship were the requirements for tight security, absolutely precise navigation, the ability to do everything in total darkness – and complete silence. Furthermore, in order not to jeopardise the location of the chosen landing pinpoint, while on passage it was essential to avoid any contact with either friendly or enemy forces, on the surface or in the air. To be spotted, let alone fired on, could give the whole game away.

Pressures upon the individual were intense and required outstanding physical and mental strength and resilience. In rough weather a helmsman could be battling for hours to keep his vessel on the right course, threading through unforgiving rocks in a very strong tideway. As for the navigator, precision was everything. 'I remember most vividly,' David Birkin recalled, 'the apprehensive excitement as the MGB crept silently towards the Brittany coast in absolute darkness, wondering whether my outward show of confidence in my calculations was going to be justified or rudely shattered.'

*

Close inshore, an exact drill was followed. No lights were shown at sea, nor was there any talking or smoking on deck (it required a stern effort of discipline to hold the French to this). S-phone contact was usually made; failing that, the beach party would flash an agreed Morse letter from a hand torch, or signal with a luminous plastic ball held in the closed fist. The MGB anchored offshore, by a grass rope instead of a chain in order to minimise noise and to be easily cut – a rating was on hand with an axe to cut it immediately. The landing party were rowed in with muffled oars in a surf-boat, and carried the last yard or two ashore by sailors after the Boat Officer had gone ahead to contact the reception committee. Agents wore waterproof capes (taken back by the sailors) over their clothes to prevent spray stains.

To launch a surf-boat without mishap in rough conditions took both high skill and fine judgement, let alone then having to load landing parties and stores aboard. The boats' crews would have anything up to two miles to row, with their oars suitably muffled, before arriving at their chosen spot, sometimes without knowing that the friendly reception committee was in place. And each time they knew the hazardous journey had to be repeated in order to return in safety to the mother ship, waiting somewhere offshore in the pitch dark. On several occasions the boat could not find the mother ship and so the crews had to land again and stay as 'guests' of the local Resistance cell until they could be rescued a few days – or even weeks – later. This happened to two surf-boat parties, as we will see later.

The procedures for this part of the operation are summarised below from the DDOD(I) Standard Operating Procedures.

General Principles:

1. Operations will be restricted to the dark moon period of each month unless otherwise stated when arranging specific operations. The dark moon period is from the last quarter of the moon to the first quarter.
2. Clandestine disembarkation/embarkation of evaders will take place at night between 2300 and 0200 GMT.
3. Signals will be required from the beach every half hour. These

should be given with a blue torch. The signal letter will be passed, together with a password, when details of the pinpoint are sent.

4. Embarking evader groups should be divided into small units to facilitate embarkation.
5. Communications with UK are all-important.
6. Should a party of evaders visit a given pinpoint and fail to make contact with the expected craft, they should, if circumstances permit, return to the pinpoint on each of the following three nights. If they have W/T communications, they should contact HQ at once. Possible causes of such a failure are bad weather, mechanical failure or enemy sea patrols.
7. Beach discipline is most important. The Senior Officer present must insist on orderly behaviour, no smoking or talking on the beach, and no rushing to get into the boats.

On the beach, agents 'should be briefed to behave as much like luggage as possible'. While waiting they should always sit down except on first disembarkation when they stand by the boats. They should never contact the outgoing party and on no account talk. No one ever wore any headgear, in case it fell off and so left a trace of the landing. Usually the MGB was at anchor for about 90 minutes; 35 minutes was the shortest and three-and-a-half hours the longest times at anchor – in the latter case, the rowing party's return was hampered by a sudden fog. The actual time spent by the seamen on the beach was only supposed to be three or four minutes. Landings were made on a rising tide to minimise footprint traces: somebody from the shore party visited the beach again at first light, to ensure that there was nothing suspicious to be seen.

Alf Harris, a Seaman Gunner in 505, remembered that, 'The procedure as we closed on the beaches was that whoever was on the sweep oar, usually a leading seaman or sub-lieutenant, gave the order "Oars – out boat" whereupon I would jump out to port and Pusser (George Hill) to starboard, run the pram up the beach and turn her bow for the return trip. The advantage of the sweep oar steering as against a normal tiller was never more apparent than when Pusser and I, with 502's cox'n Fred Smith, were at practice at Helford, Cornwall when

Smith gave a demonstration of sweep oar capability in and out of rocks with a skill that had to be seen to be appreciated.'

Described as PD surf-boats, PD1 pram dinghies used on these operations were designed by Lieutenant Pat Whinney (member of DDOD(I) staff) on the basis of a Dutch prototype that had turned up at Felixstowe. Modified to give additional stability and carrying power, they rode light in the water, being specifically built to carry a heavy load.

Occasionally an extra seaman officer was taken as a Boats Officer to take charge of the surf-boats to and from the beach, although this was normally the job of the First Lieutenant of the boat concerned. John Motherwell, the Commander of the luckless MASB 36, volunteered to join MGB 502 on an operation as an extra Boat Officer to manage the surf-boat for the beach landing.

One description of a typical surf landing was given by Lieutenant Murray 'Tassie' Uhr-Henry for the operation EASEMENT 1. Uhr-Henry was from Tasmania and was not attached to a specific boat but had the responsibility of maintaining the surf-boats and training the crews. He would often go on operations where he would lead the row into the beach.

'The objective of EASEMENT 1 was to land one male on the beach in Brittany called Beg-an-Fry,' Uhr-Henry recounted. 'A 75mm gun emplacement defended the beach together with a heavy machine gun mounted on the point to the west, which was a couple of hundred yards away. MGB 502 crossed the German convoy route without incident and we anchored about a mile from the landing point near some rocks called Le Boeufs. David Birkin our navigator provided me with courses to steer in and out but warned me that I would have to make my own wind allowances. I was given a password, "Ou est Pierre?" for the beach party and, "Pierre est dans la cuisine" for my reply. With two sailors rowing the 14-foot pram, our passenger lodged in the bow with supposedly a suitcase full of money for the underground, and myself in the stern with a steering oar and a luminous box compass and a stopwatch, we set off for the beach.

'It was an extremely dark night with cloud cover but fortunately with very little wind. As we entered the bay it was very hard to see where the shore was. The tide was ebbing when we hit the beach. We had a bit of a walk to where the reception party was supposed to be. We missed them because as it turned out they had come to the wrong beach. The underground agent then elected to go on by himself. I returned the pram and was told that they had to move it twice to keep it in the water.

'During the trip in and out, I didn't dare lift my eyes from the compass and watch. When we had run the exact time on the way out, I told the sailor to belay rowing, but we could not see MGB 502. It had turned misty and visibility was limited. I was wondering what to do next when we heard an engine start not far away. I said to my sailors, "Let's get to that sound before it leaves for England."'

Once the mission was complete, best speed was made for Dartmouth. This was usually reached at about first light, with the commanders setting back in time to ensure the boats were at least thirty miles from France before dawn came up. Just as the boats left Dartmouth to the sound of music, so their return was often sound-tracked by the on-board speaker system. In the case of 502, Handel's Water Music was the piece of choice. Once moored back along *Westward Ho*, the returned agents or POWs were met by a Conducting Officer. Having been given breakfast, they would then be escorted ashore to the London train. As the engine pulled away from Kingswear, they were suddenly just another passenger heading for the capital. Others in the carriage might notice their tired expressions, but otherwise have little idea what they'd been through over the last twenty-four hours.

*

On 31 December 1941, Lieutenant Curtis steered 314 back towards the pinpoint in the Aber-Benoît Channel again. But this time, rather than silence and silhouettes of the night before, the panorama was lit up. With a thud and crackle, the skyline was ablaze with a barrage of anti-aircraft tracer rounds. A second barrage was spotted further south east near Brest. Curtis cut the engines. The wait was interminable as the barrage continued. Should they pull back? Continue? With the light flashing across the sky, they were cruelly exposed, their hiding place in the dark given away. But Curtis held his nerve. Then, almost as suddenly as the tracer rounds had started, they stopped again. The night was plunged into darkness again. Suddenly, the late hour was so silent, Curtis could hear his own breathing. He started the single engine again. Ever watchful, the boat continued its journey to the pinpoint.

This shape of the land looked familiar now – Curtis could recognise the contours of the cliffs from the night before. But there was one important difference. The presence of a light – a faint low flash down in the water close by. A short while later, there was a new noise – the gentle splash of an oar. Then, out of the darkness came a shape. A canoe, with two figures on board. As it came alongside the 314, a scramble net was used to help the two men on board.

Yves Le Tac, one of the two brothers instrumental to setting up the OVERCLOUD network, was pleased to see them. Alongside him was Godfrey Scamaroni (FRED), an outgoing SOE RF agent, to be taken back to the UK. Scamaroni was on his way back to London having been on a long and complicated mission for de Gaulle to Dakar.[21] When Curtis asked what the barrage was about, Yves started laughing. It was no air raid, but New Year's celebrations. The British had their watches at 2300, but the Germans, on Central European Time, were an hour ahead.

'Don't worry,' Le Tac said. 'It's quite safe. The Germans will all be drunk by now.'

The swap was made. The agent for the Free French Intelligence Service (BCRA), Pierre Movreaux, followed Le Tac down in the canoe, Curtis watching them disappearing back into the darkness before turning to head for home.

Yves Le Tac and Davis had agreed on another rendezvous for the night of 6/7 January. On the 6th the BBC broadcast the message 'Aide-toi et le ciel t'aidera,' signalling that the mission was on. This time, the Le Tac brothers and five others made their way to Île

21 Exactly a year later Scamaroni went back to his native Corsica by submarine HMS TRIBUNE. He was captured on 18 March 1943 and committed suicide by taking his L Pill on 20 March. The L Pill – 'L' for lethal – was a cyanide capsule given to all those operating behind enemy lines. The individual had the option to take it rather than face torture and a brutal death.

Guénnoc. At the agreed time Yves flashed the recognition signal and the gunboat appeared out of the darkness and moored 500 yards from the island. The seven passengers were ferried to the MGB by dinghy in twos which took longer than planned. But everything else went smoothly and they were back across the Channel at first light.

314 was back on the French coast at Lannion Bay on 10 January conducting operation 'PICKAXE', arranged by SIS, to drop off a Russian female NKVD agent – Szyfra Lypszyc – cover name JEANETTE DUPONT. She was on her way to join the ROTE KAPELLE network which had a large presence in France and Belgium (in total 11 NKVD agents were infiltrated into France 1942–44). On 25 January, Curtis and 314 were back again at Île Guénnoc with three passengers for what was to be the last in the OVERCLOUD series of operations. The three passengers were the Le Tac brothers and André Peulevey.[22]

Although they were put ashore successfully, the OVERCLOUD network had been completely penetrated by the Germans via a student Resistance group called 'Les Ibériques' ('The Spaniards'). 'Les Ibériques' were in touch with the INTERALLIÉ network, which had also been exposed. Among those agents betrayed was one, code-named BOB EDGAR, who was arrested at the Café Louis XIII in Paris, carrying details of the whole OVERCLOUD network. André Peulevey was arrested in Rennes on 5 February 1942. The Le Tac brothers were both arrested in Paris and after interrogation and torture they were sent to Natzweiler and Dachau. They both survived. The rather naïve students in Les Ibériques continued operating in spite of warnings from London. Twenty-five of them were deported and fourteen of them died in concentration camps.

314 was to carry out two further operations to Brittany in February 1942. On the 12th it took part in Operation WATERWORKS and from the 19th–26th Operation ROWAN. These operations, which will be discussed in the next chapter, were to be the last that 314 was involved in. In March, Combined Operations carried out a raid on the port of St Nazaire and recalled MGB 314 to take part. This involved four MGBs escorting an elderly ex-US destroyer into the

22 Real name Joseph Scheinmann.

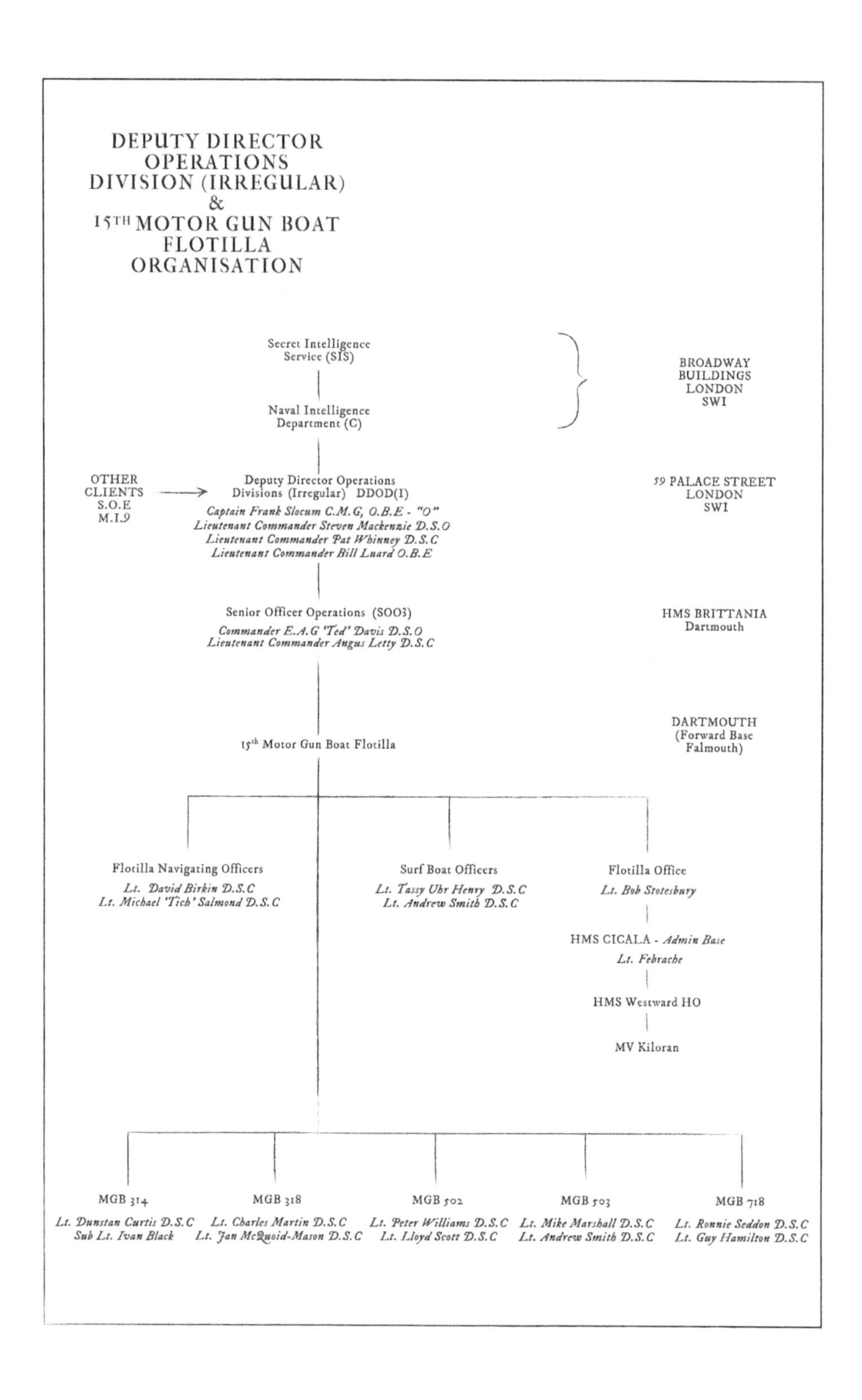
DEPUTY DIRECTOR OPERATIONS DIVISION (IRREGULAR) & 15TH MOTOR GUN BOAT FLOTILLA ORGANISATION
Secret Intelligence Service (SIS)
Naval Intelligence Department (C)
BROADWAY BUILDINGS LONDON SWI
OTHER CLIENTS S.O.E M.I.9
Deputy Director Operations Divisions (Irregular) DDOD(I)
Captain Frank Slocum C.M.G, O.B.E - "O"
Lieutenant Commander Steven Mackenzie D.S.O
Lieutenant Commander Pat Whinney D.S.C
Lieutenant Commander Bill Luard O.B.E
59 PALACE STREET LONDON SWI
Senior Officer Operations (SOO3)
Commander E.A.G 'Ted' Davis D.S.O
Lieutenant Commander Angus Letty D.S.C
HMS BRITTANIA Dartmouth
15th Motor Gun Boat Flotilla
DARTMOUTH (Forward Base Falmouth)
Flotilla Navigating Officers
Lt. David Birkin D.S.C
Lt. Michael 'Tich' Salmond D.S.C
Surf Boat Officers
Lt. Tassy Uhr Henry D.S.C
Lt. Andrew Smith D.S.C
Flotilla Office
Lt. Bob Stotesbury
HMS CICALA - Admin Base
Lt. Febrache
HMS Westward HO
MV Kiloran
MGB 314
Lt. Dunstan Curtis D.S.C
Sub Lt. Ivan Black
MGB 318
Lt. Charles Martin D.S.C
Lt. Jan McQuoid-Mason D.S.C
MGB 502
Lt. Peter Williams D.S.C
Lt. Lloyd Scott D.S.C
MGB 503
Lt. Mike Marshall D.S.C
Lt. Andrew Smith D.S.C
MGB 718
Lt. Ronnie Seddon D.S.C
Lt. Guy Hamilton D.S.C

Loire river to destroy the lock gate of the dry dock at St Nazaire: the only one on the French coast capable of taking a battleship for repair. The destroyer was packed with high explosive and rammed against the lock gates and blown up. Unfortunately, three of the MGBs were destroyed by gunfire in the approach to St Nazaire, and MGB 314 was so badly damaged that she had to be abandoned on her way home. Dunstan Curtis and his crew were brought back by the supporting force and were lucky to survive. Curtis was awarded a DSC for this action.

The loss of 314 just before she was due to be allocated permanently to DDOD(I) was a setback for Slocum. For a while it left him with just one ship at Dartmouth, MASB 36. Things started to look up when he was allocated MGB 318 as a replacement for 314, and the newly built 501, which Curtis was to take command of. But 501, as we saw earlier, was not to last long. This left MGB 318 as the Flotilla's main boat, until the arrivals of MGB 502 in summer 1943, MGB 503 in November 1943 and 718 in January 1944.

CHAPTER 5 – A DELICATE DANCE

'Treachery can't be forgiven'

Michael Corleone, *The Godfather*

On the evening of Thursday 12 February 1942, two men and a woman were waiting on the Brittany coast for a signal. Moulin-de-la-Rive in Lannion Bay was typical of this part of coastline – the sandy beach of the cove surrounded by jagged dark rocks that jutted out into the sea, the grass and rugged greenery of the headland giving ample places to hide. It was a dark, moonless night, the only sound the gentle lapping of waves as they rippled ashore.

Ben Cowburn, code name BENOIT, checked his watch. Midnight. He noticed, with a grim realisation, that it was now Friday the 13th and hoped it wasn't a bad omen for what was to come. Not that he was counting, but this was the second bad sign he'd had that evening. As with every agent who left Orchard Court, Cowburn had been given the customary leaving present by Colonel Maurice Buckmaster: a gold pen. Hiding on the Brittany coastline, he realised that this was now missing. This did not look promising. He flashed the recognition signal out to sea at regular intervals, and waited for a response.

As Cowburn's eyes adjusted to the night, he spotted a silhouette down at the water's edge. Was this the rendezvous? Had they arrived already? Cowburn cautiously made his way down from his hiding place to the beach. He could feel his heart quickening: if this wasn't the person he was there to meet, then his position would quickly be exposed. As he made his way down to the shoreline the figure, a man in gumboots, stopped. It was now or never: Cowburn whispered the first half of the agreed password. To his relief, the man responded with the second.

Cowburn explained the situation as best he could. The original plan had been for two agents to be dropped ashore, including a radio operator for him. But that plan had now changed. The two agents were to stay on board and return to the UK, along with the two agents Cowburn had with him, who needed to be extracted out of France. The man in the gumboots in turn explained that the MGB was anchored out in the bay: he'd been dropped ashore further along the beach, the boat going back to get the other agent and the radio equipment.

The water lapping at his feet, Cowburn noticed, was getting a little stronger as the tide was coming in.

Out at sea, Cowburn could see a pair of black shapes coming into focus. These were small boats, dinghies, each with a passenger being rowed ashore by a seaman. From the way that the dinghies were bobbing up and down, Cowburn could see that the sea was starting to get rougher. As the dinghies neared the beach, he called over to the two agents he had been waiting with. They scurried down to the shoreline: the woman was wearing a distinctive brown fur coat and red beret.

The waves, Cowburn noticed, were beginning to crash in with greater force now.

He waded out into the water to help secure the boats. The two passengers clambered out and as the waves crashed around them, made their way to shore. One was the second agent, the other, in Royal Navy uniform, was Lieutenant Ivan Black, second-in-command of the MGB. Cowburn explained the situation to Black, the change of plan, and that everyone needed to get back on to the boats.

By now, the waves were really rising up. The change had been swift: long gone was the gentle lapping of earlier; now there was a roaring and pounding as the waves crashed in. As Cowburn, Black and the four agents waded out towards the boats, two steps forwards, one buffeted back as another wave washed in, the seamen were struggling to keep the dinghies afloat. Before long, they were both capsized, the seamen pitched over into the foam and water.

Together, all eight fought a losing battle to right the boats, a vain attempt to empty them of water. The sea, though, was simply too strong. To make matters worse, in all of this the agents lost their luggage and the seamen their oars, drifting off into the night. Eventually, they admitted defeat. Lieutenant Black used his flashlamp to signal back to the MGB. The two seamen returned to ship, using the overturned dinghies as floats, swimming their way back into the darkness.

A larger black shape appeared. As it came into focus, Cowburn could see it was a full-size rowing boat, the MGB's lifeboat (against regulations to be used operationally). He watched as the sailors on board skilfully held its position, keeping it out of the way of the breakers and the risk of it going the same way as the dinghies. Cowburn waded out in an attempt to reach it. The waves were up to his shoulders and as they came in, he could feel himself being lifted off his feet. But try as he might the boat was frustratingly just too far – despite his best efforts, it was still an agonising thirty feet away. Cowburn couldn't make it any further out; the boat couldn't make it any further in.

Swimming back to shore, he joined the others to watch the boat pitch and fall on the waves, until it too gave up, turned away and disappeared back into the night. Cowburn knew the moment of escape had gone: without the cover of darkness, the MGB's position would be exposed. It had to leave. Whereas a few hours earlier, there were three of them ready to leave, now there were six of them, stuck in France, and debating what they should do next.

*

On 17 September 1940, the woman in the distinctive brown fur coat and red beret was having lunch with a friend in La Frégate, a busy restaurant in Toulouse, when their conversation was interrupted by the head waiter. He had a message from another customer, asking if he could join them. The stranger was young, charming and good-looking and so the offer was accepted. It was a moment that was to change Mathilde Carré's life: the start of what would lead her to being dubbed the 'Emma Bovary' of World War II espionage.

Mathilde Carré was a woman with a sense of risk. Having been married since the mid-1930s, her restless spirit led to her leaving her husband and signing up for the Red Cross in search of action. While other colleagues were terrified of finding themselves under threat, Carré seemed to revel in it: 'There's almost a sensual pleasure in

Mathilde Carré

real danger, don't you think?' she told one fellow ambulance worker. 'Your whole body seems to suddenly come alive.'

Before the defeat of France, Mathilde had been ordered to head for Bordeaux. But when she got there, exhausted and filthy, everything was in chaos. France had collapsed, and there was no Red Cross unit for her to join. Which is how she ended up making her way to Toulouse, and the chance meeting in a crowded restaurant.

The stranger who sat himself down at Carré's table was Armand Borri. Borri told Carré that he was French but had been brought up in Poland. Immediately attracted to each other, Borri suggested that she might be able to help with his French pronunciation. It was only when the pair became lovers that he revealed his true identity: his real name was Roman Czernlowski and he was both a major in the Polish Air Force, and an intelligence officer with orders to set up a clandestine network, or 'réseau', in the Occupied Zone. Czernlowski asked Carré to work with him, to which she readily agreed. He gave her the code name 'VICTOIRE' and nicknamed her 'La Chatte' ('the female cat', or, in a slightly more salacious connotation, 'Pussy').

In October 1940 Carré and Czernlowski moved to Paris. Their réseau now had a code name – INTERALLIÉ – and a headquarters in an apartment at 14 rue du Colonel Moll. They recruited a prominent lawyer, Michel Boult (MIKLOS), and persuaded him to allow them to claim to be working for him on legal matters outside of Paris. Their cover story created, they began to grow their network.

Carré was very active, crisscrossing Paris despite the risks to recruit contact after contact. These included Charles Le Jeune, a senior policeman and a vital contributor towards providing blank identity cards and police permits. A friend of Carré's introduced them to Marc Marchal, the President of the Association of Chemical Engineers, who was running a small network of his own made up of close friends he could trust. He was persuaded to bring his team under the wing of INTERALLIÉ. By the end of 1940 the réseau had 200 agents working across France. Carré typed up a weekly intelligence summary that was smuggled to London via Lisbon.

INTERALLIÉ was invaluable to SIS and swiftly became Britain's main intelligence asset in occupied France. Such was the large amount of accurate intelligence gleaned that Carré's weekly summary was quickly insufficient. The INTERALLIÉ network badly needed a radio, so they built one themselves and installed it in the top floor of an apartment near the Trocadéro. This set soon became four. INTERALLIÉ outgrew its headquarters in the rue du Colonel Moll and moved to 8 rue Villa Léandré in Montmartre.

But for all the réseau's success, the larger it got, the more its fault lines threatened its existence. Carré's tradecraft left something to be desired: her distinctive brown fur coat and red beret left her easy to remember, and no more difficult to follow. Czernlowski, meanwhile, invited a former lover, Renée Borni, to join the circuit as a radio operator. Carré hated her presence immediately and moved out to her own apartment around the corner in rue Cortot. Czernlowski rekindled his affair with Borni, while still sleeping with Carré, creating a tension at the heart of the organisation that was soon to spill over with devastating results.

On 16 November 1941, with the INTERALLIÉ network a year old, key personnel decided to have a party. They also sent a message to London: 'Tous les jours et par tous le moyens contre Le Boche. Vive La Liberté.' But the celebrations were to be proved short-lived: two days later Villa Léandré was raided. Czernlowski and Borni were in bed. The apartment was thoroughly searched, though two radio operators hiding in the roof managed to get out.

Mathilde Carré almost escaped as well. She had spent the night in another part of Paris and was heading back to her own apartment around the corner from Villa Léandré when she saw all the Abwehr activity. Without pausing, Carré made to walk quickly away, but as she was doing so, found herself intercepted by a friendly man who asked her what she was up to so early in the morning. Before she knew what was happening, she was grabbed from behind and frog-marched into a waiting van. Inside, she found herself face to face with Renée Borni, who identified her rival for Czernlowski's affections as La Chatte.

*

The man responsible for breaking the INTERALLIÉ network was Hugo Bleicher, a member of the German military counterintelligence organisation – the Abwehr. Fluent in both French and Spanish, it was Bleicher's diligent counterintelligence that had led to the capture of an INTERALLIÉ agent and persuaded him to change sides and reveal the rue Villa Léandré address.

Carré spent a night she wouldn't forget in a freezing, blood-stained cell which stank of urine. When she did manage to get to sleep, she was woken by guards who screamed at her and intimidated her. The following morning, she was taken to Abwehr headquarters, where Bleicher turned on the charm, giving her coffee, milk, bread and butter in a heated room. He offered Carré a cigarette. 'We have decided

Sergeant Hugo Bleicher of the Abwehr

that you are too intelligent and too interesting to stay in prison,' he told her.

Bleicher made Carré an offer. She could go back to prison and face the firing squad – 'You have done quite enough to be shot several times,' he told her – or she could work for him and help him to destroy INTERALLIÉ. 'We are in possession of all the documents,' he told Carré, 'but we need you, because you are known by everybody, for the remaining arrests.' Bleicher explained how he would travel with Carré to her meetings and pose as a member of the organisation before making the arrests. 'You had better save your skin and start to understand that England is beaten,' Bleicher warned. Carré nodded her assent.

That evening, while most of the key operators of INTERALLIÉ languished in Fresnes Prison, Carré joined Bleicher for dinner and then accompanied him to the Villa Harry Baur where Abwehr operators lived. Before long, the two became lovers. Carré was diligent in leading Bleicher to agent after agent. Bleicher played his part cleverly, making it look as though Carré was also being taken prisoner, pushing her around and 'arresting' her as well.

Having captured all the INTERALLIÉ radio sets, with one of the operators persuaded to change sides, Bleicher decided to play the radios back to London as if they were still operating freely: 'Funkspiel', as the Germans called it. Again, Carré agreed to play her part. She sent messages explaining a series of arrests of INTERALLIÉ members but claimed that she was free and putting the network back together. London took the bait. A stream of false and half-true intelligence was now sent back to SIS.

Britain's main intelligence asset in occupied France was now being used against it.

*

Bleicher and the Abwehr now turned their attention to an SOE circuit – AUTOGIRO. AUTOGIRO was run by Pierre de Vomécourt, one of three French aristocratic brothers from Lorraine who were all involved in the Resistance. Educated in England, de Vomécourt joined the French Army in 1939 and in 1940 was posted as a Liaison

Pierre de Vomécourt (LUCAS)

Officer to the BEF, specifically to the 7th Battalion – the Cameronians (Scottish Rifles). Evacuated from Dunkirk, de Vomécourt was recruited to F Section, and parachuted back into France on the night of 10/11 May 1941, using the code name LUCAS.

LUCAS travelled to his estate near Limoges where he met his brothers Jean and Philippe. They agreed to operate in three different areas: Jean would work in Eastern France, Philippe in Limoges and Pierre along with his radio operator, George Bégué, would go to Paris to set up AUTOGIRO, which was to be the first SOE network in France. Bégué was a skilled radio operator and pioneered the use of personal messages broadcast by the BBC to the Resistance: unfortunately for AUTOGIRO, Bégué was arrested in October 1941 (he later escaped from prison and returned to Britain).

Bégué was replaced by André Bloch who had been parachuted in on the 6/7 September 1941 with five other agents including Ben Cowburn (BENOIT). But two months later, early on the morning of 13 November the Gestapo arrested him, not as an agent, but because he had been denounced as a Jew. LUCAS was furious at SOE's ignorance of the local anti-Semitic feeling in France, and the fact it had led to AUTOGIRO losing their radio. The Gestapo, meanwhile, were delighted at their unexpected find: Bloch was interrogated, tortured and executed on 11 February 1942 at Mont-Valérien prison. LUCAS was now desperate to find a way to get back in communication with London. This led him to Michel Brault (MIKLOS), the lawyer who had been an early recruit to INTERALLIÉ, who in turn arranged a meeting with VICTOIRE (Carré).

On 26 December 1942 de Vomécourt and Brault met Carré at the Café Georges V on the Champs-Elysées, a very high-profile and popular café, not ideal for a clandestine meeting. LUCAS explained his predicament and asked Carré for her help. Carré listened carefully and told LUCAS that she might be able to assist him, but would need to talk to 'her friends'. LUCAS suggested another meeting in a few days, unaware of whom Carré was really working for. And unaware, too, that sat at another table, watching the exchange, was Bleicher.

At the second meeting, in an office de Vomécourt had rented, Carré told him the 'story' of INTERALLIÉ and the arrests. She claimed to have avoided capture and to still have a working radio link with London. De Vomécourt believed her and gave Carré his first coded message. This was transmitted to London by Bleicher and passed to F Section. Although there were some suspicions at the British end as de Vomécourt had been off the air for a long time, the message contained a code word known only to him. De Vomécourt asked for money and a replacement radio operator. The money was not a problem, but with no trained radio operators available, de Vomécourt was to use VICTOIRE's radio set.

As AUTOGIRO's communications started up again, Bleicher was able to form a picture of the circuit and started making arrests, including a contact of Michel Brault. On 16 January the Gestapo came to arrest Brault as well, but he escaped and fled to Vichy. From here, he sent a note to LUCAS asking for an urgent meeting. Brault and LUCAS met in Cannes, where Brault voiced his suspicions that something was wrong. This confirmed concerns that LUCAS himself had been having. He remembered asking VICTOIRE to procure false identity papers, which she managed to achieve curiously quickly, and of surprisingly good quality. He remembered, too, two occasions when Carré had asked him for the real names of people who were working under cover, something that was expressly forbidden under basic rules of operational security.

De Vomécourt returned to Paris and confronted Carré. As he expressed Brault's and his concerns, Carré cracked. She confessed all to LUCAS, her responsibility for destroying INTERALLIÉ, the betrayal of seventy agents, and her mission of finding out about AUTOGIRO and other networks. Carré protested that she had been forced into working for Bleicher and pleaded with de Vomécourt to let her change sides yet again, and 'get her revenge on the Germans'.

De Vomécourt should have taken steps either to have Carré executed, if not doing it himself. Instead, realising the threat that he was under, he came up with a plan to escape from France successfully. He told Carré to go back to Bleicher and tell him that she had found out that there had been a very high-level meeting of all the Resistance leaders in France, in Paris, in January, to discuss new methods of communication with SOE. Carré was to say that de Vomécourt had been at the meeting and had been ordered to go to London to bring SOE up to date, then return to Paris with him, a high-ranking member of the British intelligence community, to finalise the new procedures.

This was a high-risk strategy for de Vomécourt to deploy. Bleicher could have arrested him immediately and tortured him to find out more about the meeting. But de Vomécourt had correctly deduced that Bleicher would reach for the bigger prize: to wait for de Vomécourt's return with the senior British officer and then lead a mass round-up of the Resistance. When Carré told him that de Vomécourt intended to take her with him, Bleicher was even more delighted: here was his chance to get his own agent into the heart of SOE.

* * *

'I'm afraid I have some very, very bad news,' de Vomécourt said. 'As you know, VICTOIRE's story was that when the Polish organisation was blown, she and a few others escaped arrest. Well, that is not true ... she was caught too!' As his dinner guest paused mid-mouthful, de Vomécourt nodded at him to continue. 'Keep on eating,' he said, 'it will look more natural.'

The person de Vomécourt was dining with in a Paris restaurant was Ben Cowburn (BENOIT). Cowburn had been parachuted into France on 6 September 1941, with instructions to prepare sabotage operations of fuel installations. But having set up his TINKER network, his progress was hampered by lack of supplies. Then he met de Vomécourt by chance in a restaurant in Châteauroux, who agreed to help him get London to start delivering. Back in Paris, Cowburn was introduced to Carré who told him London would soon drop a radio operator for him, and then start dropping supplies. A drop was arranged, but when the plane came overhead nothing happened. LUCAS told him that parachuting was unreliable in winter and that he should arrange a beach landing site in Brittany. Then, as he was arranging this, Cowburn was invited to meet de Vomécourt for dinner in a Paris restaurant, where he was told that Carré had been working as a double agent.

'According to tradition, I should have felt a tingling of the scalp, a quickening of the pulse, a sickness in the pit of the stomach,' Cowburn later recalled in his book *No Cloak, No Dagger*. 'After all, it is not every day that you get this kind of news flung at you. However, I felt just nothing at all at first, and found myself stuffing another

Carte d'Identité

NOM Villeneuve
Prénoms Jean François
Etat Civil
Profession Ingénieur
Né le 12 mai 1906
Paris
Département Seine
Nationalité Française
Domicile 136 Cours de la République Le Havre

15 FRANCS

SIGNALEMENT
Taille 1m 70
Cheveux blonds
Moustache
Yeux gris
Signes particuliers néant
Dos Droit
Nez Dimensions moy.
Forme du visage ovale
Teint clair

Empreinte digitale
Le Titulaire,
Les Témoins,
Vu pour la légalisation
Le NOV 1943 19

Ben Cowburn (BENOIT)'s fake ID card

forkful of pommes de terre à l'huile into my mouth.' Digesting what de Vomécourt had told him, Cowburn concluded, 'Then they must have been following us and have found out about all our contacts.'

'Not all,' de Vomécourt replied, 'but some of course.'

De Vomécourt explained his plan to Cowburn to return to England by Motor Gun Boat and take Carré with him. They would use the rendezvous that Cowburn was setting up: but rather than the two agents, including Cowburn's radio operator coming ashore, Cowburn, de Vomécourt and Carré would instead join them in returning to England.

On the afternoon of 11 February, Cowburn, de Vomécourt and Carré made their separate ways to the Gare Montparnasse to catch the night express to Brest. It must have been a strange scene on the platform: all three studiously ignoring each other; all three being watched by Bleicher's surveillance team. The charade continued at Guingamp where the three of them boarded the local stopping train to Plouigneau, still being shadowed clumsily by Bleicher's men. From here, they walked to the coast. Stopping for lunch, they were questioned by gendarmes and threatened with fines for being in the coastal area without a permit: another incident set up by Bleicher. After further bizarre and clumsy brushes with the German military they finally reached the pick-up point at Locquirec, settling down to wait for the pick-up. Bleicher, meanwhile, was still directing affairs from afar, telling the local naval commander that the gunboat was to be given unhindered access to the pick-up point.

The only part of the entire operation that Bleicher was unable to control, however, was the weather.

*

As the MGB's lifeboat disappeared into the darkness, de Vomécourt took charge. He, Cowburn and Carré should find somewhere to stay, so that Carré could contact the Germans first thing in the morning. Lieutenant Black and the two agents were to hide in the nearby woods. The six of them would then reconvene in the same place, the following evening, in the hope that the MGB would return.

De Vomécourt, Cowburn and Carré returned to Loquirec. With their efforts to board the dinghies, all three were sodden and soaked to the skin. But when they arrived at the local hotel, it was unsurprisingly closed and, despite their best efforts, they were unable to rouse the staff to let them in. Shivering from the cold, they had no choice but to sit in the yard until daybreak. In the morning, they walked back to Moulin-de-la-Rive, the storm having now subsided. De Vomécourt and Cowburn warmed up in a local café; Carré visited the local Abwehr office to tell the Germans the agreed story. Bleicher, still, was on board.

But not everything was going to plan. Black and the two agents were found and captured by the surveillance team. Because Black was in full uniform, he was treated as a POW and would spend the rest of the war in Colditz. The two agents, George Abbot (PAUL) and GEORGE Gustave Rodding (30), would have ended up being shot by firing squad, had de Vomécourt not managed to use Carré to persuade Bleicher to intervene and treat them as POWs as well.

On the next night of 13/14 February, another attempt at a pick-up was made, but as with the night before, the extreme surf stopped anyone from making it on to the ship. A week later, a separate operation, ROWAN, was mounted on 20 and 22 February. Although the weather improved, there was no-one waiting at the rendezvous.

By this point, de Vomécourt and Carré had decided to return to Paris to wait for another pick-up date. Cowburn, meanwhile, had had the good sense to slip away. On the train back, he realised that if he returned to Paris, he would most likely be picked up, tortured and shot. He also needed to warn Virginia Hall (CAMILLE) that the Germans were on to her because of her contact with INTERALLIÉ and AUTOGIRO, and that she should disappear. Hall's capture would be a disaster, as she knew far too much about the whole set-up in France. Cowburn made contact with her and then made his way to Britain via Spain. Hall, eventually, was able to follow via the Pyrenees (a feat of courage and endurance all the more extraordinary as she had a wooden leg).

On 27 February, another pick-up at the agreed rendezvous was made and at the fifth time of asking, was finally successful. On this occasion, Buckmaster had taken the very unusual step of sending his F Section Chief of Staff, Nicolas Boddington, to go across on 314. Stranger still are the various accounts stating that Boddington went on to the beach carrying a pistol and blackjack, and wearing a white duffle coat. If true, this demonstrates a ridiculous lack of operational security – the wearing of a white coat on a night operation aside, the notion of sending the Chief of Staff of F Section to France, let alone going ashore where he could easily have been captured, was fraught with danger. What makes it all the more foolhardy was that Boddington was a Dansey 'plant' in SOE. There has been considerable speculation as to Boddington's role in SOE and his involvement in wider and more complex strategic plans. He was suspected of being in touch with the Abwehr and SD: a double or triple agent, even. So why did he end up on a French beach? Perhaps on this occasion he wanted to make sure Bleicher's plan worked. This time it did – and Bleicher and his men were there to watch it unfold.

At dawn on 28 Feburary, 314 arrived back at Dartmouth. In the harbour, they found Buckmaster waiting for them on *Kiloran*. Over breakfast he was briefed on what had been going on in Paris, and told that the radio he thought was one of his own was actually being operated by the Germans. Now fully aware of the deception, Buckmaster sent a message to AUTOGIRO saying that de Vomécourt and Carré had reached London and that de Vomécourt was soon to return with a general in the Intelligence Services.

The responsibility of interrogating Mathilde Carré was given to Vera Atkins. To win her confidence Atkins set her up in a comfortable flat overlooking Hyde Park and for the next six weeks took her shopping and wined and dined her in expensive restaurants. Carré was encouraged to talk, especially in the flat, which was heavily bugged. By the time Atkins had finished with her, Carré had revealed everything she knew about the German intelligence operation, her arrests, Bleicher and the wireless game.

With Carré's usefulness to SOE now over, she was imprisoned in Holloway and then Aylesbury prison. After the war she was handed over to the French Government, where she was charged with treason and sentenced to death; this was commuted to twenty years in prison and she was released early in 1954. She died in 2007, aged 98. As to whether the almost unbelievable saga of Carré's triple-cross had worked, Ben Cowburn met Bleicher after the war when they both happened to be witnesses at a trial in Paris. 'He then looked at me almost pleadingly,' Cowburn recalled, 'and suddenly asked, "Tell me I beg of you, La Chatte, is it true she was double crossing me?" This proved beyond a doubt that our manoeuvre had succeeded and that for once the Germans had been properly fooled.'

*

The extraction of Carré and De Vomécourt was the last operation carried out by 314 for DDOD(I). As mentioned in the previous chapter, she was called back by Combined Operations to take part in the St Nazaire Raid where she was destroyed. Curtis returned briefly to Dartmouth, where he was due to command the ill-fated 501. After she blew up and sank, he left to join Ian Fleming's 30 Assault Unit where he spent the rest of the war.

But although the operation had eventually proved a success, it had come at a cost. The Germans were now fully aware of the type of operations being mounted by gunboats on the Brittany coast. From now on, the element of surprise, so essential in clandestine operations, would not be in the method – but in the delivery. Meticulous planning and attention to detail, together with precise navigation and choice of location, would be ever more crucial going forward.

CHAPTER 6 – AN EXTRA 'TOT'

'For the things we have to learn before we can do them, we learn by doing them'

Aristotle

The operation on 6 January 1943 had already been beset with difficulties even before the sightings at 0304. This was 318's second attempt at CARPENTER II, a mission to ferry and drop half a ton of stores. The first attempt, on 4 January, had been beaten by the weather. Despite a favourable report, the snow had started falling before the gunboat had even left Dartmouth. That had been followed by deteriorating weather across the Channel and rain squalls off the French coast: without spray shields on their binoculars, the surf-boat crews were travelling blind, and gave up after two hours of trying and failing to find the drop-off point. On 6 January, the weather was no better. 'At 2035, the Atlantic, in solid form, arrived on the foredeck,' Ted Davis drily noted afterwards, 'quickly followed by the Pacific.' This time, it took just fifteen minutes for the attempt to be abandoned.

Rather than a second fruitless night, it was decided to carry on with their secondary mission to drop FH830 sonar marker buoys. One was to be dropped near the Triagoz Plateau and the other near Île Grande, as an aid to future operations. The buoys were six-foot-high steel cylinders, housing homing transmitters and fitted with an explosive charge which detonated if the buoy was dragged to the surface. David Birkin was detailed to rig the charges: 'I was sent a long way from human habitation with a pensioner rating, the two buoys, 4lbs of TNT, detonators, a do-it-yourself assembly diagram, and a rusty penknife,' he later remembered.

The weather continued to be shocking, making conditions near the coast extremely difficult. Having dropped the first buoy at the Triagoz Plateau in twenty-eight fathoms of water and checking it was working using their echo-sounder, 318 set off to drop the second

Arming the buoys – David Birkin

buoy at Île Grande. 'Of all the festering collections of rocks on this rotten coast,' Davis wrote in his subsequent report to Slocum, 'the Île-Losquet area wins the hamburger. Not one of the islands on the chart could be distinguished. The swell here was most uncomfortable and its action on the outlying reefs was most impressive. It would start as a white breaker with a rumble and develop as a white express train with about the same volume of sound.'

Davis and Birkin struggled to fix the gunboat's position. They tried to find the Commanon Bank, eventually doing so at 0200 – recording a depth of five fathoms, taking the tide into consideration. They then recrossed the bank, using time, sounding and bearing of Triagoz to give them their position. The buoy was dropped and checked that it was working properly. Satisfied, course was set for Dartmouth.

0304. With a tremor of apprehension, the sight of six silhouettes loomed in the water just over a mile away. Enemy trawlers. How long 318 had been spotted was unclear, though given they were in the Germans' moon path, they had probably been seen some time before. Now came contact. The flash of a challenge. The letter code

‘O’ for orange. Davis’s instinct held firm. Unsilenced, the MGB rang for full speed and turned south east. Every second counted: the more distance they could put between them and the trawlers, the greater their chance of escape. Smoke canisters on board were used to set up a smokescreen, slowly at first and then billowing out as the MGB sped on.

Thirty seconds. No response. A minute. Silence. Maybe, the crew thought, they had got away with it. But ninety seconds later, the firing started. The German shots were unnervingly accurate, passing down both sides of the boat. Small stuff – two-pounder – was bursting overhead. It seemed to take an age for the smokescreen to have its effect, but finally there was a sense of being obscured from view: the Germans were firing at both ends of the screen, together with several points in between, trying to pin down the location of the ship. Now it was 318’s turn to try and locate the enemy’s position. At 0308, the smokescreen was stopped to help work this out. Shortly after this they started using three- or four-inch ammunition: some of these shells burst ahead and about six metres above the water. MGB 318 restarted the smoke, turning to south to gain cover of the land and rocks. The second smokescreen seemed to confuse the enemy completely: the shooting, which had started off so accurately, was becoming increasingly haphazard. At 0314 the two enemy trawlers engaged each other. Through the screen 318 watched with delight as their tracers flew backwards and forwards at each other. The engagement was brief. The Germans realised they had lost their catch, ceasing fire about 0320. 318 altered course again for home.

It had been a narrow escape. But the night, it turned out, had not quite finished with 318 just yet.

*

After the complications of the WATERWORKS and ROWAN affair in early 1942, there was a lull in activity for the Flotilla until the end of the year. During this lull in operations much training and planning was carried out. After the shambles of WATERWORKS, where Ben Cowburn described the dinghies used for ferrying agents to shore as completely useless (‘little better than inverted umbrellas’), a lot of work was done at Praa Sands in Cornwall to develop an effective surf-boat. A fourteen-foot design was eventually agreed on and proved to be very effective.

Commander Warrington-Smyth, who worked for DDOD(I) at Helford, was the person tasked with the development of an effective surf-boat. He carefully checked the reports of all such expeditions to date and discovered two obvious weaknesses that could lead to such failures. First, he found that the First Lieutenants had been given no special instruction in the handling of open boats, and second, that they were using small yacht dinghies for landing operations. These dinghies were clearly not suitable, capsizing easily and often losing oars in the surf. As an experienced yachtsman, Warrington-Smyth was well aware of the effect even small waves in shallow water had on a yacht dinghy when approaching a beach. The many duckings he had received himself in pre-war days loomed large in the memory.

Warrington-Smyth collected a number of dinghies, a Dutch surf-boat, a Norwegian pram, and various other types of small craft. He took them down to Praa Sands in Mount's Bay, Cornwall, where there was plenty of surf to be found. With the aid of a professional film unit, he observed the behaviour of each type of boat up to the point when it finally overturned. When the footage was studied in slow motion, the actual cause of the capsize could be pinpointed. With this knowledge, Warrington-Smyth then set to work to design a special surf-boat, the length being limited by the extent of the available deck space in the gunboats which would be carrying them.

Working to this design and incorporating some additions of their own, Messrs Camper and Nicholson produced three prototypes. Trials carried out with them in very cold and rough weather at Praa Sands proved completely successful. They were clinker built of wood with an identical transomed bow and stern (both overhanging the waterline rather than rising vertically from it), obviating the necessity of a turnaround on the beach. Motor propulsion was considered, but found to be too noisy at night, not to mention that in rough weather, the propeller thrashed the air when required to bite into the water. Oars were therefore substituted, using specially lengthened crutches and a long sweep oar for the helmsman to steer. The forks of these were made of rubber, not only to muffle the sound of the oars, but because metal crutches could penetrate the human body in the event of a violent capsize. To minimise the risk of them becoming unshipped with consequent loss of oars in rough water, they were also specially shaped and secured with a lanyard. The boats were also equipped with a sea anchor which could be streamed when breakers were anticipated to avoid a surf riding or broaching to. In total, Warrington-Smyth's design could carry up to five passengers and a crew of three. Each vessel in the Flotilla was issued with four of these new surf-boats as they came into production, and a course of instruction in handling them instituted for officers and men.

Once the correct type of surf-boat had been procured, many hours were spent training with them. Not only did the crews have to be able to handle the boats efficiently, it all had to be done in silence. The final push to land involved a journey of between 1,200 yards and 2 miles from the gunboat to the shore in pitch dark across strong tidal streams and often on a lee shore, meaning that the wind was blowing the boats towards land, making them harder to control. Phosphorescence was always a worry. The return journey always involved rowing into a head sea against the wind with a heavily laden boat. Finding the gunboat was a problem which Peter Williams addressed. He developed a small hydrophone which, when the gunboat echo-sounder was switched on, the regular pulses were picked up on the hydrophone and a course steered in the direction of the sound.

Surf-boat

A lot of the practice surf-boat work was done down in Cornwall. Alf Harris, a seaman gunner on 502 and one of the surf-boat crew, remembered that, 'We did a considerable amount of boat pulling practice particularly in surf around the Helford River area in Cornwall and as a stroke oar in a prams crew formed a pretty efficient team with George (Pusser) Hill as bowman. In fact, we were both quite proud when the First Lieutenant at the time, Lloyd Bott, told us we were his best crew. George was also my number two on the twin Oerlikon turret.

'The procedure as we closed on the beaches was that whoever was on the sweep oar, usually a Leading Seaman or Sub-Lieutenant, gave the order "Oars-Out Boat" whereupon I would jump out to port, Pusser to starboard, run the pram up the beach and turn her bow for the return trip. The advantage of the sweep oar steering as against a normal tiller was never more apparent than when Pusser and I with 502's Coxswain, Fred Smith, were at practice at Helford, Cornwall, when Smith gave a demonstration of sweep oar ability in and out of rocks with a skill that had to be seen to be appreciated.'

Harris remembered how phosphorescence was a real concern: 'We all wondered during the long pull to the beach if the pools of phosphorescence from our oars and passage through the water could be seen from shore. The surprise at the contrast between the chill of the water as we leapt in to run the prams up the beach and the seeming warmth of the sand on your feet.' Once in Brittany, there were additional challenges to consider. Harris recalled, 'the sudden shock while unloading supplies for the Resistance on the beach and seeing a pair of unmistakable female legs with skirt tucked up belonging to a young girl helping to unload the pram'. He also remembered vividly, 'the uncanny rustle of feet on shingle as people came down the beach to be taken back to England; at one time we had five or six in our pram which gave us a spot of bother keeping afloat as she was only 12 feet long'.

But all the practice and preparation was to pay off: 'As far as the actual landings were concerned, I can only remember a feeling of supreme confidence in those organising the mission and a determination not to let anyone down. Our job as prams crew was to ensure

Surf-boat launch

that we reached the beach however far it may be, to get there with no splashing of oars or noise and to get off the beach with whatever load was necessary and however difficult it may seem. I think we can justifiably claim to have achieved that, sometimes with a little effort particularly on one occasion when with more passengers than the prams were designed to carry, I pulled the whole way from beach to ship with my right foot jammed under an airman's chin. I might add he was only too happy to be in that position as it was bringing him back to England.'

In addition to the surf-boat training there was an intensive period of exercises covering such things as anchoring drills and beach procedures at the pinpoint. Every chance was taken to improve navigation skills. Hours were spent on the measured mile in Start Bay, calibrating speed with engine revs and differing sea and wind conditions; and measuring fuel consumption. Compass adjustments were also carried out regularly to ensure that courses could be steered precisely.

*

Warrington-Smyth's development of surf-boats wasn't the only experimentation taking place into missions. As Harold Pickles of 318 wrote, 'Innovations were the order of the day. 318 on occasion was swarming with these "boffins" dressed in bowler hats or trilbies and bow ties, and thick glasses – entirely out of keeping with the officers and matelots surrounding them. One particular invention which intrigued us, was a device in the form of an Aldis lamp with a lens. A cable was plugged into the electrics, and the second part of the contraption was carried in the surf-boat and took the form of a long post with a circular dome fixed on top which contained perhaps a dozen prisms. The idea was that the surf-boat, after making landfall and during the return to the mother ship, could look through the prism and pick up a reflection thereby giving a directional "fix" to facilitate a safe return.'

One of the 'boffins' that Pickles describes was Geoffrey Pidgeon, a young 18-year-old radio technician who worked for SIS at Whaddon Hall, their secret communications development centre, Section VIII. Section VIII was commanded by Richard Gambier-Parry, an old Etonian who had worked for the BBC until 1938 when an unfortunate episode with a secretary led to his resignation. He was recruited by SIS to run their Communications Research and Development. Section VIII was asked to develop a radio set to enable good ship-to-shore communication on an approach to a pinpoint by the MGB and for use by the surf-boat crew.

To locate the coastal party waiting on shore, they had tried several different methods of communication. The 'S Phone' designed for the SOE was rather bulky for those on shore and for the surf-boat. They also tried the US Navy RB7 by Emerson Radio of New York – again a large set for a dinghy or a party waiting under quite perilous conditions on the beach. The SIS wireless research team in 'Hut 12' at Whaddon Hall were tasked with finding a solution. The result was a small hand-held set with a short range – exactly what was required to communicate with the incoming party.

One trip that Geoffrey Pidgeon took to Dartmouth to fit and test communications was more dramatic than anticipated:

'Dennis [Smith, his Section VIII boss] told me to pack for a week or more away, from the next day. We were to go to Dartmouth in Devon to work on MGBs – another new acronym for me! He was to go down one day by Packard, and I was to follow on the next day with a Guy 15cwt wireless van with a selection of tools and a quantity of wireless gear. The Guy was a beast to drive so thank goodness I had an army pool driver. We had only army maps and all signposts were removed or blanked out. It was little help asking the way, since you would often get a rude answer, due to the parachutist scare. It was a little easier being in an army vehicle but still you might still find it difficult. Dennis gave me written instructions.'

By the time Pidgeon made it to *Westward Ho*, 'Dennis was already there but had gone out. I was shown a cabin and told that the Sunday lunch had been cleared away long before. However, a chef came along with a metal tray with several shoulders of lamb on it with piles of roast potatoes and told me to help myself. Then a sailor asked if I would like a drink and brought me an enamelled mug half full of rum! I had never had rum before and because I was thirsty drank the lot fairly quickly. After the meal and the rum – I staggered to my cabin and do not remember the rest of the day!

'Early the following morning Dennis appeared and told me what had to be done. I went aboard the furthest MGB of the three moored alongside. This was the MGB 502, the one chosen for our work. My first task was to add a di-pole aerial to those on the mast and that meant clambering up it without much help but fortunately it was not very tall. The aerial was not part of the new telephone test but for other tests being conducted ... I was told the first test was to be off Slapton Sands – an extensive beach some eight miles west along the coast from Dartmouth. At midday, after I installed the di-pole aerial on the mast – Dennis drove off in the Packard and I followed on in the Guy wireless van to Slapton Sands.

'The area was still totally closed to civilians and we had to pass through a tight security guard before driving on. We passed through desolate villages that were quite eerie. When we arrived at the beach there was already quite a party of Naval and Army officers there including "Freddie" Cox, and Dennis joined them to explain what MI6 (Section VIII) had produced. Off the beach was MGB 502 and Dennis was rowed out to it in a rubber dinghy.

'Before he left, I was given the new wireless telephone and told to keep talking until he either waved or flashed a light. So as soon as the MGB slowly moved away – I started with the alphabet a few times then counted slowly to 100 several times but soon got tired of that – so said the following rhyme: “Mary had a little lamb she also had a bear – I have often seen her little lamb but never seen her bare” – Captain Slocum descended on me like the wrath of god – shouting at me to “Stop that bloody nonsense – immediately!”

‘I was about to be in serious trouble with the famously grim Captain Slocum but help came at that very moment – as Dennis flashed a light showing he was out of range. I gathered that the test was over and a success. It proved that the contact was good up to the rather short distance required by Slocum for the brave men manning the ships.

‘After the test off Slapton Sands, they decided we needed to do a real test of the telephone at sea. So, the following night we set off in MGB 502 from Dartmouth and into the English Channel.

‘Apparently, we were to replicate a dinghy adrift – having left the enemy shore but missing the “mother” ship waiting in the pitch darkness. It had actually happened, meaning the dinghy somehow had to find its way back to shore and the dispatch party.

‘I was on the deck as it became dark and as I was not needed at the time I found my way below and to the navy telegraphist sitting at his wireless set. He then offered me some rum – again in an enamelled mug. This time, remembering my earlier rum, I only sipped it just in case I was needed.

‘We had been at sea for perhaps an hour when there was a lot of activity above and I went out on deck. There a very brave sailor was helped into a rubber dinghy – after being handed one of our new sets. A minute or two later we moved away from him. He was supposed to be a “returning crew” out from Brittany who had lost contact with the mother ship MGB 502. It was so dark that he was quickly lost from sight. Not involved, I went down and sat beside the friendly telegraphist.

‘After a few minutes my new friend received a message in Morse “en clair” and rushed up to the deck – followed by me. He took the message up to the skipper on the bridge where Dennis and Freddie Cox were working. The skipper let out a yell as the message told of a loose mine in the Channel – just where we were cruising. Apparently, it had been spotted by an MFV and only just reported. Two problems:

MGB 503 alongside the depot ship *Westward Ho* in Dartmouth Harbour, with the Royal Naval College seen behind.

one to try to spot the mine before it hit us and second get our "lost dinghy" back on board.

'The entire crew – including Dennis, Freddie Cox and me – were positioned around the ship to try to see the mine. Several sailors had long boat hooks to push it away if it got too close. Dennis was also on his wireless set trying to get the poor sailor in the dinghy back on board. After what seemed like an age he was alongside and quickly brought aboard to everyone's relief.'

*

Even with the gap between missions, naval routine continued. Harold Pickles gives a flavour of life on board 318:

'It was regular malpractice to "dhoby" (wash) oily overalls in a bucket of petrol. As our engines were propelled by high-octane petrol, the supply from the 1,800 gallons we carried presented no problem. The day dawned when our inoffensive Stoker 1st Class was busy dhobying his overall when our dim "Scouse" came along with his box of matches and with the determination of a man with suicidal tendencies threw lighted matches towards our unfortunate Stoker. Within seconds there was an almighty "flash", and the Stoker literally kicked the bucket, which spread blazing petrol down the ship's side. We had a fire on our hands; the several layers of paint on the ship's side and deck burnt furiously until we manned the fire hose and brought the fire under control. Our scouse "Ginger" was given fourteen days' stoppage of leave and ordered to scrape and paint the ship's side, which didn't prove to be an easy job as most of the operation was performed from a dinghy tied up alongside. The crew and his immediate "oppos" were given strict instructions that no help whatsoever should be given to him.

'Dhobying was always a chore but the morale of the crew and the wellbeing and cleanliness of the individual was dependent on this chore being performed on a regular basis. The consequences of not adhering to the basic rules was an outbreak of the infestation of crab-louse known as "crabs". An insect which burrows under the skin on the human body and is attributed to the lack of facilities for washing, rinsing and drying. We had a Stoker aboard 318 who was most meticulous with his personal cleanliness, but each time an outbreak was reported, he was sure to catch them! One wonders how we survived.

'I served on board 318 for three years, four months and fifteen days, and my duties were divided into sea duties and harbour duties. I performed most of the harbour jobs on board 318 during my service, with the exception of the engine room. These included painting, cleaning and servicing guns, cook, mess caterer, flunkey, postman and supplies collection and some navigator yeoman duties plus the one hundred and one daily chores which were handed out by the Coxswain. At sea, I was the Coxswain's relief on the wheel, bridge lookout, No 2 on the two pounder pom-pom, and boat's crew reserve.

'Perhaps it is apt to recall the job of "mess caterer". Each man had a victualling allowance of 1s.1½ d per day; officers 2s.4d per day. Should the allowance be overspent, each and every member of the crew had to contribute to the overspent kitty. We were overspent when I took over, hence the reason I got the job. I must point out that we also received an allowance of tea, sugar, kye [the naval version of Ovaltine] and tinned fruit which was based on the number of hours' sea time we put in during each month. It was therefore an advantage to the wellbeing of the mess kitty to have as much sea time as possible. It was fairly easy to work out: each man had so many ounces or part of an ounce for each hour at sea – all clever stuff provided you extracted every ounce out of the system.

'The mess caterer also had the job of planning the menu, and this was dependent on the monies available in the kitty. Generally, with a well-run mess the only time one could get into debt would be after December when Christmas dictated many extra goodies. On the credit side I must point out that should a profit be made this was equally distributed in cash to crew members. Much to the surprise of everyone my first act as mess caterer was to take the tins of Libby's Condensed Milk off the breakfast table. We were using a case a day "neaters" on Corn Flakes, and I replaced it by a mixture of two and one – it almost caused a riot!!! But we were soon in the black. My time as mess caterer coincided with the arrival of the tank landing craft of the US Navy. I visited these craft on the pretext of cementing Anglo-American relations, but I usually came back with a couple of cases of bully beef or some such items of tinned good.

'When the "C" class boats were commissioned they were fitted with a paraffin stove with oven, but how the devil any cook made a hot meal on that contraption I will never know. After a short while we were fitted with a coal-burning stove, similar to the present-day Aga. The only snag was that we had to coal ship and take down the chimney whilst at sea on operations and erect it when we came back into harbour. There were advantages to being cook: I had "galley slaves" peeling potatoes, mess deck dodgers washing up the greasy dishes and best of all no watchkeeping in harbour. I particularly remember baking bread – it never did rise all that well but was always eaten with gusto by the crew!

'At sea the first eighteen months of my service on 318 were perhaps the most instructive and rewarding. Under the guidance of Petty Officer Boyle, I took over as his relief on the "wheel" and being on the bridge where the "conning" of the boat took place I was always in a position to know just what was happening at any given time. Usually the Coxswain would take 318 out of harbour and take part of the first two-hour watch, generally from 1800 to 2000 hours. I would then take over from 2000 to 2200 hours by which time we would be in mid-English Channel. The Coxswain would then take the 2200 to midnight

Petty Officers Mould and Smith

and by this time "action stations" would be sounded, and all the crew would be called to their stations. I would normally take over as bridge look-out. We would do our landings or observations and, as soon as we were outside enemy territorial waters, we would revert to normal watchkeeping procedure, two hours on and two hours off. It was pretty taxing and tiring routing particularly if your harbour duties happened to be cook of the mess, and cooking breakfast and preparation for a midday meal had to follow on after the hour early- morning watchkeeping routine.

'In our training session we were instructed not to speak of our "clandestine voyages" to the Brittany coast of France, and indeed posters throughout the country warned that "CARELESS TALK COSTS LIVES". However, our matelot who hailed from Oxford was home on leave and his father took him to the "local" pub for a drink and during the conversation at the bar he explained the operations which we undertook on behalf of SOE with the 15th MGB Flotilla. Of course, the inevitable happened – alongside them apparently taking little notice of their conversation was an Army Major who at once realised the significance of his "Careless Talk" and immediately made a report. By the time "our matelot from Oxford" returned to 318, he was arrested and charged and spent the next 180 days in the "glasshouse".'

*

Despite all these improvements and preparations, the period from March 1942 to October 1943 was a tough time for the Flotilla. This was a period when very few agents were landed or exfiltrated. The Germans had occupied the whole of France on 10 November 1942 and throughout 1942 and 1943 had considerable success in rolling up SOE networks. Such operations that were undertaken were all carried out by 318 under the successive command of Mike Martin, Eric Horner and Jan McQuoid Mason. The lack of action felt particularly frustrating because with the Battle of the Atlantic raging, Britain was fighting to maintain a flow of armaments, raw materials and food.

The imperative for SIS was intelligence on German submarine bases on the French Atlantic coast. But from the summer of 1942 when the Germans created a 15-mile Prohibited Zone along the whole of the north coast of France, SIS use of the Dartmouth boats fell away to nothing: it was thought to be too difficult for agents to penetrate in or out of the Prohibited Zone. Instead, SOE came up with an alternative plan for the gunboats to take large quantities of stores – mostly weapons, ammunition and explosives – from Dartmouth to the Brittany coast. The Flotilla would go to an agreed pinpoint, take the stores ashore and bury or hide them in a cache, for later collection by the Resistance networks.

The stores were packed up in waterproof containers with shoulder straps to be carried to the caching site – which needed to be easily identifiable to those collecting – and all traces of delivery obliterated. All this to be carried out on a moonless night, in enemy territory, with all the associated physical effort involved in loading the stores into surf-boats, man-packing the 60-pound cases to the cache site and then burying or concealing them, while clearing the site of any traces. That would have been challenge enough, but the hidden stores were all in the Prohibited Zone, making collection and transport much more difficult. One wonders whether they ever had any chance of success: it would have been far simpler to airdrop containers to a reception committee outside the Prohibited Zone. Certainly, Ted Davis and Angus Letty were sceptical and resented SOE's determination to have the Flotilla carry out these operations. To make matters worse, the winter of 1942/3 was to be one of the worst on record for the Channel with unusually cold temperatures and strong winds.

These operations were given the overall codename of LARDERING. The first in this series, codename CARPENTER, took place on 9/10 October 1942, with the aim of landing half a ton of stores on the beach at Grac'h Zu. On the first attempt on 9 October the weather was so bad off Start Point that 318 suffered a lot of damage as she was shipping seas up to the wheelhouse. On the 11th, 318 tried again. At midnight, they arrived off the coast but found themselves completely surrounded by rocks and rough water. It took an hour of manoeuvring and reversing to dexterously pick their way out of this. Navigation continued to prove difficult and the attempt was abandoned at 0230. A third attempt was abandoned early on due to a change in plan for other naval operations in the Channel.

The fourth attempt on 15 October also fell foul of terrible weather off Start Point. This time, 318 persevered and reached the Brittany coast at 2230. But the surf was extremely strong, far too strong to get the stores ashore, and the attempt was abandoned. Ted Davis, in charge of the mission, decided not to turn for home immediately as he wanted to observe the pattern of the surf for future planning. For twenty minutes, they stayed just outside the rocks, watching. At 0141 they turned back, having a most uncomfortable crossing. To compound matters further, just off the coast near Start Point, the engines failed. These were eventually restarted and they finally reached Dartmouth well after first light.

The initial failures were put down to bad weather and difficult conditions but underneath it was a good old-fashioned personality clash. SOE had recruited Pierre Guillet who at first glance appeared to be a Breton fisherman who had escaped France and joined the organisation. However, he was much more than that: not only was he an expert at coastal navigation on the Breton coast, but he had been around Cape Horn on a square-rigger and held a master mariners' ticket for steam and sail. Guillet was made a lieutenant in the RNVR and in July 1942 was awarded a DSC. He was then chosen to go on the CARPENTER operations.

No one, however, had told Ted Davis. When Davis spotted him on

318, he asked who Guillet was. As his presence was explained, Davis proclaimed that as the Navigating Officer of the QUEEN MARY he didn't need a scruffy Frenchman to tell him how to navigate. An impasse was reached, with both refusing to go to sea with the other. In the end, a solution was found by arranging for Davis to be summoned to a meeting in London. On 10 November 318 sailed with Pierre Guillet, for a fifth attempt at CARPENTER. This time, they found the beach immediately and the operation was a complete success.

*

When 318 evaded the German trawlers during the return from the second attempt at CARPENTER II on 6 January 1943, it was a triumph that proved to be short-lived. As one threat receded, so another reared its head.

Throughout the confrontation with the enemy ships, the gunboat's engines had been misfiring, with large quantities of water breaking over her. Over the next half-hour, as 318 tried to put the German threat behind them, rather than accelerating away, speed had to be gradually reduced. The wind was from the south, force 7, and the sea very rough, with a heavy swell. The boat had to be watched continuously as she took the hit and rode a swell at exceptionally high speed. On several occasions engines had to be stopped to allow the swell to pass underneath. The wind increased to force 8 gusting to 9. 318 was now battling high sea and swell, overcast and rain, with wave height rising to 30 feet. These conditions worried Martin and scared Davis 'almost stiff': 'We were all thinking about the steering gear,' he later wrote, 'but nobody dared mention it.'

The bad weather would have a final sting in the tail: when land was finally sighted at 1000 the following morning, the crew realised that rather than reaching Dartmouth, they were much further west towards Plymouth. As if things couldn't get worse, they were forced to use half speed on only one engine. Rather than finding safer harbour, 318 was in a very nasty spot: every wave had to be watched and on one occasion a wave broke across the boat behind the bridge, taking away the surf-boats and flooding the engine room.

'I was taking the early-morning watch on the "wheel",' remembered Able Seaman Harold Pickles DSM, 'and the Coxswain was taking a rest in his cabin below when the Skipper realised that to avoid running aground in Wembury Bay he would have to change course, bringing the boat round on a new westerly heading. The Skipper explained to me what he intended doing and gave me precise instructions that at his command I must immediately put the wheel over to "hard-a-port". As soon as the boat responded to the rudder I was to steady her on a new course of 30 degrees to port.'

This, however, proved easier said than done: 'A suitable wave and trough appeared, the command was given, and "hard-a-port" ordered. The boat shuddered, she started to come round and then appeared to stop and with an almighty crash heeled over at an angle of about 50 degrees. Everyone on the mess deck in the bunks on the starboard side of the ship were literally thrown out on to either the mess deck tables or the deck. The Coxswain was on the bridge post-haste and raved at me with a mouthful of choice words and told me in no uncertain terms, never to take on such a manoeuvre again without first calling him! The sequel to this tale came ten minutes later when the hydraulic steering collapsed under the strain and we had to rig the hand steering from the stern of the boat and orders from the bridge given by word of mouth.'

At 1310, after being within five miles of Plymouth for four hours, they secured to HMS DEFIANCE. They could now eat and drink for the first time since leaving Dartmouth. Davis reported that this was the first operation during which not one officer had had any sleep whatsoever. Everyone was exhausted. There was at least a modicum of reward for their efforts: 'For the third time in a period of twelve months,' Pickles recalled, 'Paddy Boyle our Coxswain persuaded the Skipper, Lieutenant Charles (Pincher) Martin DSC, that the crew were deserving an extra "tot".'

Of the twenty hours that the operation lasted, the Coxswain, Petty Officer Boyle, had been on the bridge for fifteen, and Davis considered that they owed their partly successful return to harbour to his skill, unfailing cheerfulness and sense of humour. The behaviour of the motor mechanic, Petty Officer Barker, had also been splendid:

his efforts to keep the engines running at high speed while in contact with the enemy, despite the obvious difficulties audible to those on deck, and his constant care of the engines on the return passage, when they were endeavouring to race themselves to pieces, enabled the gunboat to return safely.

*

In spite of the weather and constant pounding damage to 318 was negligible. CARPENTER II was never completed, though it was not finally cancelled until April. There was an attempt at another operation, CARPENTER III to Île Stagadon, but this also failed as there was no sand to bury the containers of stores – an example of terrible planning by SOE, resulting in a futile operation endangering 318 and her crew.

The final chapter in the LARDERING saga consisted of operations DRAPER, COOK and HAPPEN. DRAPER took 318 to Stagadon again, where whey managed to establish a small cache in a secluded cave. COOK was the last fruitful operation to the Aber-Benoit Channel to bury arms on the Île Guénnoc. This time they landed successfully but found there was not enough sand to bury the cases. There were fifteen cases each weighing 80 pounds, a total of half a ton. In the end, the crew were able to hide twelve of the fifteen cases in the rocks. Operation HAPPEN was scheduled for 27 September 1943, but failed to live up to its name: the operation was abandoned when 318 was nearly lost in a force 7 gale.

Even the semi-success of Operation COOK almost ended in disaster, when seaweed gatherers subsequently found some of the containers. The containers not only had weapons and ammunition inside but also food, whisky, sweets and biscuits. Thanks to the seaweed gatherers' find, many of the sweets found their way to local children who went about openly munching this unheard-of and obviously British luxury. Once the local Lannilis Resistance leaders – Louis Bodiger, Amédée Rolland and the gendarme Derrien – heard what was going on they acted quickly to move the containers. Keeping the children and their chattering mothers quiet, however, was another question. Here, the Resistance leaders enlisted the help of

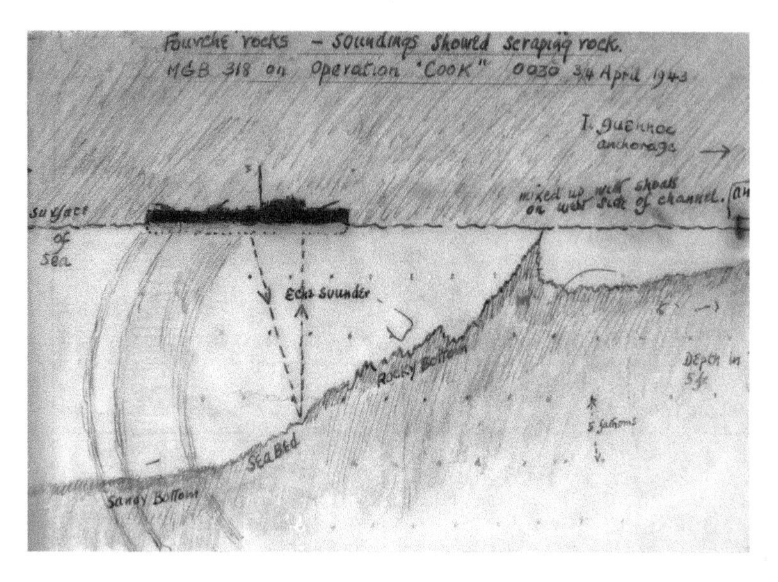

the Curé of Landéda, the 75-year-old Abbé Saliou. This brave man told his congregation that if British provisions were discovered in their possession, they would find themselves visiting the Gestapo in St Brieuc. This risky strategy worked, and no more illicit groceries were seen in the streets or schoolyard.

Overall, the LARDERING operations were not a success. They were considered again for implementation prior to D-Day but were not implemented. One particular worry was that the numerous attempts at LARDERING operations had alerted the Germans to the interest in this part of the coast. Some involved considered the operations to be ill thought through and poorly planned, not only alerting the Germans but endangering both ships and crews in the process.

But for all the failings of the LARDERING project, there remained positives for Slocum and his teams to take away. In particular, the training value for the ships' crews and surf-boat teams, not to mention to the navigational experiences, would prove invaluable for future operations. The 15th MGBF now had a really strong team spirit, centred round the crews which had worked together during that winter.

CHAPTER 7 – L'ABER-WRAC'H

> 'A brave captain is a root, out of which as branches, the courage of his soldiers doth spring'
>
> Sir Philip Sidney

At first glance, it seemed an everyday scene at Café de la Place on the main square of the Breton market town of Lannilis. Apart from the presence of German soldiers, who had recognised its charms and chosen to frequent it, it was a snapshot in time that could have taken place at any point in the previous decades. Sat outside the front, Amédée Rolland, the café's owner, and his friend, Pierre Jeanson, were chatting, drinking a glass of wine, and passing the time of day.

Jeanson, however, was also known as SAROL, in command of the Brittany part of the Secret Intelligence Service JADE FITZROY circuit, and second-in-command of the escape line set up and run by Pierre Hentic (code name MAHO). And rather than idly chatting, Jeanson and Rolland were carefully keeping watch. They weren't the only ones. Perched in a tree opposite, hiding among its branches, was another member of the Resistance, Robert Jestin. All three were keeping look-out for the sight they all dreaded: German radio detection vans.

Amédée Rolland's café showing the attic where the radio was hidden

Amédée Rolland

Robert Jestin

Rolland's café didn't just attract customers for the quality of its coffee. While German soldiers relaxed downstairs, up above in the attic was the advance headquarters for Hentic's team.

It was here that Hentic and Jeanson would join radio operators Eugène Lorion (JEANNOT), and Jean Bougier (JACQUES) tapping out messages to London and anxiously awaiting the replies which came as coded messages in French at the end of the BBC's overseas news bulletins.

On 3 November 1943, those crouched around the radio were listening out for one very specific message: 'Les faux-cols de George-Henri sont prêts à la blanchissière' ('The detached collars of George-Henri are ready at the laundry'). When this was broadcast just after 1800 hours that evening, it was the sign that the operation was in motion.

The operation was a vital one for two reasons. Its first aim was to collect fifteen Allied airmen escaping back from France. Its second was to pick up some highly important top-secret mail: among the letters were the details of the V1 and V2 launch sites. Earlier that day Jean-François Derrien, the gendarme from Lannilis, had been asked to find transport for the evaders. He arranged with Louis Bodiger, in charge of a local fifty-man réseau, to use one of his vans to move them.

Bodiger's van had transported the passengers to the peninsula of Sainte-Marguerite at Landéda, the agreed rendezvous point, where the boatmen Joseph Mouden, Théophile Jaouen from Tréglonou, Amédée Rolland, the café owner, François Coum and the coastguard

Le Guen from Landéda had been waiting. Under the watching eyes of German sentries, the team made for the Île Tariec at low water in small groups, under the pretence of being shellfish gatherers. It was a nerve-wracking transfer, but Hentic thought it safer to do the journey by day 'au nez et à la barbe des Allemands' – under the German's noses. From the Île Tariec, Job Mouden transported the seventeen clandestine passengers to the Île Guénnoc in his boat.

Having dropped the airmen, the team returned to the café in Lannilis to await developments. At 1800, came the confirmation they were waiting for: 'Les faux-cols de George-Henri sont prêts à la blanchissière.' By the time the message was received, 318 had been en route for just over an hour. Operation ENVIOUS was a go.

*

During 1943 the fortunes of war were finally turning in the Allies' favour. The submarine menace in the Atlantic was receding, America was firmly in the war and planning for the invasion of Europe was well underway. For SIS, the intelligence priorities were changing. Now the focus was on the acquisition of intelligence on the coastal defences in France and the German order of battle, and on the emerging V1 rocket threat to London and the invasion build-up.

After a pause of some twenty months, the winter of 1943 also saw the beginning of the heyday of DDOD(I) and the 15th MGBF. Slocum finally had a properly supported and organised set-up at Dartmouth with a planning staff, air liaison, and three gunboats in 318, 502 and 503 (there were soon to be four with the arrival of 718 in early 1944). At the same time, SIS were 'back in the fold' as far as maritime insertion of agents was concerned. SOE, too, had recovered from the reverses of 1941 and 1942 and was now ramping up its activity: with the invasion of Europe at an advanced stage of planning, SOE would have a big part to play. As well as all of this, there was a need to evacuate the growing number of downed aircrew on the run in Brittany – an increase due to the Allied air attacks on French Atlantic ports.

One of the key SIS networks tasked with the collection of strategic

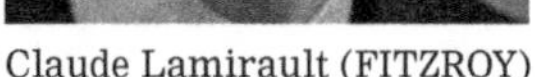

Claude Lamirault (FITZROY) Pierre Hentic (MAHO)

intelligence was the JADE FITZROY circuit. Pierre Hentic, code name MAHO, had joined the Resistance as second in command of JADE FITZROY in January 1941. In 1942 Hentic had been arrested at a Lysander pick-up that went wrong. Luckily, he had been in the unoccupied zone and was sent to prison in Périgueux. In November 1942 he managed to escape and make his way to London. He was then parachuted back into France on 27 May 1943, following the arrest of Claude Lamirault (FITZROY) in December 1943, to set up a new network, to conduct parachute and air landing operations for SIS.

It had been Lamirault who had recruited Hentic in the first place – the pair knew each other from the time they served together in the Chasseurs Alpins. Lamirault, described by Bill Cordeaux, Deputy Director SIS Naval Section, as 'tough as any gangster', had been recruited by SIS to set up JADE FITZROY, a country-wide intelligence network, on behalf of Biffy Dunderdale. A member of the extreme right and a fervent Catholic, Lamirault had escaped to Britain in October 1940. He parachuted back into France in January 1941, with cash and a radio, to set up the network. Initially he recruited his family and old comrades from the 27th Regiment of the Chasseurs Alpins, including Hentic. Hentic, as a young communist, could not have been more different from Lamirault, but the partnership was to work very well.

To begin with, JADE FITZROY was a sub-network of the successful JADE AMICOL network. JADE AMICOL had been set up by Claude Arnould and Phillip Keun. Phillip Keun's father, George, was

British[22] and his mother, Germaine Tarbierre, Anglo-French, and both were very close friends of Biffy Dunderdale. Phillip himself attended Blundells School in Devon from 1925–1930. Described by Bill Cordeaux as an 'international adventurer with more than his fair share of charm and cunning', he was recruited by SIS, and worked on several missions for them in Turkey, Hungary and Bulgaria. By 1940, he was in Paris and Biffy Dunderdale asked him to stay there to set up an intelligence network.

Co-founding JADE AMICOL with Father Claude Arnould, the pair set up their headquarters in the Convent of the Sisters of Sainte-Agonie in rue de la Santé in Paris. But when they were betrayed through penetration of other networks, including INTERALLIÉ and ALLIANCE, Arnould was arrested. Keun escaped, and although JADE FITZROY and JADE AMICOL had gone their separate ways in 1942 after a dispute between the two leaderships, he and Pierre Hentic (MAHO) pulled together the remnants to work together. These included AMICOL members Mathurin Branchoux and André Le Cun in Guingamp, whom we will meet later. Hentic took control of operations and Keun was the network organiser.

JADE FITZROY's mission was to collect strategic intelligence including troop movements, submarine activity from the Atlantic ports and anything on V1 and V2 rockets. One of JADE FITZROY's early recruits was Alice Coudol who in 1940 had set up her own network 'Le Mouvement Violette' in Brest to gather intelligence on submarine bases. This network was absorbed into JADE FITZROY. Coudol also worked for the ALLIANCE network and initiated the local Resistance network in the Aber-Benoît/Aber-Wrac'h area, centred around the towns and villages of Lannilis, Tréglonou, Landéda, Kernilis and Plouguerneau. She had seen the potential of the area and had initially approached Théophile Jaouen in April 1943. After his initial concern that her approach might be a Gestapo 'sting'

22 In Keith Jeffrey's official history of MI6, and Pierre Hentic's *Agent de l'ombre*, he is described as Anglo-Dutch. Keun's father divorced his mother in 1913 when Keun was two, remarrying Eugina Sfiatslàvona von Gunther, daughter of a White Russian officer. His mother remarried a French banker, Raymond Tortière. George Keun was a leading European trader in pharmaceutical opium, and lived in great splendour in Paris and at the Villa Tanah Merah on Cap d'Antibes, where Dunderdale was a regular house guest.

Phillip Keun

Alice Coudol

Edmond Calves

operation, he accepted that she was genuine. Jaouen in turn thought of his close friend Amédée Rolland, in Lannilis. Rolland agreed to help, telling Jaouen 'tu peux compter sur moi' ('you can count on me').

Coudol also suggested the formation of a fifty-man réseau. Together with Jaouen, they went to see the local head of the Gendarmerie, Jean-François Derrien. This was a considerable risk as he might have arrested them on the spot. Derrien was the only one in the police station, his colleagues being out on patrol. After a long conversation Derrien agreed to join the Resistance and promised to coopt the other gendarmes. This was to prove particularly useful as they could pass through roadblocks, provide security for clandestine movement and give advance warning of German operations. Coudol thought Derrien as a gendarme would inspire confidence in others if he was seen to be with the Resistance. She encouraged him to begin recruiting a group of 400 men in the Lannilis, Landéda and St Marguerite area. One of her early recruits was a draughtsman Edmond Calves (PHILIPPE). He worked in the Brest Arsenal. He was trusted by the Germans and could rove around freely noting every detail without being noticed: 'I methodically counted, measured and memorised everything I saw. Every evening I worked at my draughtsman's table, noting everything on hand-copied maps. Urgent messages were sent by radio, the rest microfilmed and sent to London.' Sadly, just as she was getting into her stride, she was arrested on 4 October 1943 in Lesneven, taken to the Château Trouzilit, severely tortured, deported and executed on 30 November 1944 at Pforzheim

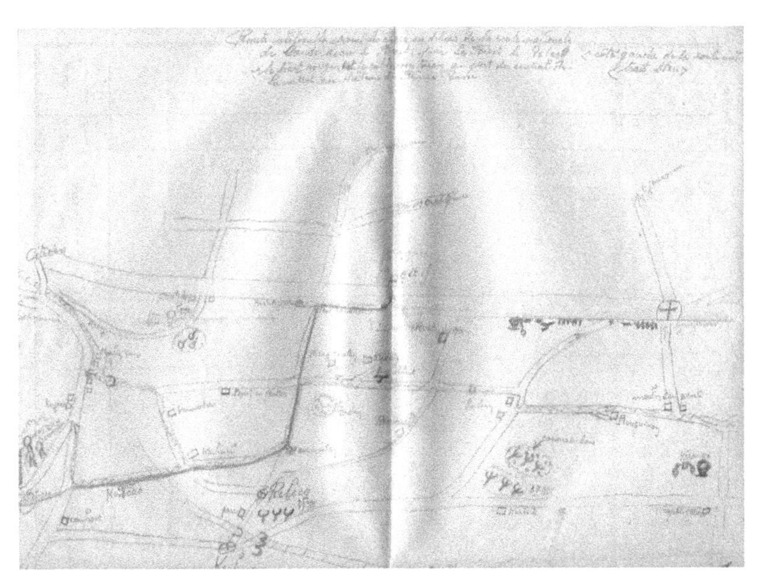

One of Calves's sketches showing German defences in Brest

in Germany. She was shot in the back of the neck by Julius Gehrom, Head of Gestapo in Strasbourg.

Despite her torture, Coudol gave nothing away and the réseau stayed intact. It was run by Louis Bodiger and Amédée Rolland. Bodiger owned a transport company, running the local bus service. Other key members of the group were Claude Tanguy who provided transportation, assisted by his son Edouard,[23] Robert Jestin, Louis Bodiger's son-in-law, Guillaume and Joseph Le Guen, Job Mouden, Louis and François Coum, Jean Galliou, Joseph Pronost and René Le Gall.

In addition, a number of families in Brest and throughout the area were providing safe houses when needed. So many were the helpers that, when Hentic arrived in the summer of 1943 to study the possibility of maritime pick-ups, it seemed that much of the population was devoted to the Allied cause.

Hentic had been arranging Lysander pick-up operations for agents and secret mail since 1941, but due to the increasing number of airmen on the run and the need to repatriate them urgently,

23 Edouard Tanguy was fifteen at the time. His school had been closed by the Germans. In a recent conversation with the author he described his Resistance work as 'my summer holiday job'.

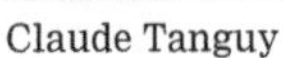

Claude Tanguy

Louis Bodiger

Michel Hollard

more transport capacity was needed. Hence Hentic had travelled to Brittany to try and set up maritime pick-ups. Briefed on the Le Tac/ OVERCLOUD operations to the Aber-Wrac'h when in London, he arranged with DDOD(I) to use the Aber-Benoît estuary as a pick-up point for JADE FITZROY/AMICOL and AGIR mail to be sent to SIS.

Among the mail Hentic had to send safely to London was crucial intelligence on the V1 and V2 rocket launching sites, which had come from Michel Hollard who ran the AGIR network. Hollard was a sales representative for a company that made gas generators for motor cars (a job which allowed him to travel all over France), and had offered his services to the British assistant military attaché in Berne in January 1942. He was at first rejected, but the report he made on the French motor and aero industries was graded so highly that, when he turned up again in May, SIS recruited him at once. With Victor Farrel his controller in Berne, Hollard built up a network that included many railway workers. He began by reporting economic intelligence and the German order of battle in France. Then in August 1943, one of his agents drew attention to a site near Rouen where the Germans were imposing unusually precise specifications on the French building contractors. Masquerading as a labourer, Hollard investigated for himself and found mysterious 'miniature runways' being constructed – all of which were carefully aligned on bearings pointing towards London and the D-Day assembly areas of Southampton and Portsmouth. The Berne station was not particularly impressed by the information, but when it was sent to London it was realised that they

Pierre Tissier (PIERROT)

were launching-ramps for the V1 flying bomb. Hollard was instructed to concentrate exclusively on locating other such sites, which he and his colleagues did with extraordinary success.[24]

So in October 1943, keen to establish this maritime link, Hentic escorted his first group of airmen to be repatriated, from Paris to Brittany. Hentic travelled to Brittany with his number two, Pierre Tissier (PIERROT) and one of his radio operators Eugène Lorion (JEANNOT). Hentic made contact with Louis Bodiger at the beginning of November via one of his agents Monsieur Broc'h (FLORETTE),[25] he discovered a second burning issue: they were completely preoccupied with gathering, hiding and feeding large numbers of British and American aircrew who had been shot down and were now evading capture. Hentic fully realised the value of these airmen, and the need to get them out of France and to allow the Resistance to concentrate on other work. He contacted Dunderdale with a proposal: to use the gunboat connection for his mail and also to evacuate the first fifteen evaders. DDOD(I) agreed, and so began what David Birkin described as 'The Aber-Wrac'h Saga'. The initial operation for Hentic – code name ENVIOUS – was planned for the night of 3/4 November.

*

Preparations for the operation began on both sides of the Channel. Hentic's first task was to tighten up the structure of the local network to ensure operational security. He divided them into four teams: his own command group, and three further groups for providing safe houses for the escapees, transport and the guides and reception committee for the beach operations. Back in Dartmouth, 318 was still the only boat immediately available for operations. Lieutenant Jan McQuoid Mason, newly appointed, was in command. Mike Pollard

24 Hollard was eventually betrayed, arrested and tortured, but gave nothing away. He was sent to Neuengamme Concentration Camp, but survived.
25 Broc'h worked as Assistant Mayor in Guissény. He would supply all the false papers to the evaders.

was his First Lieutenant, David Birkin was the Navigating Officer and Ted Davis in overall command of the operation.

The pinpoint chosen was Rosservor, the most westerly of the three isles (Île Tariec and Guénnoc). It was one David Birkin may have had some apprehension about, having been the location for the ill-fated LARDERING operation – CARPENTER – earlier in the year. It was 110 miles from Falmouth – the furthest of the pinpoints from England – and under favourable conditions took six or seven hours' steaming time. The double journey plus waiting time off the pinpoint could take up to twenty-five hours if weather conditions were poor.

The area was well-known to both the men of 318 and Bretons alike. The locals called it 'La Côte des Naufrageurs' – Shipwreck Coast. They were fully aware of the navigational difficulties and the fact that gales could blow up in a very short time. From the sea, the first indication of approaching land, with luck, was a sudden lessening of the echo-soundings as the MGB passed over the western tip of the Le Libenter bank and then, with more luck, the appearance of La Petite Fourche Buoy marking the seaward end of the Aber-Benoît Channel – left there by the Germans to guide local fishing boats, though night fishing was not allowed and the buoy was not lit. From the buoy, the gunboat had to make its way, into the Aber-Benoît Channel, in some places only 100 yards wide and often with breaking water on either side, to the rendezvous anchorage ninety yards off the south-west tip of Île Guénnoc.

David Birkin's sketch of the approach to Guénnoc

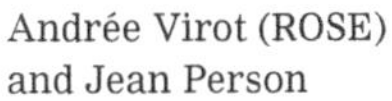

Andrée Virot (ROSE) and Jean Person

The Roué farm. The radio was operated from behind the top left shutters

Aside from the natural dangers, the area selected for the pinpoint was in the middle of a very heavily defended part of the coastline: it featured two batteries of heavy artillery firing seaward from block-houses and numerous smaller pillboxes with heavy machine guns. The foreshore was mined, and the minefields covered by searchlights and machine guns. In addition, there was a notice displayed in every town hall, police station and village square:

> *'Any help given to enemy aircrew by a Frenchman will be reason to shoot him immediately. Women found guilty of the same offences will be sent to concentration camps in Germany.*
> By order of General of Infantry Stülpnagel, 22 September 1941'

The method of repatriating escapers by MAHO and his group was fraught with dangers. Allied airmen from far afield were brought to Landerneau railway station, in the care of an agent who had boarded the Paris–Brest Express at Rennes. On disembarking, they were taken over by members of the group, assisted by station staff who were sympathetic to the Resistance. From there, they were distributed to 'safe houses' in Landerneau and surrounding villages including the Roué farm, which was also used for radio transmissions, or taken by car to Brest. The operation in Brest was run by Doctor and Madame de la Marnierre with assistance from Andrée Virot (ROSE), Colonel Scheidaur and his two daughters Ghislaine and Christiane. Then they began the nerve-wracking wait for sea transport to England and the really tricky part of the operation.

Despite the German warning notices, the whole area around L'Aber-Wrac'h was full of willing helpers and in particular the villages of Kernilis, Plouguerneau, Treglonou, Landéda, and the market town of Lannilis. Help took the form of transport by vans, cars and even horse-drawn carts, food and accommodation, and a rowing boat with oarsmen for the final six hundred metres between Île Tariec and Île Guénnoc when that was the chosen rendezvous.

As 3 November approached, the weather for once seemed on 318's side. There was a south-west wind force 3–4, producing a slight to moderate sea and swell – enough to confuse the German surface radar detectors. Best of all, the sky was overcast, which cut down the likelihood of phosphorescence – always a danger on starry nights. As well as Davis, Birkin, Mason and Pollard already mentioned, the crew also included Tassie Uhr-Henry as Boats Officer, in charge of the landing party, and Petty Officer Mould the Coxswain. If conditions on setting out seemed too good to be true, they were. Halfway across the Channel, the centre engine started spluttering. A quarter of an hour later it completely stopped due to fuel starvation. From that moment onwards until 318 reached harbour the next morning, one of the crew had to pump the petrol by hand.

By 2000 hours the sudden appearance of very low cloud and drizzle greatly reduced visibility. Two hours later it had become very misty. At 2225 hours, the spluttering engines were silenced to pass through the German Coastal Convoy route ten miles off the coast. Speed was maintained; time was always a precious commodity. Visibility, meanwhile, was getting worse, just as the MGB was approaching the rocky coastline. Right on course they picked up a prominent rock – Le Relée – which Birkin was using as his first marker. At 8 knots, MGB 318 started nosing towards the land. Visibility was now down to two hundred yards or less as the patchy mist swirled around the gunboat. At 0010 the mist cleared for a second: before the blanket of fog came down again, an island became vaguely visible a quarter of a mile ahead. 318 anchored, Tassie and his crew went in a dinghy to identify that the island was indeed Rosservor. But no one was there waiting for them.

Unbeknownst to 318, the fifteen airmen awaiting rescue, together with the details of the V1 and V2 launch sites, were sat two miles away on Île Guénnoc. Due to a misunderstanding between London and the Resistance Headquarters in Lannilis, the two sides had come away with differing ideas of where the pinpoint was. To make matters more galling still, at midnight the airman had seen the MGB in the mist. There followed a frantic flashing of torches in her direction, but to no avail. On Rosservor, 318's two dinghies were duly landed with stores for the Resistance which were hidden in the rocks. At 0245 Tassie and the two rowing dinghies returned. By 0306, as the mist was clearing, they were en route for home again. They arrived back in Dartmouth at 1000 very disappointed – though not half as disappointed as the airmen they'd left behind.

Later that same morning, MAHO and his group returned to Lannilis. That night they tried in vain to establish contact with London by radio. By 5 November, concern was growing about how long they could leave the airmen on Guénnoc. At the very least, they needed to be provided with food and water. This was done at considerable risk during the afternoon, once again in full view of the German look-outs and once more with MAHO and his group playing the role of seaweed and shellfish gatherers. The airmen – by now ravenous, freezing and soaked to the skin – devoured the food. But in spite of protests, they were told to remain where they were in case a rendezvous could be arranged for the night of the 6th. But once more, contact with London could not be established. On 7 November, MAHO decided that the fifteen airmen must now be brought back to the mainland: they were too at risk from the weather, from possible exposure and from the likelihood of being discovered by the Germans. Guénnoc was an inhospitable place at the best of times, but in very bad weather it was not sustainable. It is more or less flat, with no trees, bushes or cover from the elements of any sort. That night they were evacuated back to the mainland. The gendarmes provided security and safe passage to the safe houses.

MAHO decided he needed to go to London to consult with Dunderdale and Slocum. He left by Lysander from a site near Reims on the night of 11th/12th,[26] with the return trip to be by MGB on the

26 David Birkin managed to squeeze in his wedding on 9 November, between operations ENVIOUS I and II.

next attempt to pick up the airmen. This could now not take place until the night of 26 November, which was the beginning of the next non-moon period. But operation ENVIOUS IIa was no more successful than the first. At 2300, they found themselves in among the very dangerous Grande Fourche rocks and went rapidly into reverse. Then, looming out of the drizzle, they found the Petite Fourche buoy. 318 crept up the Channel and anchored off Guénnoc. The boats were launched but returned an hour and a half later empty-handed. Guénnoc was deserted. They went back up the estuary to La Relée Rock where they dropped MAHO to head back to his team.

MAHO had been insistent on going ashore to get operations going. He canoed to the island of Rosservor, making it ashore both freezing cold and soaked to the skin. Not only that but he found himself in the middle of the German defences – barbed wire and, unknown to him, a newly laid minefield. It took him four hours crawling carefully to extract himself, lightly brushing the sand with his fingertips to detect the mines. It was morning when he reached the garage of Gaston Boursier, a member of JADE FITZROY who was astonished at how he had made it through the German defences. While that was going on, 318 had set course back for Falmouth at 0315. Once more the journey was marked by terrible weather and engine trouble, with the boat not getting back until midday.

The next attempt, ENVIOUS IIb, was to take place on the night of 1/2 December 1943. Again, transport was arranged by Derrien, the Lannilis gendarme, to take the airmen from the safe houses. By 27 November, all was arranged both locally, and with DDOD(I) for the night of 1 December – as well as land transport for the airmen, a flat-bottomed boat and boatman was arranged to ferry the airmen the six hundred metres between Tariec and Île Guénnoc.

On the afternoon of the 1st, the twenty airmen assembled at Landéda, about two miles from Tariec. In small groups, with some of the airmen carrying long-handled pitchforks, they moved off to the pinpoint headed by Mouden, MAHO, Person, Rolland and Coum. The groups had to cross a fairly wide minefield before reaching the shore; in addition to barbed wire covering the area, look-out posts seemed to be everywhere. Nevertheless, the airmen were guided past

The beach crossing to Île Tariec

the obstacles and on to the beach. Once more, the airmen and their guides became seaweed gatherers or shell collectors and this pretence, under the scrutiny of the German sentries, lasted until they reached Tariec a mile and a quarter across the sand. Progress was painfully slow.

Later that afternoon, MAHO and JEANNOT were installed once more in Amédée Rolland's attic in Lannilis, sending out the message 'the radiator is holding well, and the Loin is a long river', at intervals of an hour. After the second transmission, London sent the eagerly awaited reply on the 2115 GMT BBC News bulletin: the operation was 'on' and MGB 318 had already left. MAHO and JEANNOT allowed themselves a celebratory drink in the bar below, before MAHO set off for Tariec to join the airmen, and ensure that all was going according to plan.

DDOD(I) had decided that in view of the number of passengers a second gunboat should be coopted for one operation only, with MGB 329 joining 318 for the mission. The weather in the Channel had been force 5 as the two gunboats sailed across. At 2345, 318 spotted La Petite Fourche buoy. 329 was at first nowhere to be seen but was eventually spotted heading straight for Grande Fourche rocks. Radio silence was broken, and disaster avoided. At midnight they reached the pinpoint and dropped anchor. Three boats were landed: Uhr-Henry in the first, 318's First Lieutenant Mike Pollard in the second and the Coxswain of 329 in the third.

At the same time, with the rendezvous fixed for Île Guénnoc, MAHO had set off for Tariec in a single-seater canoe at about 0030 to intercept the MGB and pass on the news that the airmen were on Tariec. Soon, though, MAHO was in bad trouble owing to the rising wind and heavy surf. After an hour of being lost, he suddenly saw a distant red light flashing through the spray. MAHO paddled furiously towards it. It took a supreme effort, but spent and exhausted, he finally managed to land on Tariec to discover the gunboat's dinghies already there.

At 0045, Tassie Uhr-Henry had also seen the flashing red light on Tariec. Having reported on the walkie-talkie that he had combed Île Guénnoc with no sign of life, he was told to investigate. Twenty-five minutes later, he announced that there were twenty escapers ready and waiting. Uhr-Henry was told to load up and get back to the MGB as fast as possible in view of the deteriorating conditions.

Back on ship in the rolling chart room, David Birkin had noticed that the barometer was plummeting. At 0200 a violent squall of wind and rain hit them. At the same time a radio message had been received from England saying: 'Weather deteriorating rapidly, gale force 6–7 approaching your area.' The warning was too late: the wind had already increased to force 6 and was now howling through the rigging. Great waves rolling in from the Atlantic were smashing themselves on to the reefs and rocks around them, the sea was a mass of foam and the engines had to be started to take the strain off the anchor cable. It was a most awe-inspiring and frightening sight. MGB 329 was having her own troubles and at one ghastly moment she managed to foul 318's anchor cable with her propellers.

At 0220 Uhr-Henry reported that all three dinghies with twenty escapers were starting back to the mother ships. That, though, was substantially easier said than done. Even getting the escapers on board the dinghies was difficult enough, with the boats rolling and pitching in the powerful surf. The crossing from Tariec to Île Guénnoc was dangerous at night, even for the local fishermen who knew the whereabouts of all the submerged rocks and were well acquainted with the fierce current which runs between them. For the dinghy crews on that stormy night the crossing was a nightmare. On Tassie Uhr-Henry's boat, the bung was knocked out on a rock and he had to stuff his naval cap into the hole to stop it from sinking.

From Uhr-Henry's message that they were on their way, and with the sea getting worse by the minute, no further word was heard from him over the walkie-talkie. If nerves weren't jangled enough, at 0335, 318's electrics were short-circuited from deluges of sea water and pelting rain. This was marked by its gun-buzzers blaring out in unison and the navigation lights switching themselves on. The only way to stop the noise and extinguish the lights was to cut the wires.

0418. The decision was made that with dawn coming up, they could wait no longer. Not only would everyone get caught, but the pinpoint would be forever compromised if they were spotted by the Germans. But just as they weighed anchor and began to turn for home, one of the dinghies was sighted astern. With the heavy seas breaking over her, she was making no progress at all. 318 dropped astern towards the helpless boat and the reef which she had just negotiated. A line was thrown. The wind hurled it back. Scrambling nets were lowered as the gunboat and dinghy bumped into each other. With all available hands on deck, and with the jagged reef getting closer every second, the men were finally dragged out and the sinking boat pulled on board.

In total, seven out of twenty escapers had been rescued, with Lieutenant Henry and his two oarsman safe. But that success had come at a heavy cost: thirteen escapers, two agents and five sailors, including Mike Pollard, the First Lieutenant, were left behind, and two dinghies had been wrecked in the process. As MGB 318 started up the Aber-Benoît Channel at 0450 on the long run back to England, they could see a red lamp flashing from the island behind. At least they could return home knowing that those left behind were safe.

For those who had made it on board 318, they were treated to a nightmarish return journey in the worst possible weather. With the MGB caught in the full force of the wind and sea, it was not until 0530, with dawn breaking, that they got clear of the French mainland. David Birkin wrote in his logbook: 'Wind west-south-west force 7, sea very rough, heavy and confused swell, sea covered with streaks of foam.' The movements of a small flat-bottomed, top-heavy ship in such conditions almost defy description – suffice it to say that seasickness was the least of their worries. 318 and 329 altered course to

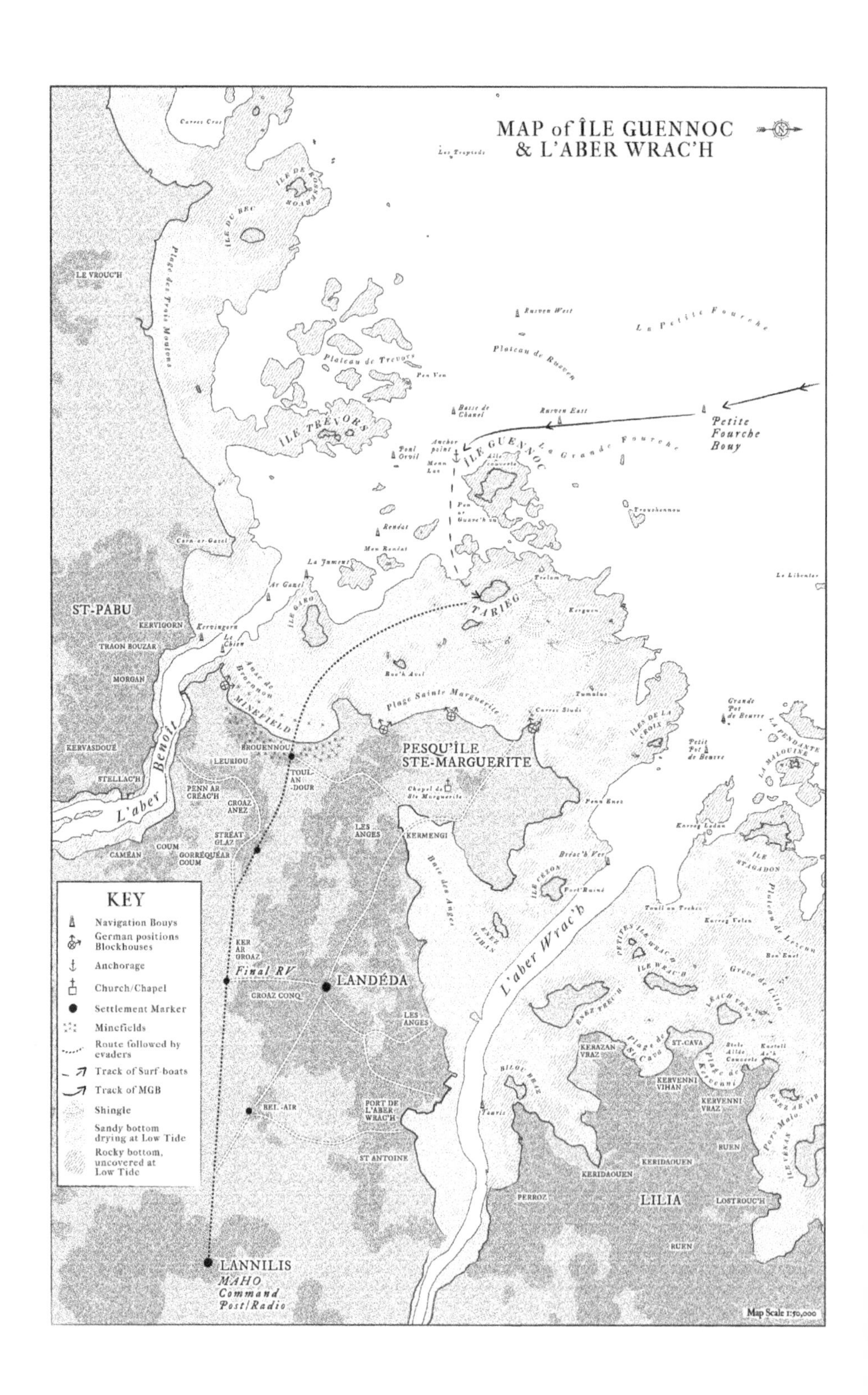

MAP of ÎLE GUENNOC
& L'ABER WRAC'H
KEY
Navigation Bouys
German positions Blockhouses
Anchorage
Church/Chapel
Settlement Marker
Minefields
Route followed by evaders
Track of Surf-boats
Track of MGB
Shingle
Sandy bottom drying at Low Tide
Rocky bottom, uncovered at Low Tide
Map Scale 1:50,000
Petite Fourche Bouy
ÎLE GUENNOC
ÎLE TREVORS
Plateau de Trevors
Plateau de Ruaven
La Petite Fourche
La Grande Fourche
Plage des Trois Moutons
ÎLE DU BEC
LE VROUC'H
ST-PABU
KERVIGORN
TRAON BOUZAR
MORGAN
KERVASDOUÉ
STELLAC'H
L'aber Benoît
MINEFIELD
TARIEG
Plage Sainte Marguerite
PESQU'ÎLE STE-MARGUERITE
BROUENNOU
LEURIOU
TOUL-AN-DOUR
PENN AR CRÉAC'H
CROAZ ANEZ
STRÉAT GLAZ
COUM
CAMÉAN
GORRÉQUEAR COUM
LES ANGES
KERMENGI
Baie des Anges
KER AR GROAZ
Final RV
LANDÉDA
CROAZ CONQ
LES ANGES
BEL-AIR
PORT DE L'ABER WRAC'H
ST ANTOINE
LANNILIS
MAHO
Command Post/Radio
L'aber Wrac'h
ÎLE WRAC'H
ÎLES DE LA CROIX
ÎLE STAGADON
LA MALOUINE
KERAZAN VRAZ
Plage de St Cava
ST-CAVA
KERVENNI VIHAN
KERVENNI VRAZ
RUEN
KERIDAOUEN
PERROZ
LILIA
LOSTROUC'H

the east, parallel with the French coast, to avoid being capsized by a beam sea.

By 0930, and now in full daylight, the two boats were still only thirty miles from the Breton coast and not making much headway. Crisis point seemed fast approaching: neither MGB had enough fuel to carry on making no headway homewards for too long; the rolling of the boats, which was estimated at the time to be in the region of 50 degrees, was causing considerable concern. Lashings parted and heavy objects started rocketing across the deck. Conditions in the chart room became chaotic and David Birkin had to wedge himself against the chart table to remain standing. The chart table itself was an indescribable mess of vomit, rusty water cascading down the voice pipe from the bridge, and blood from the cuts on Birkin's head which banged against every kind of projection. With sodden charts slithering in every direction, pencils and notes flying through the air, and parallel rulers careering madly across the table and on to the deck, navigation was difficult to say the least.

At 1000, with the wind veering slightly, the opportunity was taken to alter course northwards and begin to bash their way home. Just to add to the growing problems, at that moment four unidentifiable fighter planes swept out of the mist and spray, creating further concerns. Action stations were manned but, thankfully, the fighters didn't reappear.

To conserve fuel, one engine was now cut. On the boats crept, more like semi-submerged submarines than MGBs, with personnel on the bridge hanging on to the side rails and their legs clear of the deck. From now on, starboard and port engines competed with each other for stopping. It was not until 1720 that 318 and 329 were secured alongside the jetty in Falmouth harbour. For the crews on board, this was the end of twenty-five continuous hours in extremely rough conditions without a break of any sort. Emotions were a mixture of exhaustion and sadness at having left two dinghies and their occupants behind. But almost immediately, the question of what happens next reared its head: when and how were they going to rescue their fellow crew members, and bring them and the missing airmen back to Britain?

CHAPTER 8 – CHRISTMAS DAY 1943

'The call sign for tonight's operation is Zulu. Hotel. Delta'[27]

While the majority of the MGB 318 crew were recovering from the efforts of ENVIOUS IIb on return to Dartmouth, First Lieutenant Mike Pollard was enjoying a somewhat different experience, having been left behind in France, and with the events of the night of 1/2 December still fresh in his mind.

Pollard later wrote that having found the airmen, 'The boats started back in company for the MGBs and we found that, although Nos 1 & 2 boats were keeping well together, No 3 boat was lagging behind. The wind had freshened by now to force 5 with frequent gusts up to force 6. Nos 1 & 2 boats reached Guénnoc together. As we rounded the reef on the south western side of the island, we felt the full force of the wind and tide, and after a while found that No 3 boat could no longer be seen. It found it impossible to make any further headway. Communication between the boats was now impossible and in a heavy squall when the visibility was nil, we parted company.'

Pollard was experienced enough to know that getting back to the MGB was now unlikely: 'During this squall my boat shipped quite a lot of water, being close in to the reef at this time. Owing to this extra weight, and the exhausted condition of the boat's crew, even with the additional help of the airmen on the oars and bailing with shoes and hats, I considered that, as headway was impossible, the best thing to do would be to land on Guénnoc, tell 318 of our predicament and, with the boat emptied of water and the crew a little rested, to have another attempt if time permitted.'[28]

The surf-boat landed back on Guénnoc at 0455. Unbeknownst to

27 From the original OP FELICITATE operation order (National Archive SOE history 14 vol. IV HS7/25).

28 The original notes of Pollard's report to DDOD(I) of his experiences were written in pencil on a series of naval signal pads. The original is held at Dartmouth Museum.

Pollard, MGB 318 had already started up L'Aber-Benoît Channel five minutes before. 'I crossed over the island to the hillside overlooking the gunboats and endeavoured to obtain v/s contact to explain our movements and predicament. However, as the boats could not be seen, and no answer was obtained from our signals, I presumed that they had left, the time then being 0510.'

The question was what to do now. 'Returning to the P.D. I talked the situation over with PIERROT, a French agent who had taken passage in my P.D. We decided that the best thing would be for him to get into contact with the other agents on the mainland and for them to arrange for our dispersal until the gunboats could return. With this end in view, I left the seven airmen on Guénnoc and started off for Tariec with PIERROT – considering that the boat was easier to handle with four on board and that, should we fail to contact the agents on shore, the airmen would be better off on Guénnoc, which is seldom visited by the Germans, than on Tariec where they go nearly every day.'

By now the wind freshened to force 6 and had gone round to the south-west – 'a fact which I had not noticed', Pollard admitted: 'I was carried too far to the north (the tide was setting north as well), so that instead of passing to the west of the first reef between the two islands – on the south of the Plateau de Guénnoc – we came to the centre of it. Visibility had dropped right down and was nil during the rain squalls which were fairly frequent and the reefs could not be seen from Guénnoc.' Whichever way Pollard turned presented difficulties: it was impossible to get to the south of the reef due to the wind and tide. But going to the north of the reef left them in a ring of surf. Pollard broke through on the leeward side, crossed over one line of rocks and, finding more rocks ahead, presumed he'd reach the mainland. But with visibility down, he'd mistaken the mainland for Trelam Rock and Kerquinn. He went ashore on Kerquinn for a rest, the boat crew having rowed hard for ninety minutes by this point.

It was now 0900 and with little darkness left, there was little time to pause. PIERROT told Pollard that they could walk to the mainland from their position, so they landed the boat on to the reef, turned her over and hid her under a pile of rocks and pebbles. The tide was starting to drift at about 0900 and by later morning, the local fishermen were appearing on the sand, gathering clams and picking up seaweed. 'By 1200 the reef we were on was only separated from the mainland by two small channels some 3 feet deep and 30 yards wide,' Pollard remembered. 'A fisherman came quite near to our reef and Pierrot went over to him and explained our case. The fisherman agreed to take us inland and went away, returning at about 1400 with a cart and a friend. By this time, we had worked our way towards Tariec and remained behind a large rock where we destroyed anything that might give us away – badges, gold braid, uniform buttons etc.'

Able Seamen Clancy and Bently took the cart, while Pollard and PIERROT walked to the mainland by a different route. From here, the four of them walked a further couple of miles to a farmhouse near Landéda where food and a roaring fire awaited (the farmhouse belonged to Guillaume Le Guen, appropriately enough a seaweed gatherer). Also at the farmhouse were the crew and passengers of No 3 boat. They'd landed on a small island south of Tariec at around 0500, and had been led to the farm by another local fisherman. The next day, the seven airmen left behind on Guénnoc made it to the farmhouse as well. In the meantime, Pollard had arranged for the two boats to be disposed of.

The following evening, 3 December, the cohort of twenty-five airmen, agents and boat crew travelled cross-country for four miles to a lorry that was waiting for them. This took them to Lannilis, where Pollard, Clancy, Bently and the French agents hid in a garage. The rest of the men were driven to Brest, where they were split and hidden in small groups. Pollard's group were picked up in a small van by the local gendarme and taken on to a safe house in Landernau. After a night here, it was decided that Clancy and Bently would stay, but Pollard would be taken to Paris, 'in readiness for the first "pick-up" operation'.

'The agents supplied me with the necessary papers to pass any check-up,' Pollard wrote afterwards: 'identity cards, permit to be near the coast, birth certificate etc. making me out to be deaf and dumb to overcome the language problem, for, although I can understand a conversation fairly well, my French is not nearly fluent enough to pass for a Frenchman.' Pollard caught the overnight train

Commune de Guisseny
CARTE D'IDENTITÉ N° 610
Nom : GOALABRE
Prénoms : Jean
Né le 1.5.1915
à Névez
Département Finistère
Domicile Bourg de Guisseny
Profession ouvrier agricole
SIGNALEMENT
Taille 1m74
Cheveux cha
Moustache rase
Yeux bleu
Teint clair
A Guisseny, le 7 Janvier
MAIRIE DE GUISSENY

Navy Form S.1511
NAVAL
IDENTITY CARD No. 47274
Surname POLLARD
Other Names Michael John
Place of Birth Exeter
Year of Birth 1921
At Southampton
Date 3. 11. 44
FLAG OFFICER SOUTHAMPTON

Pollard's Naval ID card and his fake ID produced in France

to Paris without incident, arriving in the French capital at 0700 on 5 December. 'We crossed Paris by Metro and went to a small flat owned by a friend of PIERROT where he and I stayed for our entire stay in Paris ... I was lent clothes more suitable for wear in Paris than the flannel trousers, large reefer and big white sweater in which I had come ashore and had been wearing up to now.'

*

While Pollard and the others were recovering at Guillaume Le Guen's farmhouse, SAROL and Derrien, waiting in Lannilis, were told of the mission's failure. MAHO, meanwhile, was on his way to Brest. To everyone's consternation the Germans had found one of the wrecked dinghies and had put up road blocks on all roads leading from Sainte Marguerite: thus, only Derrien, because he was a policeman, could reach Le Guen's farm.

Falmouth 1943: L to R Ted Davis, RAF Liason Officer, Philip Schniedaur (SIS), Steven Mackenzie, David Birkin.

Seaweed gatherer's cart used for transporting the classified mail

MAHO, never daunted, immediately began arranging another rendezvous with London. A new attempt was fixed for the night of 23/24 December. The orders for the operation had been hand carried from London by Steven Mackenzie and Philip Schniedaur.[29] By this point, so much secret correspondence had accumulated since Operation ENVIOUS on 3/4 November that it had to be carried on a horse-drawn cart by Amédée Rolland. A key advantage over the previous operation was the S-phone supplied by London. It allowed direct communication between those on shore and the gunboat when it was in range.

In Paris, Pollard and PIERROT prepared to leave. They caught the night train back on to Landeneau on 21 December. Pollard and others were taken to a house where two of the American airmen were staying, before being moved to the village school for the night. On 23 December, the BBC broadcast the message 'Les Troènes sont en fleurs' ('The wild Privet is in bloom') indicating the operation was on. Claude Tanguy, in his lorry, picked up MAHO, SAROL, Pollard and the other shipwrecked sailors, the airmen, JEANNOT and PIERROT. They all got off at Bel Air in Landéda from where they were to be guided by Guillaume le Guen and François Coum to the beach and then across to Tariec.

For the first mile or so to the beach, the party kept to cart tracks and fields, the only incident en- route being a barking dog at a nearby

29 Philip Schniedaur DSO from SIS, Biffy Dunderdale's Liaison Officer with DDOD(I).

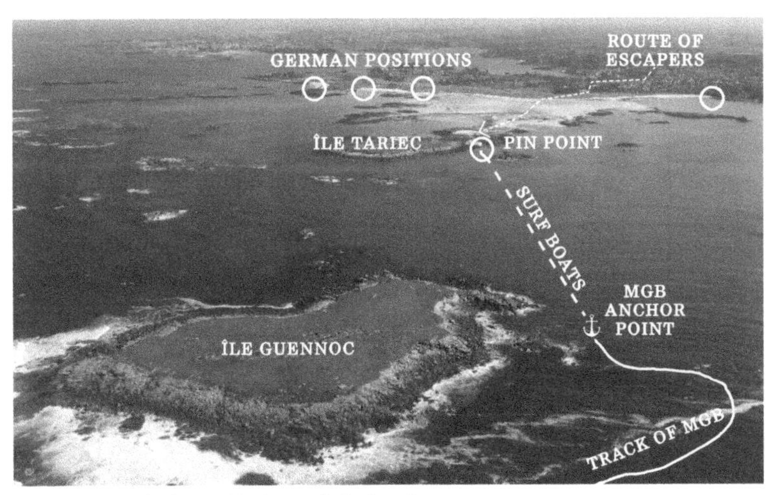

Aerial view – Guénnoc, Tariec and the beach

farmhouse. The mile-and-a-half stretch of sand to Île Tariec was, as usual, the most dangerous part of the journey. The first obstacle was a newly laid minefield in the sand above the high-water mark which had to be crossed. Each mine consisted of a canister of explosive buried under the sand with its detonator, three metal prongs, showing an inch above the surface. Guillaume Le Guen had watched the Germans laying them, so he volunteered to lead the column, bent double, passing his hand gently over the sand. The men followed in a long line, each holding on to the shoulder of the man in front, eventually passing safely through the minefield and on to the sand where the groups re-formed. For the next mile and a half everyone once more adopted their cover of seaweed gatherers – again under the noses of the German look-outs who manned the three observation posts guarding that stretch of beach. It seems quite amazing that this continued to fool the Germans, particularly now they were on alert following the dinghies that had been found smashed on the beach.

When the party of thirty-two reached Île Tariec in safety, the weather seemed reasonable and hopes were very high. At 2300 contact was made with MGB 318 and the message came back over the walkie-talkie that the dinghies were on their way.

MGB 318 had left harbour at 1600 earlier that afternoon (with

Lieutenant Commander Ray Guest[30] of the US Navy as observer from the PT Boats newly arrived in Dartmouth). Heading for La Petite Fourche Buoy, the journey across was comparatively uneventful, though the swell was greater than forecast (easterly wind force 3, confused sea, moderate south-westerly swell) and seasickness was rampant.

By 2045, however, the reasonable weather was evaporating. Visibility was becoming poor owing to a continuous drizzle and the QH position-finding equipment was again causing trouble. Courses were altered several times and at 2125 engines were silenced for crossing the coastal convoy route. At 0040 La Petite Fourche Buoy was sighted, the course was altered, and speed reduced to 8 knots. 318 proceeded once more down the Aber-Benoît Channel with an increasing wind and breaking water on each side. At 0050 she anchored off Guénnoc. A quarter of an hour later, however, the wind had increased to force 5 and trouble seemed to be brewing once again.

At 0125 contact via walkie-talkie was established with the shore party. They reported that a dinghy landing was tricky, but possible. Encouraged, MGB 318 moved in closer to Île Guénnoc and dropped anchor. A few minutes later the anchor's grass line broke and a new anchor with a stronger line was dropped; this time it held. At 0215 the two dinghies, with Tassie Uhr-Henry in the first with his crew and the second in tow, left for Île Guénnoc.

Now the weather started to play havoc with the operation. Five minutes later, owing to bad weather, 318's second anchor was lost. From then onwards, position had to be maintained using the engines. At 0420, with wind and sea increasing in strength every minute and anxiety on board increasing similarly, Tassie reported that he was returning but could make no headway against the sea and swell. He was ordered to sink the dinghy he had in tow.

On the bridge of 318 the remaining crew could just see the dinghy struggling to reach the MGB, with great waves breaking over her. 'Pull, Tassie – for God's sake, pull!' the US observer Ray Guest

30 Raymond Guest, wealthy businessman, horse breeder and polo player. Appointed Head of Naval Department OSS. Awarded the Bronze Star and Legion of Merit, an OBE and Croix de Guerre. Became US Ambassador to Ireland 1965–8.

was shouting into the walkie-talkie. 'Good lad, Tassie – you'll make it – pull…!' Tassie and his crew pulled for their lives as wave after wave broke over the sinking dinghy. By 0438, they had made it and were hauled aboard, battered and exhausted. It had been a very close shave indeed.

MGB 318 set course for home and after a very rough and at times dangerous Channel crossing, tied up at 1315 after a very testing twenty-one hours. Though they had again failed to bring out the escapers, every single man on board was resolved that next time they would succeed. And next time would come very soon indeed – just one day later.

*

The weather on Christmas Day, grey and miserable, echoed the mood of the 318 crew. Everyone who had been on board felt dispirited with the failure of the previous day. Moreover, they were exhausted. As it was Christmas, a 'make and mend' and a 'splicing of the main brace' was the order of the day: a rest day, in other words, with the crew carrying out their tasks with gusto. Once finished, the officers and crew set about cheering themselves up. There followed a Christmas lunch of turkey, Christmas pudding, all washed down with lots of gin, and a turning in for a well-earned afternoon 'kip'.

This bonhomie was interrupted at 1500, with a telephone call from DDOD(I) in London. Jan McQuoid Mason and David Birkin made their way rather shakily along the quayside to the office where the secure telephone which had been installed for the Flotilla while using Falmouth as an advance base. Jan picked up the receiver, with Birkin putting the extension to his ear.

'FELICITATE is on for tonight,' Slocum told them. 'The weather report is reasonable, force 3–4 wind, no moon and a cloudy sky, twenty-eight bodies and one is an agent with the Gestapo hot on his heels. You sail in an hour. Good luck to you both and your crew.'

The weather report might have been reasonable, but the operating conditions and state of the crew after a large lunch were somewhat less than favourable. Even those with the toughest constitution quailed at the prospect of twenty hours-plus tossing and rolling in the Channel. 'Everything came with a rush,' David Birkin recalled. 'No time for calculations and only just time to change into seagoing clothes. My insides, never quite sure of themselves at sea, turned over several times in anticipation of the night's work on top of turkey and gin, consumed in the fond belief that Christmas would be spent in port.' As Jan McQuoid Mason began preparing the ship for sea and David Birkin set about working out the night's course, many a head went under the cold water tap in an attempt to get back to a state of mental alertness.

Fifty minutes later, in the fading light of Christmas afternoon, MGB 318 slipped unobtrusively from her moorings and nosed slowly towards the Channel. Although daylight was falling fast, there was still enough to see that smoke from the chimneys of the houses near the harbour entrance was flattening: an ominous sign that the wind was rising. Whether to encourage or simply rouse the crew, the ship's radio was at full blast until the moment they set course for France – Vera Lynn's voice rose from the mess deck with 'We'll Meet Again' bringing a lump to many a throat: '... but I know we'll meet again some sunny day.' Guns were tested with a shattering roar.

Despite the short notice and the disappointment of the night before, there remained a sense of optimism among the men on board. It felt a matter of honour for the ship's company to succeed this time. The fact that this was Christmas Day felt a good sign: surely nothing would go wrong this time. Certainly, the weather to begin with felt like a late festive present: it was not as bad as feared. Under a starless sky and with a north-westerly force 3 wind behind them, they headed south east for Brittany.

*

TP NR 0014 Op Felicitate

TELEGRAM FOR JADE TRAVEL VIA CHARLESTON 11 HORNPIPE

III. VI.

CXG 55 MOST IMMEDIATE – TO BE SENT ON CONTACT

OPEARTION MARITIME AURA LIEU A PARTIR VINGT ET UN RPT VINGT ET UN STOP SIGNAUX POSITIFS OU NEGATIF PAR PLAN CHARLESTON DEUX A ONZE HEURES TRENTE OU TREIZE HEURES TRENTE GMT JOUR DE L'OPERATION CHOISISSEZ STOP SI GUENNOC OU ROSSERVOR IMPOSSIBLES ET VOUS ETC FORCE UTILISER MEME POINT QUE DERNIERE FOIS ENVOYEZ CHIFFRES SUIVANTS STOP QUATRE HUIT ZERO SIX RPT QUATRE QUATRE HUIT ZERO SIX STOP PREFEREONS GUENNOC OU ROSSERVOR STOP VOICI MESSAGES BBC STOP LE LOING EST UNE RIVIERE RAPIDE RPT LE LOING EST UNE RIVIERE RAPIDE STOP L'ODEUR DES TROENES EST DELICIEUSE RPT L'ODEUR DES TROENES EST DELICIEUSE STOP DONNEZ VOTRE ACCORD EXTREME URGENCE STOP NOTE. HORNPIPE III. HAS A CONTACT TODAY AT 1400 HOURS GMT

Back in Lannilis, MAHO had sent a message to London on the morning of 24 December, asking for a return of 318 on Christmas night. He was delighted to receive confirmation that the MGB would try again. *'Maritime operation will take place as from 2100,'* the telegram read. *'Positive or negative signals will be sent on Charleston Two at 1130 or 1330 GMT on the day of the operation choose. If Guénnoc or Rosservor impossible and you are obliged to use same point as last time send following figures. 44806. We prefer Guénnoc or Rosservor.'* The telegram finished with the all-important BBC messages to listen out for: *'Here are the BBC Messages stop. "Le Loing est une Riviere rapide. Repeat Le Loing est une Riviere rapide. L'Odeur des Troènes est délicieuse repeat L'odeur des Troènes est délicieuse." Give your agreement extremely urgent.'*

On the evening of Christmas Eve, some of the escapers gathered for a celebration party at the house of Mme Pailler in Lannilis. After plenty of wine and food had been consumed, and despite the fact that the Germans occupied a building close by, the strains of 'La Marseillaise' and 'It's a Long, Long Way to Tipperary' filled the house. The escapers made such a racket that Derrien, the gendarme, who happened to be passing by, came in and told them to quieten down. The Germans, even if they noticed, didn't intervene.

Pollard remembers meeting Phillip Keun that night: 'I only met Phillip once, on the night of Christmas Eve 1943, which we spent together with an RAF pilot in the stables of a farm outside Lannilis, prior to our return to the UK on the following day. He was a very able and charismatic man, bilingual in French and English – and probably other languages as well. Rumour had it at the time that he was on his way back to London from a trip to Germany, which was probably correct, since I now know he carried information about the location of the V1 and V2 rocket launching sites. He must have had a long and dangerous journey, for although not standoffish in any way, he seemed never able to relax. Only once, when we were in the cart in the farmyard and starting off for the last journey to the beaches did the mask slip for a minute. He produced a pistol from his pocket and called out, "Now we are going to carry the mail over the Rocky Mountains!"'[31]

On Christmas morning, the message, 'Les Troènes sont en Fleures' was sent to London from Lannilis. The reply came back: 'Joel aura un an au mois du Juin.' Operation FELICITATE II was 'on'. The assembly point for the escapers, as before, was Bel Air at Landéda. Doctor de la Marnierre arrived with some escapers housed further afield by ambulance, being the most likely transport to get through the German road blocks: only emergency vehicles were allowed to travel on Christmas Day. The night was so dark that the leader of each group softly whistled the tune of 'La Madelon' to establish their identities.[32] But everything worked like clockwork, except that at the last minute the Germans banned all vehicle movement and bicycles had to be found for the escapers. The thirty-two people in two groups reached Île Tariec again without attracting the attention of the German look-outs.

MGB 318, meanwhile, had continued its trouble-free crossing: the weather was ideal, and she had maintained a speed of 15½ knots. At 2112 engines were silenced for crossing the convoy route and courses were altered to offset the coastal tidal stream. At 2300 land was sighted, and at 2310 La Petite Fourche Buoy, with which everyone

31 Keun had been meeting Admiral Canaris, the chief of the Abwehr, whom he'd already met on two occasions in Paris. JADE AMICOL had established communication with Canaris on behalf of SIS, in support of the plot to kill Hitler.

32 'La Madelon – I'll be true to the whole Regiment' was a popular WWI song written by Louis Bosquet and Camilla Robert. It was revived during WWII and popular with the Resistance.

was now very familiar, lay dead ahead. 318 headed down the Aber-Benoît Channel at a steady 10 knots, and had reached the anchorage after fourteen minutes, very close indeed to the southern tip of Île Guénnoc. The watchers on Tariec saw MGB 318 drop anchor a few hundred yards away and contact was made via the S-phone.

According to Pollard, 'R/T contact was established at 2355 with MGB 318. Information as to the number of people to leave, and the amount of courier we had, was passed and the airmen were divided up into 4 groups, 7 in each, there being 28 people to get on board all told, and being told by 318 that she had 4 boats. Actually only 1 P.D. and the SN2 came in but we managed to get 14 in the SN2 and 7 and the courier in the P.D. The SN then returned for the remaining 7.' By 0152 the operation was completed, with thirty-two escapers and the huge load of mail safely on 318. 'It was a very nice feeling to clamber on board,' Pollard wrote. The last transmission from ship to shore was also from him: 'Good luck MAHO, thank you.'

The return journey to England in the early hours of Boxing Day gave everyone on board 318 a tremendous sense of achievement and satisfaction: after five attempts, rescuing the airmen had finally been a success. Indeed, such was the feeling of relief that no one really cared when, at 0600, all three of the MGB's engines began spluttering and then, an hour later, stopping altogether, with the boat still twenty-five miles from England. By 0800 they were underway again, and at 0945 318 stopped off at the Helford River to transfer the night's 'takings' to the motor launch from SOE's Helford base.

Congratulations were in the air: these would include a message from General Eisenhower, for the detailed information about the V1 and V2 rocket sites. MAHO, meanwhile, had arranged with 318 that a message would be transmitted on the BBC on 30 December, as a 'thank you' and encouragement for his team. 'Salut Bretagne,' it read, 'terre héroïque au sol de granit, recouvert de Chênes' – a rare acknowledgement that there were hearts of oak on both sides of the Channel. A second message followed: 'Jean Maurice a sauvé la prestige de la Gendarmerie Française.' JEAN MAURICE was the code name of Jean-François Derrien. The message let them know in Brittany that everyone had arrived safely. It also acted as an encouragement for the other gendarmes of Lannilis – Clouarec, Guillou, Pedan and Carré.

As the official report put it, 'This operation will long be remembered by those on board, not (only) because it took place on Christmas Day, but because of the smooth way in which the internal organisation of the ship ran. All officers and men fulfilled their duties in a highly effective manner.'

*

The seven sorties of the Aber-Wrac'h Saga were to be the last operation in that treacherous area. But though they culminated in success for the Flotilla, for the Resistance workers, the end of the Flotilla's visits to Île Guénnoc and Tariec heralded the start of a disastrous period.

Buoyed by the success of FELICITATE, the gallant MAHO and Guillaume Le Guen had started planning another escape operation for mid-January 1944. But on 6 January MAHO was arrested by the Gestapo in Paris, taken to the Gestapo offices at 101 Avenue Henri-Martin, but miraculously avoided torture and was deported to Dachau.[33] The same fate befell SAROL a few weeks later. Dr de la Marnierre and his family were also caught, but after imprisonment and torture were eventually released. Andrée Virot (ROSE) was caught and sent to Ravensbrück, then Buchenwald (Virot survived and eventually settled in England. She died in 2010.)

Joseph Mouden, the farmer who had guided escapers across the beach, was also arrested on 31 May 1944 and subjected to ghastly tortures at the Château de Trouzilit in Tréglonou, by Sergeant Herbert Schaad, the leader of the Kommando Landerneau. He was deported first to Dachau – where he briefly saw MAHO, then to Neuengamme. It is generally believed that he died there, but it is possible that he was killed when being transported at the end of the war on the liner *Cap Arcona*, which was mistakenly attacked by Allied aircraft. François Coum was killed on 5 August 1944 while taking part in an attack on a German strongpoint at the Château de Kerbabu, south east of Lannilis.

The Kommando Landerneau was one of seven anti-Resistance

33 Although beaten up, Hentic was spared further torture by the intervention of an SS Colonel.

Joseph 'Job' Mouden

'Kommandos' the Gestapo had set up in 1943. These were small groups of thirty men, a mixture of Gestapo, German Military and Milice collaborators whose mission was to penetrate, interdict and destroy Resistance networks. Kommando IC 343, also known as 'Kommando Landerneau' or 'Kommando Schaad', operated out of Le Manoir de Colleville in the centre of Landerneau. As well as its headquarters, it contained a number of cells and what the Gestapo called 'the kitchen' or torture chambers where members of the Resistance were 'cuisinés' or 'cooked'. Herbert Schaad, its leader, was highly intelligent, ruthless and vicious. He had studied at the Sorbonne before the war and spoke fluent French. He reported directly to the head of the Gestapo in Rennes, Willy Kruger. His key collaborators were Breton Nationalists André Geffroy, Jean Corré, Gabriel Poquet and Hervé Botros – the most vicious torturer of the group.[34] On 31 May 1944 they arrested Henri Prouistic, the regional head of the ALLIANCE network, Job Mouden and Jean Le Gall. All three were horrendously tortured and deported, and all died in concentration camps.

Back in UK, Mike Pollard wrote a report for DDOD(I), with a list of suggestions for future operations:

SUGGESTIONS

1. Although a P.D.1 seems very suitable for weight carrying in calm water she does not seem too good when there is any wind and swell. Her high free board and lack of grip of the water, especially forward, make it hard to keep control all the time.

2. I think they should always be used with a crew of 4 wherever possible as the 2 extra hands would make a lot of difference to your speed in a long pull. When laden the stern ships water rather

34 Herbert Schaad was tried in Paris in November 1951. He was convicted of murder, torture, pillage and arson and sentenced to forced labour for life, but released in June 1954. Hervé Botros was condemned to death and shot on 7 November 1945. André Geffroy was shot on 17 July 1946. Corré and Poquet were sentenced to forced labour for life.

excessively, I think some trials in a seaway of weight distribution might be worthwhile. Communication between the boats is essential, not only between the leading dinghy and the G.B. but also between each dinghy. I feel that to achieve this it is worth going to a lot of trouble and even making sacrifices in the dinghies, for, without proper communication they are apt to become a great danger.

3. Each boat should be equipped with an RAF Grid Compass, RAF type torch binoculars, bailers and a boat's bay for repairs. The Captain of the boat should have a watch with a luminous face. I also think that the question of buoyancy apparatus for the boats is well worth considering as it would make them a lot steadier when in a swamped condition – a thing in which a boat crowded with people and full or nearly full of water is singularly lacking.

4. Should the worst ever happen again, and a boat's crew be left behind I know it would greatly help the agents in supplying identity cards if each member of the crew had his photograph, taken in his plain clothes, with him. These have already been taken and I think, if possible, it would be a good thing to issue out the men with the escape kit and purse.

After completing his report, Pollard was sent on leave. While he had been on the run in France his mother had died, and the family were very concerned as to why Pollard had seemingly ignored this tragedy. In Pollard's words 'the reactions of those in charge of the Flotilla to my position was sensible and considered. Before I went on leave, Jan (McQuoid Mason) told me that providing I obtained prior promises of secrecy from my family, I was allowed to tell them about the work of the Flotilla, and where I had been.'

On his return from leave, however, Pollard was told that as he knew so much about JADE FITZROY and the local Resistance in Brittany, it had been decided that he could not go on any future operations. There is some debate about the exact reasoning. It has been suggested that Slocum was furious with him for leaving the other sailors and going to Paris for a possible Lysander pick-up. However

Pierre Hentic (right middle row) with veterans of JADE FITZROY at the end of the war

the move and pick-up was not initiated by Pollard. Pierre Hentic subsequently wrote to Pollard after the war saying that he had cleared the Paris move and pick-up with Biffy Dunderdale, who as we know worked very closely with Frank Slocum. The source of this initiative remains unclear. In any event the fact remained that Pollard had been exposed not only to the local Resistance in Brittany but also to the wider JADE FITZROY networks' Paris structure. Pollard's time on operations was over: he was given a friendly and sympathetic send-off from Ted Davis over drinks in the wardroom of the *Kiloran*.

CHAPTER 9 – FULL THROTTLE

'A spy carries his life in his hands. His existence is one long hazard, joyous or the contrary'

Go Spy the Land, George Hill

The first time that Suzanne Warengham was stopped by the police, she escaped arrest by swallowing the plans she was carrying. Warengham had joined the Resistance when she was just seventeen, and assisted with escape line and courier work. On the first occasion she was stopped by police, she was taking plans of an airfield near Paris to Lyon, for onward transmission to London. Approaching the house she'd been sent to, she noticed some suspicious activity and with some difficulty, managed to digest the plans before the police stopped and arrested her. Taken to police headquarters, she was questioned and searched, but without any incriminating evidence, was let go.

The second time Warengham was arrested, this time by the Gestapo in January 1943, she was not so lucky. Her particular misfortune had been to meet and marry Harold Cole, a sergeant in the BEF who became a black marketeer and helped early Resistance activity. Cole became involved with the PAT escape line, but in 1941 the PAT Line leader, Albert Guérisse, confronted him about the theft of Resistance funds. With Guérisse determined to shoot him, Cole escaped, handing himself in to the Germans and agreeing to work for them. Cole went on to betray 150 members of the Resistance of whom fifty were executed. It was while he was working out of the Gestapo headquarters at 84 Avenue Foch in Paris that he met and married Suzanne Warengham. When Warengham discovered Cole's treachery, she fled to Marseille. She tried to keep one step ahead of Cole and the Gestapo, but by January 1943, they had caught up with her.[35]

35 Harold Cole was caught in Germany in 1945 by MI5. He escaped from custody and hid in Paris. On 8 January 1946 the French Police, acting on a tip-off, raided his hideout above a bar on the rue Grenelle. He tried to escape but was shot and killed.

Suzanne Warengham

Warengham was interrogated and tortured for two months. Although she did not crack, she was sent to Castres prison. While in Castres, Warengham met Blanche Charlet (JAPONICA, VENTRILOQUIST). Charlet had arrived in France in September 1942, taking over a lot of the work begun by Virginia Hall. She worked with Brian Stonehouse (CÉLESTIN), acting as his courier, distributing his radio messages, and finding safe houses from where he could transmit. On 24 October 1942, radio direction finders found Stonehouse: when Charlet arrived at the house a few minutes later she was also captured and sent to Castres. The prison was where Resistance fighters were held pending their execution: Charlet and Warengham knew that if they did not manage to escape, they would not leave that prison alive.

On 16 September 1943, the pair took part in a carefully planned breakout. 'Some of the prisoners had got hold of pistols through one of the warders who was in the Resistance,' Warengham later recounted. 'They also had duplicate keys of all the cells. About 1800 one evening when half the guards were out having their dinner the prisoners held up the other half, knocked them out and locked them in their cells. The prison was in the centre of the town and we had to get out by little groups of three every five minutes, so as not to arouse suspicion. In the meantime, some of the guards had been coming back from dinner. They would ring the bell, one of us would open the door and whilst he was closing it, two of the prisoners would jump on the guard with a blanket, knock him out and put him in one of the cells. We were very lucky that none of the guards happened to ring the bell while one of the groups was escaping – it was a chance we had to take.'

As well as Warengham and Charlet, fifty men escaped that night (five of whom were recaptured and tortured to death). Warengham and Charlet were among those who found their way to a Benedictine Monastery, at En Calcat, where they stayed in a guest house in the grounds for two months. From here, they were able to contact a network near Toulouse. One of the officers, Captain Paul de la Taille, arranged for them to be taken to the Pyrenees but the weather was so bad on their attempt they were unable to cross. Instead, Warengham and Charlet returned to Paris where they continued their Resistance work until London sent a message arranging for their return from Brittany by MGB.

Just before leaving Paris, Warengham was asked to meet Jean Mauricheau-Beaupré from the ALLIANCE network. She met him in the Tuileries Gardens, where he gave her a roll of microfilm containing fifty pages of details of the Atlantic Wall defences – critical information for the planning of D-Day. Warengham agreed that if she got it safely to London the BBC would broadcast the message, 'Onesime a une belle bobine.' Beaupré also asked her to take a paper plan of the German radar station at Jouy-en-Josas. Remembering her previous experience of digesting information, Warengham insisted it was put on really thin paper. She was told that if the plans fell into German hands, it could be traced back to the one person at Jouy who could have passed it to the Resistance, putting their life at stake.

On the night before she left for Brittany, Warengham went on a final shopping spree and bought a sexy black nightdress, an exotic hat with white feathers and a bottle of Chanel No 5. She also had a farewell dinner with Captain de la Taille, where they agreed a code for the BBC that would confirm she was in England: 'Patrick fait toujours pipi au lit.'

Together with three airmen also escaping, Warengham and Charlet travelled the standard route from Paris Gare Montparnasse to Rennes, where they were collected, taken to a grocer's shop, and hidden for an hour. From there, a baker's van came to collect them for the run into the Forbidden Zone. The baker had smuggled many people into the Forbidden Zone via a policy of 'hiding in plain sight'. With all the roads watched and any lorries with closed doors stopped and searched, the baker used his little bread delivery-van which had no rear doors at all, only a wildly flapping loose tarpaulin over the back. The German sentries never supposed that anyone would have the nerve to smuggle clandestine passengers in a van which was not even closed. Hidden behind a pile of freshly baked loaves,

Warengham and her fellow escapees held on as firmly as they could to the sides of the van as it rattled around the narrow Brittany roads.

As part of the conceit, the baker continued on his regular deliveries around the villages. As he stopped and disappeared inside one village shop, Warengham and the others heard the unmistakable crunch of military boots on the pavement. They came closer, stopping just by the van. Warengham held her breath and tried to keep as still as possible: suddenly the tarpaulin she was hiding under seemed very thin indeed. Any noise or movement would give them away. The silence in the moment seemed to stretch out for ever until, finally, Warengham heard the scratch of a match, the flicker of a flame, and the waft of tobacco smoke. With her heart pumping ninteen to the dozen, she heard the footsteps start up again, the crunch receding as the soldier walked on, unaware of their presence.

The van reached the coast, driving straight into the garage of a fisherman's house north of St Brieuc. With the garage door closed, Warengham and the others were allowed to get out and stretch their aching limbs. They were taken into the house to join the other escapees whom the baker had smuggled in earlier. In total, there were at least sixteen people, men and women, and a boy of fourteen, who were due to cross the Channel that night. The organisation was impressive: the fisherman's wife had a fine meal of roast pork, potatoes and red wine for everybody, and afterwards Warengham fell asleep.

In fact, there was only one mishap to set the nerves on edge. Charlet accidentally dropped Warengham's precious bottle of Chanel No 5. The pair of them tried to wash it away, but the perfume managed to infuse the whole house. However much they scrubbed and cleaned, the smell just wouldn't go away. If the Germans came calling, there was no hiding from it – as soon as a soldier stepped over the threshold, their presence would be clear. As the hours ticked by, the arrival of the gunboat couldn't come quickly enough.

*

Of the fifty-seven operations carried out by the Flotilla during the war, thirty-six were carried out between January and September 1944.

Peter Harratt, second from right, after the Dieppe raid

This was by far the most concentrated period of activity and was due to the impending invasion of Europe. This required Strategic Intelligence, the build-up of SOE networks with agents, equipment for the role in the invasion and its immediate aftermath, and the increasing need to evacuate aircrew and others for MI9.

Fortunately, the Flotilla was in good shape. It now had four boats: 318 (Jan McQuoid Mason), 502 (Peter Williams), 503 (Mike Marshall) and 718 (Ronnie Seddon). MASB36 was detached for D-Day duties. Having cut its teeth on the exceptionally difficult operations of 1943, the Flotilla was also more than ready for action. Its planning, battle rhythm (the daily routine of mission planning, briefing and maintenance) and battle procedure was tried, tested and slick. All the crews were now highly experienced and their ability to navigate to an exact pinpoint in difficult and dangerous conditions perfected. Ted Davis and Peter Williams had trained them into a highly formidable team.

In the winter period of 1943, the Flotilla was involved in a series of operations for SOE's VAR Line. The VAR Line was originally the creation of two people – Peter Harratt and Erwin Denman. Harratt, a regular soldier in the Queen's Own Hussars in the 1920s, had retired to south-west France to farm, before fighting for the Republican side in the Spanish Civil War. In 1939 he made his way to England and was recruited by SOE. Erwin Denman was Jewish. Born in Vienna, he had been a businessman in Lisbon before the war. He joined the French Army in 1940, was taken prisoner, escaped and joined the

French Foreign Legion in North Africa. This did not hold his interest for long and he deserted, making his way to Britain. Speaking fluent French, English and German, Denman was immediately taken on by SOE.

Because of the in-fighting between SOE, SIS and NID(C) DDOD(I), Leslie Humphrey's DF Section bypassed the SOE chain of command and arranged for Harratt and Denman, one of the DF agents, to be trained in Dartmouth by the Flotilla, with a view to DF setting up their own sea line to Brittany. This was approved by Slocum, who saw it as a way of gaining further control, but infuriated SOE.

Harratt and Denman went to Dartmouth and lived on a yacht on the River Dart while they underwent training. They became experts in navigation, beach reconnaissance, surf-boat landing and pinpoint procedures. Harratt, known as Captain 'Peters' to the Resistance, was described by David Birkin as 'one of the most remarkable men I have ever met'. 'I remember him best sitting hunched up on the MGB's deck en route for an operation in battle-dress,' Birkin remembered, 'with an oilskin over his head and shoulders, looking wretched and being, more often than not, sick, with his head bowed and an almost translucently green face. He would remain motionless like a dying gnome until the MGB anchored. From that moment onwards he became a model of controlled action – efficient, tireless and, I suspect, entirely ruthless. I always felt a twinge of sympathy for any German he might encounter.'

According to Birkin, Harratt 'behaved more secretly than any agent – it was always penetrating whispers, which could be heard over a considerable distance with a hand shielding the mouth in a too obviously secret gesture; I think he thoroughly enjoyed his clandestine calling. One night I remember particularly well, outside the bar of the Dartmouth Raleigh Hotel, where we had been for a final drink before setting out on one of the CARPENTER operations. Within earshot of at least a dozen people Peter hissed at me in needless French "Prenez garde ce soir David"! As we were always "Prenez-ing garde" as much as possible his public warning was not necessary.'

Before the launch of the VAR Line, Harratt had already been on an operation with the Dartmouth Flotilla – Operation MIRFIELD on 9/10

March 1943 to conduct a reconnaissance of the beach of Clogouren and to inspect the CARPENTER I cache of weapons. As 318 was on another operation – DRAPER – DDOD(I) borrowed another gunboat, 324, for their operation. Peter Williams had intended to take the surf-boat crew from 318 whom he had told to stay put on *Kiloran*. He was furious when he found they had sailed with 318. At very short notice, Tassie Uhr-Henry volunteered to go. David Birkin was the Navigating Officer and Peter Harratt went along from SOE.

324 left Dartmouth at 1823, crossed the boom ten minutes later and picked up their air cover of two Beaufighters. They left their departure positions half a mile south off Start Point at 1912. The crossing was calm but punctuated by technical problems. At 2340 they sighted the Île de Bas and anchored but had problems with a dragging anchor. Lowering the dinghies at 0100, Birkin and Uhr-Henry went ashore with Harratt. They came back at 0255 having found no one on the beach. A corner of the cache was visible and was recamouflaged. At 0305 they headed for Dartmouth, and as Ted Davis put in his operational report '…324 entered Dartmouth at 0856, the end of a very pleasant, if a little disappointing, night's cruise.'

Harratt, meanwhile, had been very impressed with both Birkin and Uhr-Henry. In his own report he wrote, 'I wish to bring to notice the fact that Lieutenant Uhr-Henry and Sub-Lieutenant Birkin both volunteered for the job. On landing both these officers remained in the breakers holding the boats off the beach for a period of one and a half hours with the thermometer colder than I have known it at any time during the previous six months. During the one and a half hours I visited them on three occasions to see how they were getting on and on no occasion did they utter words of complaint. In fact, Lieutenant Uhr-Henry encouraged me in further efforts in my reconnaissance and said, "We will stick it just as long as you want us to."'

This mission cemented the relations between Harratt and the 15th MGBF.

Six weeks later, on 29 April, the Flotilla attempted to land Erwin Denham on the Clogouren Beach to begin the set-up of the VAR Line. Operation MANGO failed due to bad weather and it wasn't until

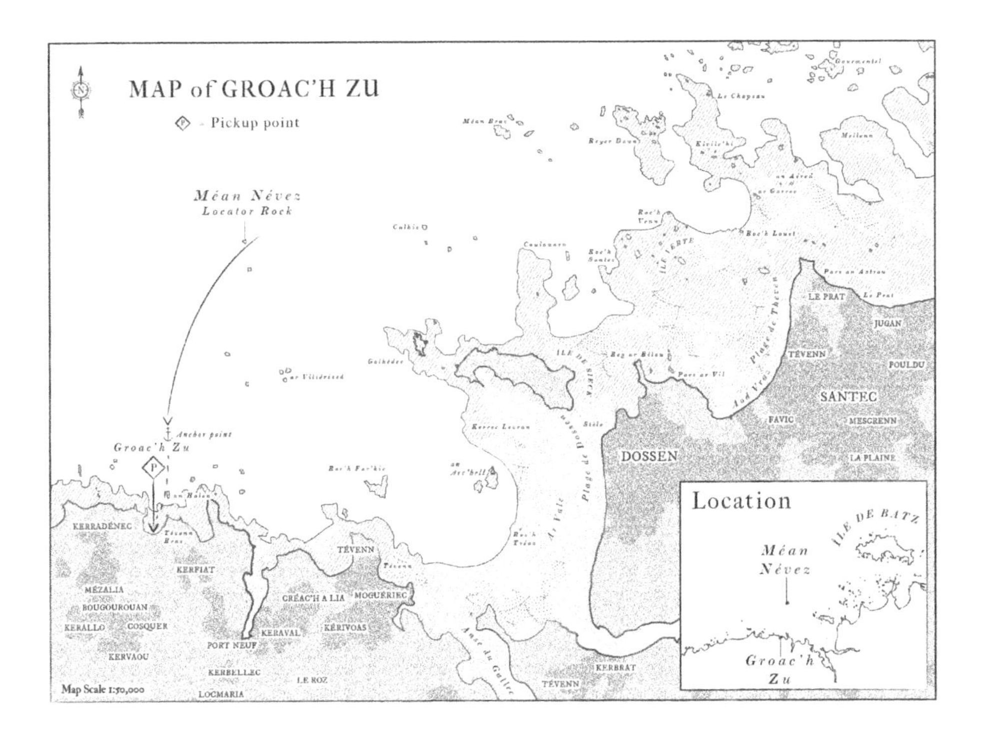

20 August that he was air landed in France to begin the process instead. The aim of the VAR Line was to become an escape and communication line across the beaches of the Breton coast in the winter and spring of 1943/44. Harratt briefed Denman to investigate a landing beach where agents could be landed, and agents and escapers taken out.

Harratt had a friend in SOE whose sister had an old nanny, Madame Jestin, who lived in Rennes. Denman was given half of a letter that Madame Jestin had sent from France to England to serve as a fool-proof introduction. Denman made contact at once and Mme Jestin's two unmarried daughters, both in their early forties, entered enthusiastically into the plan. While they organised safe houses, suggested further contacts, and arranged reliable guides and couriers, Denman went off to reconnoitre the two beaches. One of these, at Beg-an-Fry near Morlaix, Harratt had heard of from the French proprietor of a West End restaurant who often spoke about his pre-war seaside holidays there with his daughter. The second beach for Denman to explore was one Harratt had been told about by an F Section agent, Cicely Lefort,[36] when she was under training. She suggested the use of a little beach below her villa 'La Hune' at St Cast, west of Dinard. Lefort gave Harratt an ancient Irish ring which he passed on to Denman as it would establish his bona fides if shown to the housekeeper at her villa.

Within eight weeks Denman had established an excellent cover as an insurance agent in Rennes and had his organisation ready. Harratt flew over to have an air-to-ground S-phone conversation with him, to confirm that all was ready for the next phase. Denman told his team that he was taking two weeks' holiday from 'the insurance business' and went via the VIC Line across the Pyrenees to Gibraltar. He got back to London in a record seven days. Here, he settled details with Harratt and the RF Section and was in Rennes, having been put ashore by MGB, by 29 October. The VAR Line was up and running.

Inevitably, it wasn't long before the VAR faced problems. Felix Jouan, the miller of Bédée, west of Rennes, provided a van in which journeys to and from the coast could be made. In January 1944 he was pulled up by a German policeman for having dirty number plates; the sharp-eyed officer, shining his torch into the back of the van, recognised suitcases in it as of SOE type. Jouan was arrested on the spot; his companion, Denman's beach lieutenant at St Cast, slipped away. Jouan spun so plausible a story about an unknown man who had asked him to carry the suitcases for a favour that his own connection with SOE was never divined. VAR had by then acquired so much momentum that Denman had no trouble in finding another driver, but the alarm of Jouan's arrest forced the Jestin sisters to move away to Paris.

VAR did not long survive their transfer, for as often happened, the circuit snowballed. As its activities grew wider, and as more people became involved, it ceased to be secure, and had to be reorganised completely. Denman fell by the wayside. He came back to England – using his own route – on 27 February 1944, taking with him Langard, his excellent wireless operator (DINU) and his beach Lieutenant

36 Cicely Lefort (ALICE) went into the field in June 1943 as a courier for the Jockey Network. In September she was arrested by the Gestapo, sent to Ravensbrück and executed.

Astride Sicot (JEANETTE), a St Cast fisherman's son. Langard and Denman returned to France, again by sea, on 18 March. By now, the Jestin sisters were spreading the network far and wide from Paris, with contacts both in Brussels and far down the Rhône valley. Langard moved from Redon to Quimper near the south-west Breton coast, where local possibilities seemed excellent, and no one in the circuit could understand why operations to beaches in the neighbourhood were not feasible.

As the short summer nights imposed a pause on sea crossings, Denman was again summoned to England for consultation: he returned once more on the last and most crowded VAR sea operation, arriving on 16 April. Back in England, he had been instructed in some detail on the need to keep his circuit from expanding too fast and was sent back through Spain to take it over again from Louis Lecorvaisier (YVES), the discreet Rennes insurance agent who was in charge in his absence. Denman's nerves were becoming increasingly frayed, and his equanimity did not survive a series of exasperating hitches in his journey across Iberia. Fortunately for everybody, his false papers were lost by one of the guides early in his attempt on the Pyrenees, and he was recalled.

In his absence, Lecorvaiser, Langard and Emile Minerault of OSS (RAYMOND) turned the VAR Lline into an efficient SOE land escape route during the summer. This continued operating until after the D-Day landings. Langard, unfortunately, was arrested while transmitting on 8 June 1944; he kept silent under torture and died in Buchenwald eight months later.

*

The VAR operations carried out by 15th MGBF were part of the JEALOUS, EASEMENT, SEPTIMUS and SCARF series of operations.

The nights of 28, 29 and 30 January were busy. Three operations were carried out. On the 28th, MGB 502 attempted to carry out EASEMENT I, 503 carried out the first BONAPARTE operation for the SHELBURNE escape line. (In all there were eight operations for SHELBURNE, which are covered in a later chapter.) 318 successfully

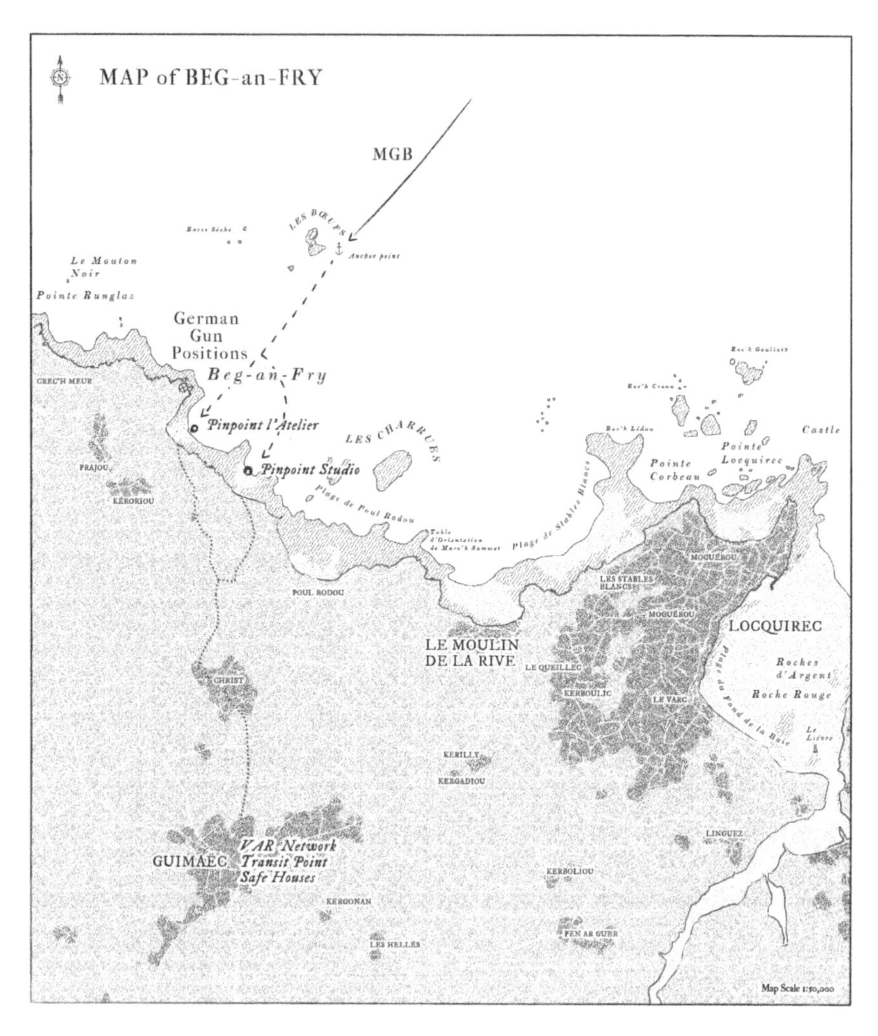

carried out operation FLANNEL FOOT for SIS/BCRA to put an agent ashore at Île d'Er.

Before beginning full operations across the beaches at Beg-an-Fry, Erwin Denman wanted to make a quick trip to London to consult Peter Harratt. It had been arranged that he would be picked up from Beg-an-Fry on the night of 28/29 January. EASEMENT I was to a pin-point at Beg-an-Fry that had been selected and accepted as suitable by DDOD(I), but at some point, confusion arose, as the team on the ground wanted to use one point and London another 300 metres away.

The tabac at Guimaëc owned by Yvonne Jacob and used as a transit for agents

The local team, not having the training or experience in pinpoint procedures, erroneously believed that, in any event, the MGB would see their signal whichever part of the beach they were on, and the surf-boats would home in on them. They were wrong.

502 was given the job with David Birkin as Navigating Officer. Peter Harratt went along as SOE Conducting Officer. Weather conditions off Start Point were not ideal but improved as they made good time towards the French coast. Birkin had chosen Les Boeufs – a distinctive group of rocks – as his marker point. At 0015, 502 anchored and the surf-boats under Tassie Uhr-Henry launched. Uhr-Henry had been involved in many of the previous years' operations. He was now 502's First Lieutenant and Boats Officer. The surf-boats landed without incident and Harratt searched the beach. Unfortunately, he couldn't find the reception committee and went back to 502.

At 0210 they left and returned without incident to Dartmouth.

The reception committee had in fact been on the wrong part of the beach some three hundred metres to the east. The muddle was put down to lack of training and enemy pressure on the network. The VAR Line team at Beg-an-Fry was commanded by Doctor and Madame Le Duc. Two young sisters Raymonde and Alice Jacob worked in the beach landing team, and their elder sister Yvonne, who ran the Bureau de Tabac at Guimaëc, provided a safe house for those transiting in or out. Having failed to make contact with 502, the group waiting to be evacuated had to lie low until the next attempt could be made. They were hidden in an empty house in Guimaëc opposite Yvonne Jacob's shop.

EASEMENT II went ahead on 25/26 February. Again 502 undertook the operation and they dropped anchor off Les Boeufs. The surf-boats went ashore, and there was almost a nasty moment when the wrong recognition signal was given by the reception committee on the beach. As it was, the three agents landing disembarked and those embarking got on. One of the three agents going ashore was 'MORLAND' – the code name for François Mitterrand, future President of France. Among those going to England was a young Frenchman called Andre Hué, who had been born in Britain but lived in France. Andre Hué had been a merchant seaman. His ship was sunk at the outbreak of war. Determined to fight back, he got a job in the railway yards at Guer in Brittany where he was noticed and recruited by the PARSONS SOE circuit centred on Rennes. He helped OSCAR, the leader of the circuit, with many acts of sabotage. OSCAR was impressed with Hué and arranged for him to go to England for further training. And so it was that he joined the party heading out to 502.

On the way back to 502 from the beach the surf-boats were suddenly engulfed in a very thick fog. After a worrying hour or so they gave up trying to find 502 by stealth and switched on a torch and shone it at sea level below the fog. It worked and very soon 502 lowered their scramble net and they climbed aboard. Hué was delighted to be taken below and given 'kye', Pusser's rum and above all cigarettes. Four hours later they were in Dartmouth having a very welcome breakfast in the wardroom of *Westward Ho*. That completed, the 'passengers' were ferried ashore to Kingswear station and the train for London. Hué was somewhat bewildered but was soon taken in hand by an SOE Conducting Officer. Six months later on 31 August he was parachuted back into Brittany. Mitterrand was first taken to the house of a retired gendarme at Kergoriou and then on to the Jacob sisters in Guimaëc where the local fish merchant Louis Mercier picked him up in his truck and took him to Morlaix where he was to catch a train for Paris.

Henri Frager
(JEAN MARIE)

Ange Defendini
(JULES)

Alex Schwatschko
(ALBERT)

Three nights later on 29 February, Peter Williams and 502 went back to Beg-an-Fry to drop three F Section agents: Henri Frager (JEAN-MARIE, DONKEYMAN), Ange Defendini (JULES, PRIEST) and Alex Schwatschko (ALBERT, POLITICIAN). These agents were not lucky. Frager, on his third mission to France, was tasked to organise attacks on railway targets for D-Day. He was captured by the Abwehr on 2 July 1944 at the Duroc metro station, tortured by the Gestapo at Avenue Foch and deported to Buchenwald.

Ange Defendini was a Corsican who had been a professional soldier and, before the war, an Intelligence Officer. He was an early Resister, assisting in the liberation of Corsica and joining SOE in June 1943. His mission was to attack rail targets in the Verdun area in the run-up to D-Day. Unfortunately his arrival had already been 'blown' as a result of Abwehr penetration of the ARCHDEACON circuit. He was arrested on 8 March 1944, imprisoned in Fresnes and, though tortured, gave nothing away. He too went to Buchenwald where he was hanged on 9 September along with Phillip Keun and Peter Tissier.[37] Frager knew that he, too, was scheduled to die, and knowing that Defendini had died by slow strangulation, persuaded the camp authorities to execute him and three other F Section agents,

37 This group of prisoners were categorised under the 'Nacht und Nebel' order – to disappear without trace. The victims were taken into the hanging room in pairs while the Buchenwald Orchestra played to cover the screams. SS guards clubbed them with heavy mallets. A thin wire was put around their neck and they were hung on hooks to slowly strangle. The bodies were then burnt.

Buchenwald execution chamber

Barrett, Mulsant and George Wilkinson, by firing squad. Buckmaster admired him very much, noting on his file, 'An absolute first class Frenchman ... He achieved a remarkable series of sabotage actions.'

Alexandre Schwatschko, meanwhile, had been recruited by SOE after escaping from France, arriving in June 1943. His mission on return to France was to organise Lysander pick-up sites. On 7 June 1944 he was reconnoitring a target at Barrage d'Eguzon. While being driven through the town centre by Jean Traversat, they were stopped by German sentries after taking a wrong turn. Traversat remained in the car while Schwatschko was taken into the Hôtel de France for questioning. Traversat panicked and ran for it, immediately giving the game away. Schwatschko still had his pistol and decided to shoot his way out. He shot his German escort but was himself wounded. Knowing the game was up, he shot himself.

During March there were three other successful operations to the Beg-an-Fry pinpoint. On 17/18 March, 503, under the command of Mike Marshall, conducted Operation SEPTIMUS to pick-up the VAR Line organiser Erwin Denman and deliver Gilbert Védy (MÉDÉSIC) for SOE RF. The landing operation went very successfully. Védy was an important organiser for the Resistance Council. He was well known in France – some thought, too well known. Having returned to France, he travelled from Morlaix to Paris. Checking in to a hotel, a terrible stroke of bad luck meant he was given a room recently

Charles Rechenmann (JULIAN)

Virginia Hall (DIANE)

vacated by a black-marketeer, whom the police were after. Védy was arrested and taken to police headquarters where he was recognised by the very zealous collaborator, the head of the Police Counter-Terrorism Unit. Knowing he was about to be handed over to the Gestapo, he took his suicide pill.

Four nights later on 21/22 March, 501 conducted Operation SEPTIMUS II (on the same night 503 was unsuccessfully conducting Operation GLOVER II for SIS, finding no reception committee on the beach). SEPTIMUS II involved the landing of six SOE F Section agents. These included Charles Rechenmann (JULIAN) who had previously worked with Ben Cowburn (Chapter 5). Rechenmann was caught on 12 May 1944 at the Hôtel Cheval de Bronze in Angoulême having been betrayed by his previously loyal assistant René Bochereau, who was subsequently executed by Rechenmann's group. He was taken from Angoulême to Paris and held in Fresnes. On 8 August 1944 he was deported to Buchenwald where he joined Frager and Defendini. He was also among the first group to be executed by strangulation on 9 September 1944, on the same day as Defendini.

Five days after SEPTIMUS II, 503 was back at Beg-an-Fry on 26/27 March for SEPTIMUS III, another successful and uneventful drop off for F Section of one agent, Yvonne Fontaine (MIMI). They embarked an agent from the VAR network. The night before 318 had carried out FLANNEL FOOT II for SIS at the Île d'Er pinpoint, with a successful drop of three agents, Theodore Doare, Louis Marec from the TURQOISE network and Pierre Serandour from the DRAX network.

*

One of the other agents landed as part of SEPTIMUS II was Virginia Hall (DIANE). Virginia Hall was one of the most successful F Section agents of the entire war, who later became a CIA legend. It was Hall whom Ben Cowburn had travelled across France to see after the shambles of the VICTOIRE (La Chatte) exfiltration. Cowburn was determined not to be captured, as VICTOIRE was working for the Germans, and LUCAS was clearly 'blown'. LUCAS had told Ben that it was imperative that he get away from them on the trip back to Paris, and to get to London at all costs as a back-up plan to warn London about VICTOIRE if LUCAS was arrested.

Virginia Hall was an American. She had studied French, Italian and German at university. Wanting to finish her studies in Europe, she got a job at the US Embassy in Warsaw. Transferred to Turkey, she then lost the lower part of her left leg in a shooting accident: her lower leg was replaced by a wooden leg she named 'Cuthbert'.[38] Hall resigned from the US Consular Service in 1939 and took a job as an ambulance driver for the French Army. She escaped to Spain in 1940 and eventually found her way to London where she was recruited by SOE in 1941. Sent back to the unoccupied zone in August 1941, her cover was as a reporter for the *New York Post*. This gave her licence to interview people, gather information and file stories filled with details useful to military planners. Based in Lyon, she abandoned her chic Parisian wardrobe to become inconspicuous and often quickly changed her appearance through make-up and disguise. She had to learn quickly the 'exacting tasks of being available, arranging contacts, recommending who to bribe and where to hide, soothing the jagged nerves of agents on the run and supervising the distribution of wireless sets'.

Hall's lengthy stay in France without being arrested illustrates her extreme caution. In October 1941, she sensed danger and declined to attend a meeting of SOE agents in Marseille, which the French police raided, capturing a dozen agents. After that débâcle, Hall was one of the few SOE agents still at large in France and the only one with a

38 The French nicknamed her 'la dame qui boite' and the Germans put 'the limping lady' on their most wanted list. Klaus Barbie, the exceptionally vicious head of the Gestapo in Lyon, is reported to have said, 'I would give anything to get my hands on that limping Canadian bitch.'

means of transmitting information to London, George Whittinghall, an American diplomat in Lyon, allowing her to smuggle reports and letters to London in the diplomatic pouch. In the absence of an SOE wireless operator, her access to the American diplomatic pouch was the only means the few agents left at large in France had of communicating with London.

Hall continued building contacts in southern France. She avoided contact with an SOE agent sent to Lyon named Georges Duboudin and refused to introduce him to her contacts. She regarded him as amateurish and lax in security. When SOE headquarters directed that Duboudin should supervise her, she told SOE to 'fuck off'. She also avoided contact with Philippe de Vomécourt, who, although a genuine Resistance leader, she felt was too grandiose and maintained poor security procedures. Hall also took on the task of helping British airmen escape and return to England. Downed airmen who found their way to Lyon were told to go to the American Consulate and say they were a 'friend of Olivier'. 'Olivier' was Hall, and she helped dozens of airmen escape from France to Spain and from there back to the UK.

Hall learned that twelve agents arrested by the French police in October 1941 were incarcerated at the Mauzac prison near Bergerac: wireless operator Georges Bégué smuggled out letters to her. Too well known to visit the prison herself, Hall recruited Gaby Bloch, wife of the prisoner Jean-Pierre Bloch, as an ally to plan an escape. Bloch visited the prison frequently to bring food and other items to her husband, including tins of sardines. She smuggled in tools and keys fashioned from these sardine tins, enabling Bégué to make a key to the door of the barracks where the prisoners were kept. A priest smuggled in a radio to Bégué, and from within the prison, he began transmitting to London. On 15 July 1942 the prisoners escaped. After hiding in the woods while an intense manhunt took place, all of them had met up with Hall in Lyon by 11 August. From there, they were smuggled to Spain and onwards back to England.

The Germans were furious about the escape from Mauzac prison and the laxity of the French police in allowing it. The Gestapo flooded Vichy France with 500 agents and the Abwehr also stepped up operations to infiltrate and destroy the fledgling Resistance and the SOE networks. The Germans focused on Lyon, the epicentre of the Resistance. Hall had always counted on contacts she had with the French police to protect her. But under pressure from the Germans, she found her police contacts were no longer reliable.

On 7 November 1942, the American Consulate in Lyon told Hall that an Allied invasion of North Africa was imminent. In response to the invasion, on 8 November, the Germans moved to occupy Vichy France. Hall anticipated correctly that the suppression by the Gestapo and Abwehr would become even more severe and she fled Lyon without telling anyone, even her closest contacts. She escaped by train from Lyon to Perpignan then, with a guide, walked over a 7,500-foot pass in the Pyrenees to Spain, covering up to fifty miles in two days in considerable discomfort. Hall signalled to SOE before her escape that she hoped 'Cuthbert' would not trouble her on the way. The SOE did not understand the reference and replied, 'If Cuthbert troublesome, eliminate him.' After arriving in Spain, she was arrested by the Spanish authorities for illegally crossing the border, but the American Embassy eventually secured her release. She worked for SOE for a time in Madrid, then returned to London in July 1943, where she was awarded the MBE.

On her return to London, SOE leaders declined to send Hall back to France as an agent despite her requests, saying she was compromised, and too much at risk. However, she took a wireless course and contacted the American Office of Strategic Services (OSS) suggesting she work for them. She was hired and on 21 March 1944, as part of SEPTIMUS II, returned to France.

Hall's mission was to organise sabotage in support of D-Day. She was disguised as an older woman, with grey hair, disguising her limp with a shuffling gait. Landing with her was Henri Lassot, at 62 years old, unusually old for an agent. Hall and Lassot were the fourth and fifth OSS agents to arrive in France. Lassot was the organiser and leader of the new SAINT network (it being too radical an idea that a woman could lead an SOE or OSS network of agents), with Hall his wireless operator. Hall, however, quickly separated herself from Lassot, whom she considered totally inexperienced and a security risk: she even instructed her contacts not to tell him where she was. Aware that her accent would reveal that she was not French, she engaged a French woman, Madame Rabut, to accompany and speak for her. Virginia Hall went on to become a very successful Resistance leader in the Haute Loire.

*

On 15 April 1944, the Flotilla undertook Operation SCARF. The operation was the first for MGB 718 under command of Ronnie Seddon with Guy Hamilton as his First Lieutenant. 718 also had Jan McQuoid Mason, Commanding Officer of 318, on board as overall Mission Commander and Lieutenant Salmond as Navigating Officer. Mason also brought with him a surf-boat crew from 318. 718 was accompanied on the mission by 502. 318's First Lieutenant was on board 502 as Surf-boat Officer and there were two Navigating Officers, Lieutenant Connor Smith and Sub-Lieutenant Fraser. The Flotilla was deploying in force. Before sailing, Ronnie Seddon gave his crew their briefing for the first operation, concluding with '...and if any of you are feeling a bit scared, well you are not alone.'

502 carried six agents, two of whom, Captain Rendier (ADOLFE) and Felix Duffour (AMÉDÉE), were tasked with sabotaging and delaying the German forces in Brittany that would be moving to counter the D-Day landings. They would prove to be very successful. On the night of 5/6 June, they carried out sabotage operations which delayed a German armoured formation from reaching Normandy for nine days. 718, meanwhile, was carrying suitcases and a tyre for the local Resistance group. The crossing was uneventful until they saw some unusual lights which they assumed was an aircraft beacon. They moved ahead slowly and at 0145 sighted the Les Boeufs rocks. They anchored and four surf-boats were lowered – under the command of Sub-Lieutenant Miller. For those on the bridge of 718 this was an uncanny experience, feeling exhilarated by the sheer audacity of it. The beach landing was made without difficulty but took longer than normal as there was a lot of chattering and farewells: among those embarking were Erwin Denham of the VAR Line, nine airmen,

and the two F Section agents, Suzanne Warengham (CHARISE) and Blanche Charlet (BERBERIS).

A few hours earlier, back at the farmhouse now smelling distinctly of Chanel No 5, Warengham, Charlet and the rest of the waiting party had been gathered round the radio set to listen to the BBC news bulletin in French. It had been agreed that a code sentence, read at the end of the bulletin, should tell them whether the gunboat was en route to pick them up. There was a tense moment as the news bulletin ended and the announcer began to read the code messages. But finally, they heard the message they had all been waiting for: 'Onesine a une belle bobine' – confirmation they were leaving that night.

Around 2200, the escapees began the three-hour walk to the pinpoint at Beg-an-Fry. Warengham insisted on wearing the new hat she had bought in Paris, tying it securely on her head with a dark scarf, in case it blew off. As the party left the house, a number of revolvers were handed round. The fisherman explained that, if a passing German patrol came upon the party in the dark in the 'zone interdite' there would be no choice but to shoot it out with them. 'If there is any trouble,' they were told, 'kill as many Germans as you can before you get killed yourself.' For anyone surviving, there would be a rendezvous for all survivors at the Paris Métro station Passy the following Friday afternoon at three, and every Friday afternoon after that for the next ten weeks.

The escapees started on their way, walking in single file in the darkness, along with three Breton guides and half a dozen local volunteers. The volunteers were going to the beach to help unload the arms, ammunition and radio sets of the agents who simultaneously were due to be landed that night. Every quarter of an hour or so, the chief guide halted the column to pause and listen. Warengham was on full alert: checking and rechecking the film in her pocket and holding the plan of the radar stations in her hand, ready to eat it if there was any trouble.

Around 0100, the party reached the pinpoint. The whole party was assembled on the beach in the darkness, not talking, not smoking, hardly daring to move for fear of making a sound. After what felt like an interminable wait, the surf-boats were seen approaching the beach. Now there were whispered exchanges, men splashed in and out of the sea carrying packages. Warengham felt herself grabbed by two powerful arms and the distinctive voice of a British sailor said, 'You come along with me, Miss. You don't want to get those pretty feet of yours wet.' The gallant sailor carried her through the waves and deposited her in his dinghy – for all the attempts of keeping her dry, she found herself sitting in about six inches of water. Meanwhile, as Blanche Charlet was getting into the surf-boat, a sailor noticed her rather shapely legs and muttered 'ici mademoiselle' as he tried to help her board. 'It's OK, Jack,'[39] she replied sharply, 'I've been on one of these boats before.'

Soon after that, the boat rowed silently out to 502 and 718. Warengham and Charlet scrambled to a net and on to the deck. They and their companions were led silently below to a cabin which, for security, was in pitch darkness. For some time they stood bunched together there, hardly daring to move, since they could see nothing around them. Then they heard the low throb of the ship's engines and knew they were on their way.

Though the pick-up had gone smoothly the events of the night were not quite yet finished with them. At 0336, 502 spotted three ships on the port bow about 800 metres away. They were undoubtedly German, probably armed coasters. Peter Williams ordered both boats to increase speed. They came up to the enemy shipping at a range of 500 metres. The enemy sent a challenge signal to 718 – a flashing 'V'. 502 replied with a 'KA' – 'I am taking instructions' in order to buy time.

There was a pause and then the enemy opened fire.

Signalman College, who was on the bridge of 502 with Williams and the Coxswain Petty Officer Smith, described what happened next:

'By this time, we were doing about 20 knots, very steady in fact and the bluff had to begin very soon, eight Jerry boats were there, we knew later that they were R boats. They were five on our port bow

39 She had been landed in the south of France from a felucca on 1 September 1942. 'Jack' is military slang 'Jack Tar' for a sailor.

when we were challenged, I do not know to this day whether it was V… or B … it came so fast I was not the only person to feel his blood race that night. Anyway we were ready for such a challenge and the Captain told me to send KA, which I did, this told the German to wait as would another German ship who had to look up the reply, all of the time we were drawing closer to the gap and away, the longer we could confuse and delay him the better our chances to get home. He finally got fed up of my lamp, he knew who we were anyway, and they opened fire.

'One second I was looking at his lamp, the next to hundreds of tracers moving slowly at first and then terribly fast, it was a dark night and then to have all the tracer, did not help one's vision. The Captain called for emergency speed and ordered open fire. I pressed the open fire button to all guns and told them over the phone to fire, NOTHING happened, not a shot in reply, a dreadful moment I shall never forget, we felt sure on the bridge that all guns had been hit, the D boat (718) didn't fire because we didn't and she fell slightly behind because of our increases in speed, I was not able to tell her of this. We were now thundering along and level with them when they stopped firing as suddenly as they began, seconds later we were on our way home out of it. I was detailed to go visit the guns and check what happened, I didn't know what I would find so it was a surprise to find only one man had been killed and no one wounded, in fact what had happened was that they could not see to open fire, the tracer after the dark and so close to them had made them blind for some seconds. This fact saved us because Jerry had real doubts as to who we were when no firing came his way.'

The firing lasted about fifteen seconds and then stopped abruptly. A damage and casualty report was called for from the bridge of both ships. Neither was damaged except one hit on 718 which did not incapacitate her in any way. Sadly, however, there had been one casualty on 502: a young eighteen-year-old Able Seaman, William Sandalls, had been badly wounded in the arms, chest and stomach.

Remembering the incident, Seaman Alf Harris recalled, 'The First Lieutenant then told me to take over my guns and I suppose it could only have been a minute or so before I saw the seemingly slow climb of tracer coming towards us which at the last moment sped across the ship. What I can say with absolute truth is that I heard the cannon shell that killed Sandalls, it was the same sound as a large dry twig snapped close to one's ear. The CO ordered the guns to hold fire. I always respected his coolness under stress and it certainly proved the right decision on the night.'

William Sandalls died before Sub-Lieutenant Miller and a rating could get him into the Charthouse to treat his wounds. The boats reached Dartmouth at 0848 – with 502's White Ensign at half-mast. 718 headed to *Westward Ho*, whilst 502 went to Dartmouth Railway Jetty to hand over Sandall's body.

Sandalls was the only casualty suffered by the Flotilla in all 57 missions[40] and is buried at Charlbury in Oxfordshire. His was a sacrifice that was anything but in vain: the intelligence brought back by Suzanne Warengham almost certainly contained much detail about the Normandy coastal defences, essential for planning D-Day. Frank Slocum's report dated 2 May 1944 confirmed that she also brought out intelligence on CROSSBOW targets, the V1 and V2 rockets.

40 At the end of the war 502, redesignated 2002, hit a single floating mine in the Skagerrak, killing all but two on board (see Chapter 12).

CHAPTER 10 – 'UN PISTOLEUR'

> 'The measure may be thought bold, but
> I am of opinion the boldest are the safest'
>
> Horatio Nelson

The airman was terrified. Shot down over France, he'd been picked up by what he assumed was the Resistance. He'd been transported to Paris, where he'd been taken to hide high up in an attic, in anticipation of news about his return home.

'Name? Rank?'

The man asking the questions was short, tough and articulate. He was a forceful personality, not someone to mess with.

'Number? Date of birth?'

The questions were relentless and kept coming. The interrogator was joined by an equally tough-looking Frenchman who also questioned him in English.

'Using your fingers show me the number one.'

The airman was bemused, but did as he was asked. The Frenchman offered him a cigarette. For a second, the airman felt touched by the gesture, but then realised the two interviewers were watching him closely, to see how he was holding it. He tried to stop his hand shaking as he lit it. A third interrogator arrived, a very attractive woman who introduced herself as Claudette. She spoke with an American accent which at first threw the young airman, but he answered her questions as best he could.

Finally, the original interrogator offered his hand. 'I am Captain Hamilton from British Intelligence,' he said with a tight smile. 'You passed the test.'

The airman blew out a sigh of relief. 'And if I hadn't?'

'You'd have been shot as a Gestapo infiltrator.'

Lucien Dumais, 'Captain Hamilton' or 'LEON' as his French contacts knew him, was born in Montréal in 1905. At the outbreak of war, he had joined the 1st Battalion Les Fusiliers Mont Royal where he

Lucien Dumais

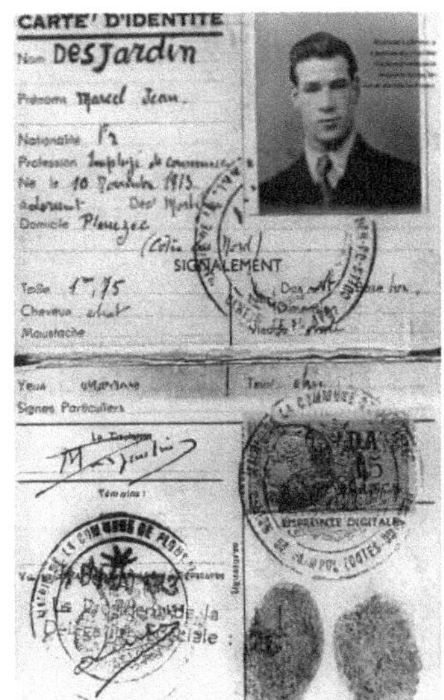

CARTE D'IDENTITE
Nom Desjardin
Prénoms Marcel Jean
Nationalité Fr
SIGNALEMENT
Taille 1m75
Cheveux
Moustache
Yeux
Signes Particuliers
EMPREINTES DIGITALES

Raymond Labrosse

rose to the rank of Sergeant-Major. He took part in the Dieppe raid in August 1942, was captured by the Germans but managed to escape by jumping from the train taking him to a German POW camp. He made his way to Marseille where he had helped Georges Rodocanchi, the doctor who had helped Jimmy Langley return to Britain. From here he returned to England himself where, as an escaped POW, he was interviewed by MI9. They liked what they saw, and Jimmy Langley offered him a job. Dumais declined, preferring to return to his old unit in North Africa. But once back there, he did not get on with his new Platoon Commander. He decided to get back to London and get in touch again with MI9.

MI9 believed that with special training in naval night embarkation procedure and the other skills needed for clandestine operations in France, Dumais would be ideal to set up exfiltration operations in Brittany. His French-Canadian accent, too, would not stand out in Brittany as it resembled the Breton accent. He was described by Job Mainguy, one of the members of the network he was to run, as, 'attentive au moindre detail, avait une grande autorité militaire ... un pistoleur' ('paid attention to minor details, he had an authoritative military manner and shot from the hip ... a real gunslinger').

Dumais's attention to detail led to him studying the security weaknesses in other evacuation lines. He was determined to prevent the same problems with his own. As with the airman described above, all rescued aviators would be questioned rigorously as they passed through Paris. Those who passed their 'test' would be outfitted with appropriate clothing and shoes, furnished with false ID cards and German Ausweis (permits to travel within restricted coastal zones), and generally taught to act like Frenchmen. Two guides (convoyeurs) would then accompany the 'packages' (colis) – as the airmen were called – by train to St. Brieuc, at the south-east end of the Côte d'Armour. There, a local agent would meet them and disperse them among safe houses in the vicinity. While on the train, the airmen would feign being deaf-mutes if someone spoke to them or pretend to be asleep. Both were highly risky strategies, but no one could think of a better one.

A few days after the airman was first questioned by Dumais, he met him again, this time in the attic of a farmhouse in Brittany, along with several other escaping aviators. Although they had all passed Dumais's test, his tone was no more friendly.

'You will be leaving for England tonight,' he told the assembled airmen. 'From now on, you do exactly as I and my team say. Absolute silence is essential. Many lives have been risked to bring you this far. There is just one mile left, and it is the most dangerous mile you will ever travel. There are enemy sentries and patrols in the area. If it becomes necessary to kill any of them, you are expected to help.' He glanced round the room, making sure to catch the eye of each airman. 'Be quick and above all, be quiet. Your lives and ours depend on it.'

*

The SHELBURNE Line, despite coming quite late on in the war and of short lifespan, was one of the most successful of MI9's escape lines, in that it was never penetrated or rolled up. This was despite the best efforts of the Gestapo, and the Abwehr, which is why those attempting to enter the line were so rigorously interrogated in order to identify potential plants. In total, SHELBURNE repatriated 130

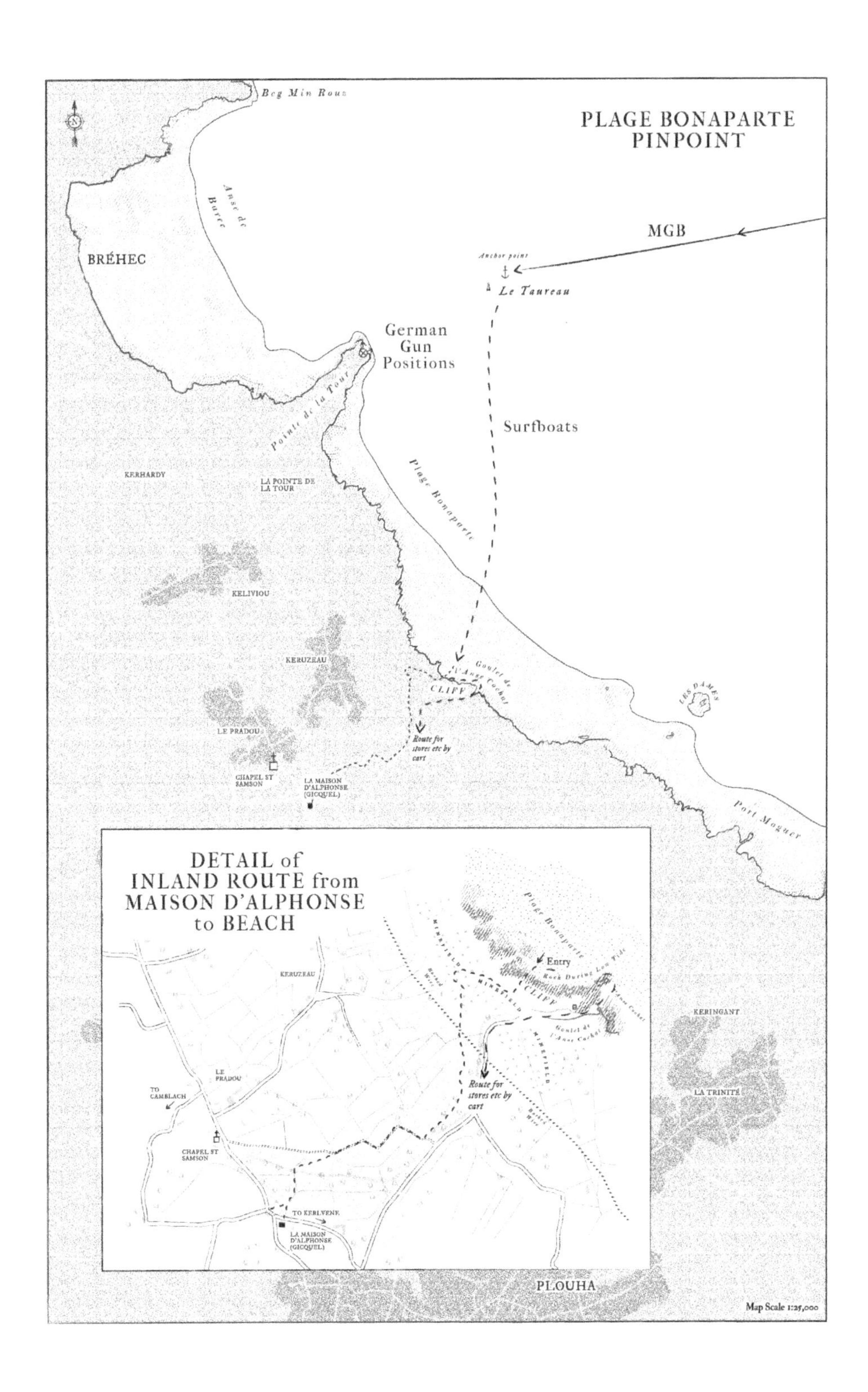
PLAGE BONAPARTE
PINPOINT
Beg Min Rouz
Anse de Bréhec
BRÉHEC
MGB
Anchor point
Le Taureau
German
Gun
Positions
Pointe de la Tour
Surfboats
Plage Bonaparte
KERHARDY
LA POINTE DE LA TOUR
KELIVIOU
KERUZEAU
Goulet de l'Anse Cochat
CLIFF
LES DAMES
LE PRADOU
Route for stores etc by cart
CHAPEL ST SAMSON
LA MAISON D'ALPHONSE (GICQUEL)
Port Moguer
DETAIL of
INLAND ROUTE from
MAISON D'ALPHONSE
to BEACH
Plage Bonaparte
Entry
KERUZEAU
MINEFIELD
CLIFF
LE PRADOU
TO CAMBLACH
CHAPEL ST SAMSON
TO KERLVENE
LA MAISON D'ALPHONSE (GICQUEL)
KERINGANT
LA TRINITÉ
PLOUHA
Map Scale 1:25,000

The Anse-Cochat beach and Pointe de la Tour

aircrew vital for the continuing war effort, as well as many other evaders and returning agents. This was primarily due to Lucien Dumais's firm discipline and meticulous security arrangements.

In total, 15th MGBF conducted nine operations in support of the SHELBURNE Line to a beach at Anse-Cochat, near the town of Plouha, which became known as Bonaparte Beach. The MGB operations consisted of BONAPART I–V (January – March 1944), REFLEXION (June 1944) and CROZIER I–III (August 1944). In the next chapter, we will look in detail at these operations, but here we will turn our attention to how SHELBURNE first came about and how it was so successfully structured.

SHELBURNE was the successor to the first attempt to set up an escape line from the Brittany coast, the OAKTREE Line. The need for an escape route by sea from Brittany had long been discussed by MI9. Two early attempts in cooperation with the Free French had not been successful. On each occasion, French naval officers were sent to Brittany via the Spanish frontier and a long journey through Vichy France to organise evacuation by ship. One was recognised and denounced by a former colleague, the other shot by a German officer in a café brawl.

During the latter part of 1942, MI9 had one solitary contact in Brittany. This was François le Cornec, of Plouha, a village on the north coast fifteen miles from St Brieuc and two miles from the shore. Le Cornec was a dedicated patriot and a clear-headed organiser. He had obtained his release from a prisoner-of-war camp in 1941 by posing as an agricultural worker and soon formed a Resistance organisation consisting of friends in the region and the local gendarme. Among the organisation's activities was the hiding of airmen. This little group of Breton fishermen and farmers formed the base for a series of brilliant sea operations at the end of 1943 and the first months of 1944.

In the autumn of 1942, Jimmy Langley began plans for a naval rescue service from the coast near Plouha. His choice for the mission was Vladimir Bouryschinke, whom he gave the cover name 'VAL WILLIAMS' after Valentine Williams, an author of adventure stories of the 1930s. Bouryschinke was born in Moscow in 1913, but had grown up in the United States, where he became a basketball champion. In 1940, while working for the American Red Cross, he met the Reverend Donald Caskie in Marseille after both had escaped from the German occupation of Paris. Caskie encouraged him to remain in France and help evaders and escaped POWs return to England.

Williams evolved an ingenious 'cover story' for this work: he obtained the job of coach to the basketball team of the Principality of Monaco. Using this cover he facilitated escapes from the Fort de la Revère at La Turbie near Monte Carlo. On 13 September 1942, he was evacuated to Gibraltar by the trawler TARANA and distinguished himself by swimming excitedly to the dinghy as it came to fetch the party on a clear Mediterranean night. He caused considerable annoyance to the crew, who made loud complaints about his lack of security awareness when they arrived in port. They claimed that had the coastguards or gendarmes seen or heard him in the water, it would have endangered the entire operation.

Although Williams arrived in London with a small blot on his copybook, this did not deter MI9 from recruiting him. He was deemed to have considerable possibilities as an agent in the future, if he were given the necessary coaching. Throughout the autumn, Williams received special training on how to organise links between Paris and Brittany. The final objective was to create an escape route from the coast to Dartmouth, though at this time the Navy had not decided on a suitable beach. Williams was trained in parachuting and night landing by Lysander and took a special course in the organisation of naval rescue operations over the beaches of occupied France.

At the beginning of February 1943, Williams was asked whether he would return to France. This would be in the face of the chaos and danger posed by Gestapo successes against existing escape lines, particularly the treachery of Roger le Neveu, known as Roger le Legionnaire, and the arrest of Louis Nouveau. Williams was asked if, in spite of these arrests, he was still prepared to go. Langley warned him that the original organisation was 'blown', and no contact could be made with any of O'Leary's group who were still free: Williams would have to start a completely new line. It was a big ask, but Williams agreed.

Under the code name OAKTREE, Langley's orders were to establish a base in Brittany for sea operations. Using charts of the Brittany coast and aerial photographs taken by the RAF, Langley explained that the Navy had selected a beach near Plouha, fifteen kilometres from the port of Paimpol and twenty-five from the railway station at Guingamp. Williams was to create a new system for hiding men in Paris, bring them by train to Guingamp and from there to the beach. A series of safe houses would be needed near Plouha, where there were a number of people, including Le Cornec, who had hidden airmen in the past.

Langley told Williams to make contact with François Le Cornec and his friends at Plouha. He was to take as his wireless operator Ray Labrosse, a volunteer recruited by Langley from Canadian Military Headquarters in London, who had just completed his training. Labrosse was a quiet, tough, French-Canadian and a good counterpart for the volatile and enterprising Williams. He was a man of courage and good sense who would prove to be an excellent agent for MI9.

Right from the start, there was difficulty in getting 'Operation OAKTREE' started. An attempt to land Williams by Lysander failed owing to the absence of the reception committee. He was, therefore, transferred with Labrosse to RAF Tempsford, so that they could be parachuted 'blind' to a field near the forest of Rambouillet, fifteen miles from Paris. During the last fortnight of February 1943, they were forced to return to England on nine separate occasions because the pilot could not find the drop zone. Each trip carried a substantial risk that the Halifax bomber used for the mission would be shot down. At last, their persistence was rewarded, and on 28 February they were dropped near Rambouillet.

For several weeks London did not know of their safe arrival since Labrosse did not come up on the air. Williams, however, had managed to make contact with Paul Campinchi, a Paris lawyer who was an MI9 agent. Within a week of his arrival in France, he was on a visit to Brittany and making his first reconnaissance at Carhaix, taking with him a large quantity of Players cigarettes for recruiting helpers. Near Paimpol he found what he later described as a 'whole regiment' of American and British airmen, hidden in the Château de Bourblanc, by Comte and Comtesse de Mauduit.

Williams visited the Château de Bourblanc on 10 April. His intention was to mount a sea operation from the Anse-Cochat near Plouha at the end of May, but he was still out of wireless contact with London. Labrosse 'borrowed' a set from the French intelligence group 'Mithridate', and eventually sent a message requesting his own set: the news was received with many misgivings about the security of OAKTREE. A message was sent through an SIS network telling Labrosse that a set would be left in the left luggage office at the St Jean station at Bordeaux, where it was duly collected by Labrosse. Whether he ever used it is unclear, as events were soon to overtake the fledgling network.

In May, an abortive operation was planned to pick up airmen from the beach, at Le Palus-Plage a few miles east of the Anse-Cochat. Williams and his friends waited on the beach, but on the night of 29 May, the message 'Denise est morte' was heard on the BBC, indicating that the operation was cancelled. It was deemed that the absence of proper radio communications made it too risky. As a result of this failure, Williams's situation was becoming dangerous. At least ninety airmen had been collected in Brittany, of whom thirty-nine were hidden by the Comtesse de Mauduit. Williams's only alternative, until a proper sea evacuation could be organised, was to take the airmen through to Spain. He recruited guides and, taking two

Polish and two American airmen, travelled by train to Orthez, near Pau, in the Pyrenees, close to the Spanish border. On 4 June, the compartment where he was sitting with the airmen was suddenly filled with German police: the party were arrested and taken to Paris.

Meanwhile, after a search by the Gestapo at the château, Comtesse Betty de Mauduit was arrested on 12 June 1943, and sent to Ravensbrück concentration camp, but she survived. There seems little doubt that she was betrayed by 'Roger le Legionnaire', who by now was attached to Gestapo headquarters at Rennes. Unsurprisingly, the local Resistance was becoming suspicious. A number of arrests followed but the main Brittany organisation remained intact.

Williams's arrest was the last that was heard of him until December 1943. He was kept at Fresnes prison in Paris for one month and later taken to Rennes to be thoroughly interrogated by the Gestapo. The amount of information they had on Williams was alarming. The Gestapo had a dossier dating from the previous year when he took part in the escape from Fort de la Revère. They also displayed a disconcerting knowledge of MI9, including full personal details of Jimmy Langley, together with a photograph of him, as well as an understanding of the MI9 training syllabus.

Williams felt compelled to tell them that he had been trained as a 'British Officer', but he maintained his cover story. He told his interrogators that as Squadron Leader Valentine Williams of the RAF Ground Staff, he had been persuaded by Langley to volunteer for an escape mission in France. Before he could be transferred to MI9 he had flown as a passenger in a bomber aircraft which had been shot down. He had then decided to remain in France and join the Resistance. It did not seem very convincing, but the Gestapo were unable to break his story. He was tortured and then with Teutonic correctness, they had him medically examined and declared 'fit to be shot'.

Before this could happen, Williams made a spectacular escape from the Jacques Cartier Prison in Rennes on 20 December 1943. Williams accomplished this feat with 'Ivan' – a Russian officer named Bougaiev, who had been recaptured after escaping from the Germans while a prisoner-of-war working on the Channel defences known as the 'Atlantic Wall'. Having been born in Moscow, Williams had the advantage of speaking both Russian and French, and made full use of it. In addition to Ivan, other Russians were imprisoned at Rennes whose duty was to serve the noon-day soup. When his cell door was opened Williams talked to them in their own language. Ivan was thus able to pass him a saw hidden in a bottle of red wine.

The first attempt to escape was a failure. Williams was caught trying to cut through a bar in his cell and was thrown naked into the punishment cell or 'cachot' for twenty-four hours. Fortunately, Ivan continued to serve the soup and they were able, in Russian, to continue planning their escape.

During an air raid alarm, some days later, Ivan stole the key of the 'cachot'. The two men climbed down ladders left behind by workmen, to the moat of the prison. At eight-thirty on the evening of 20 December, they reached the top of the outer wall and jumped. Williams miscalculated the height and fractured his leg, but despite this, was able to make his way to a hen-house, where he hid with Ivan till dawn. The pair were nearly captured by a search party with dogs but employed a useful trick which Williams had learned during his security training in England. As the dogs approached them, they urinated. This caused the dogs to urinate too and thus lose the scent. At dawn the next morning, Williams leaned on Ivan's arm and hobbled to a potato field, where they persuaded a farmer to drive them in his lorry under sacks of potatoes to the safe address of Madame Dubois at Bain de Bretagne. Here they remained while Williams's leg was put in plaster.

Through Madame Dubois, contact was regained with Campinchi: the Parisian lawyer Williams had met when he first reached Paris. The difficulty of getting Williams back to Paris was enormous and it says much for Campinchi's resourcefulness that he succeeded. He arranged that two French gendarmes in his pay should board the train from St Brieuc at Versailles and 'arrest' Williams. They escorted him handcuffed through German controls at the Gare du Maine/ Montparnasse. On arrival in Paris, Williams found that Labrosse, who had escaped to Spain after his arrest, had returned from Britain a second time and was now radio operator to a new chief. This new organisation was already preparing for naval operations beginning in January 1944 and its leader determined that Williams, so recently escaped from the Gestapo, should leave France immediately.

The name of the new chief was Sergeant-Major Lucien Dumais.

*

Dumais and Labrosse were considered by MI9 to be a perfect match to set up the new network.

Labrosse, calm and unflappable, was already known by Resistance groups in Paris and Brittany as 'CLAUDE'. Together with Dumais's leadership, they were felt to be a formidable team.

In London both men underwent specialist training including several days spent with Steven Mackenzie and Sir Colville 'Collie' Barclay of DDOD(I) in a room at St Ermin's hotel, next door to SIS headquarters at Broadway (Barclay had joined DDOD(I) in early 1943) Mackenzie and Barclay talked Dumais and Labrosse through the necessary naval problems and requirements: they explained how to describe beaches and pinpoints with accurate coordinates to London; the use of BBC messages; procedures for light signals; the surf-boat management of passengers; and how to remove all traces after a landing had taken place. At one stage during this training Dumais was asked to write out a wireless message describing a pinpoint on the coast. He wrote, 'at 5 km due east of there is a small bitch 50 metres long between two headlands of rock. This bitch has a sandy bottom.' Mackenzie and Barclay, stifling giggles, did not correct his pronunciation.

From the off, Dumais and Labrosse liked and respected each other. Both knew that they would be able to work together successfully. At midnight on 14 November 1943, two RAF Lysander aircraft departed London for a drop at a small, clandestine, dirt landing strip 60 miles north east of Paris. Aboard the lead aeroplane were Lucien Dumais and Raymond Labrosse. Their drop mission was code-named MAGDALEN II. Two previous attempts to land them in France had failed due to fog and muddy conditions at the landing site. This time, it was a case of third time lucky.

Setting up the SHELBURNE Line would be a two-part process. One was to organise the Paris end; the other was to travel to the Breton town of Plouha to meet the local Resistance leader, François Le Cornec – who had been approached previously by Val Williams – and study a nearby beach as a potential pick-up location.

Paris came first. Dumais and Labrosse planned to meet with Paul Campinchi, the lawyer, like Le Cornec, who had been contacted by Val Williams during the failed OAKTREE operation. Fearing that Campinchi might have been compromised by Williams's arrest, MI9 had told Dumais not to contact him immediately. However, Labrosse, who had worked closely with Campinchi during his previous stint in France, trusted him implicitly and convinced Dumais that they should contact him as soon as possible.

Although happy to reconnect with Labrosse, Campinchi was wary of Dumais. The lawyer had been forced into hiding for six months with his family after Williams was caught and needed convincing to help again. The men initially met in a café where Dumais described his plans for the Paris end of the proposed SHELBURNE operation. After an evening of heated discussions, Dumais had convinced Campinchi of his motives and integrity. Dumais asked Campinchi if he would lead the Paris component of the evacuation line: Campinchi, remembering the Williams experience, wanted time to think it over before he gave his answer. He told Dumais about Williams's total lack of security, saying that the OAKTREE chief had talked about his mission to anyone who wanted to listen. In Campinchi's opinion, it had been just a matter of time before Williams got caught, forcing many other agents to go into hiding. Despite his concerns, a few days later Campinchi agreed to assume responsibility for the Paris end of the SHELBURNE line. His tasks would consist of locating safe houses in which to lodge the evaders and training his operators to interrogate them.

With the Paris end of SHELBURNE arranged, Dumais and Labrosse travelled the 250 miles to Plouha to meet François Le Cornec. Two miles from the coast, Plouha was home to approximately 4,000 people. Le Cornec owned a café and butcher shop in the town and served as head of the local Resistance organisation. Mobilised in 1939 at age 34,

François le Cornec's café and shop in Plouha

he had been captured by the Germans soon after the occupation in 1940 and sent to a POW camp in Germany. As a prisoner, he managed to falsify his military papers to show that he had served in the Great War in 1918. Convincing his captors that he was too old to be held as a POW, he was sent back to Brittany to work as a farmer. France provided much of Germany's food needs during the war, and Le Cornec claimed he would help produce French wheat and vegetables for German consumption.

Le Cornec's own preference, upon returning home to Plouha, was to escape and join the Free French forces in London. However, his attempts to escape to England by boat were unsuccessful, so his desire to fight was transmuted into the organisation of a Resistance group consisting of friends he knew he could trust. Most importantly, the group included two local Plouha gendarmes.

Dumais and Labrosse explained their needs for the Breton component of SHELBURNE, and Le Cornec agreed to put together a local group to support the evacuation operations. His responsibilities were numerous. He would have to find and train guides to help in the evacuations, find safe houses in Plouha and the surrounding area in which to lodge the airmen, locate a means of transportation for those housed beyond the vicinity of the town, and find someone who could obtain legitimate documents or could falsify and print them if necessary. Dumais explained that priority for evacuees would be

Left to right: Frank Slocum, Jean Tréliou, Ted Davis, François le Cornec 1946

as follows: pilots first, then navigators, other crew, and last, agents in danger, or others who were needed for additional training and/ or jobs in England. He assured Le Cornec that MI9 would provide money to help the host families pay for food – much of which could be obtained only at high prices on the black market – and that the weapons, ammunition, explosives and equipment for local Resistance operations would be brought in by the British boats with each pick-up operation.

Le Cornec took Dumais to study the adjacent coastline. Jagged and steep, the Plouha stretch follows a general east–west direction and includes some of Brittany's highest cliffs – some 60 metres (200 feet) or more. In spite of this, the Royal Navy had determined from maps and aerial photographs supplied by the RAF that a nearby cove, Anse-Cochat, might be a suitable location for discreet night-time pick-ups off the beach with the surf-boats that the 15th MGBF had. Getting escapees down there would have to be done under the nose of the enemy: the cliff above was patrolled by the Germans and guarded by a coastal gun and searchlight which could be seen in the aerial photograph. But there appeared to be a steep path down to the beach and a cave where the men could be hidden while they waited to be embarked. It should be possible to signal from the beach to the incoming ship without being seen by the Germans on the cliff above.

Two of Le Cornec's friends in Plouha – Pierre Huet, a former

Pierre Huet

'Job' Mainguy

French military pilot, and Joseph ('Job') Mainguy, a merchant navy captain – were both familiar with Anse Cochat and convinced Dumais of its suitability for the evacuation operations. The shingled beach at the bottom – which would be given the code name 'BONAPARTE' – blended into a wide expanse of sand at low tide, acceptable for surf-boats. There were also several caves in which men could be hidden while waiting for the boats. This was crucial with the cliffs above patrolled by the Germans: they had constructed a strongpoint on Pointe de la Tour, a rocky promontory that jutted out into the sea a mile north west of Anse-Cochat. The pillboxes were manned by White Russian conscripts – anti-Stalinists known as Vassov Russians, who sympathised more with Nazi ideals than with Soviet Communism – and their strongpoint housed quick-firing cannons, machine guns and searchlights. They lived on site and had plenty of ammunition. A second and smaller German outpost lay about a mile south east of Anse-Cochat, but out of sight of BONAPARTE beach.

Halfway between Anse-Cochat and Plouha was a small stone cottage that could be used as a collection point for the airmen hidden in the town and surrounding area prior to each 'BONAPARTE' evacuation operation. Code-named 'La Maison d'Alphonse' the cottage was uninhabited, but belonged to fisherman Jean Gicquel, another of Le Cornec's trusted friends. Gicquel and his pregnant young wife Marie (Mimi) agreed to move into the cottage and provide a cover for the SHELBURNE group's activities. Both the relative seclusion of the Maison d'Alphonse and its proximity to the beach proved to be vital to the success of the SHELBURNE operation. The path to the beach led through a six-foot-high 'tunnel' of foliage that opened up a half-mile later on to farmers' fields. It then crossed a cliff-top path to the edge of an almost vertical scree-slope. At the foot of this drop, just above the high tide line, was an indentation and a cave where the evacuees would be able to hide just out of sight of the pillboxes of Pointe de la Tour.

Visiting the site with Le Cornec, Dumais voiced concern about the descent. In rain or snow, the condition of the path was potentially dangerous. Le Cornec replied that before each evacuation, local guides would instruct the airmen on how to make their descent. 'If the guides can do it,' he countered, 'I'm sure the rest of us can.' Le Cornec explained that at low tide, a long gully running up from the beach could serve as an alternate route for the returning guides whenever equipment sent from London was too heavy to carry up the scree-slope. At high tide, the entrance to the gully was impassable from the beach, but Le Cornec assured Dumais that, as with the scree-slope, they would manage somehow.

For Dumais and Labrosse, Le Cornec's confidence meant that the plans for the entire SHELBURNE Line were now in place. Leaving Le Cornec in charge in Plouha, Dumais and Labrosse returned to Paris in late November 1943, where they sent a signal to London and awaited orders from MI9 to carry out the first evacuation operation.

MI9 had told Dumais to prepare for the first evacuation in December. Large numbers of airmen were known to be hiding in both Paris and Brittany, posing an ongoing danger to the people who housed them. MI9 were also aware of the possibility of an Allied invasion the following year. This meant it was essential to evacuate as many men as possible in the months ahead, though they did not inform Dumais of this for security reasons.

Before Dumais and Labrosse left London, it had been agreed that when MI9 was ready to schedule an evacuation, a message would be sent via the BBC in December 1943. For the Anse Côte operations, the message 'Bonjour tout le monde à la Maison d'Alphonse' ('Good evening to everyone at the house of Alphonse') meant an evacuation operation was to take place that night. 'Yvonne pense toujours à l'heureuse occasion' ('Yvonne always thinks of the happy occasion') meant the evacuation was postponed for twenty-four hours. 'Rigoulet has a good head', meanwhile, meant the operation, if scheduled, was cancelled.

December arrived, and so did bad winter weather. Every night the message was read out over the BBC: 'Yvonne pense toujours à l'heureuse occasion'. In London, Paris and Plouha, everyone involved with the SHELBURNE Line was getting frustrated with the appalling weather and the increasing numbers of evaders. After nine days of gales the operation was cancelled. It wasn't until January 1944 that the first operation could take place.

*

The structure of the SHELBURNE network and the way the operations were enacted is described as follows:

The Paris part of the network was commanded by Paul Campinchi, code name FRANÇOIS (Campinchi was deservedly awarded an OBE in 1945). He and his wife Thérèse lived at 19 rue des Ursins on the Île de la Cité in the 4th Arrondissement. They worked at the Prefecture of Police where Paul was responsible for issuing identity cards and Thérèse was a nurse in the STD clinic. François ran his réseau completely independently from Dumais for security reasons. The réseau's main work was gathering airmen, hiding them and moving them to Brittany in time for the pick-up.

Genevieve de Poulpiquet (Mme la Comtesse Genevieve de Poulpiquet de Brescanvel – aka GILBERTE) and her husband, Le Comte Césaire, had sheltered six evaders in their home at the Château de Trefy near Quéménéven near Finistere, before Césaire's arrest on 29 March 1943 – he was deported to Germany where he died. Genevieve, who was fortunate to avoid the same fate, contacted Campinchi and moved to Paris where she stayed with the Campinchis at rue des Ursins.

One day in September 1943, when Mme de Poulpiquet returned to rue des Ursins for lunch, she found the concierge in a panic because there were Gestapo in the flat. She left immediately to warn the Campinchis who were celebrating a friend's wedding. They arranged a rendezvous that evening at the brasserie la Closerie des Lilas on boulevard du Montparnasse, where Mme de Poulpiquet told Paul Campinchi she had been offered the services of 'une femme du monde'. Not quite getting the joke, Campinchi was finally persuaded to go with her to meet Olga L'Hoir-Sivry, widow of an artist. She sheltered Genevieve and the Campinchis in her apartment at 6 rue Nicolet, 'un hôtel particulier' until the liberation of the city.

Dr Yves Jean Marie Porc'her of 1 rue Cabanis, in the 14th Arrondissement, took on the task of printing false papers for the evaders. A pre-war friend of Paul Campinchi, he was a pathologist, and head of section in a large psychiatric clinic in Paris. He was arrested on 7 February 1944 following the capture and torture of Marie-Rose Zerling. Porc'her was one of the very few réseau FRANÇOIS helpers who knew where Campinchi was living but his training and experience enabled him to convincingly feign madness during his own interrogation and he was transferred to Fresnes. Porc'her was handed over to the French Red Cross just before the liberation of Paris (he was later recommended for a KMC). Following Dr Porc'her's arrest, his group of 'logeurs' were taken on by Mme Suzanne Guelat (ALINE) of 68 Boulevard Auguste Blanqui, 18th Arrondissement.

Dr Jean Albert Peiffert was responsible for photographing many of the evaders and providing them with identity cards. He was a small, quiet man of deceptively weak appearance who also happened to be an excellent racing driver. A friend of Paul Campinchi since his student days, in addition to offering medical support to the network, Dr Peiffert put his physics laboratory, securely located behind iron gates in the basement of the Faculty of Medicine, at the réseau's disposal.

Dr André Le Balc'h lived at 1 Quai aux Fleurs, about 200 metres from the Campinchi home. He was a useful point of contact first in Paris and then in Brittany. A doctor at Saint-Denis hospital, Le Balc'h had been introduced to Paul Campinchi by his colleague Dr Peiffert. In early 1943, Dr Le Balc'h let Ray Labrosse use the balcony of his sixth-floor apartment to try and contact London. With the demise of OAKTREE, Campinchi suggested that Dr Le Balc'h return to his native Plouzec (just north of Plouha) and take over from a former OAKTREE contact, Dr Meynard, who had had to leave his surgery in Paimpol following a tip-off that he was going to be arrested. When Lucien Dumais told Campinchi he was looking for a base in northern Brittany, Campinchi suggested he contact Dr Le Balc'h, and gave him a letter of introduction. It was then Le Balc'h who recommended Henri Le Blais at Saint-Brieuc as local chief, and François Le Cornec at Plouha as 'beach-master' to Dumais.

Marie-Rose Zerling (CLAUDETTE) first became involved with helping evaders in May 1942. She lived at 12 rue Saint-Ferdinand, 17th Arrondissement at weekends, and taught biology at Valenciennes during the week – where she also worked for the local organisation. When her chief was arrested, CLAUDETTE took three months sick-leave from the school and moved back to Paris. In May 1943, a friend in the Resistance, Jean Texcier, introduced her to Doctor Porc'her, who in turn introduced her to Campinchi. Having spent a year at Wellesley College in Boston, she became Campinchi's 'collaboratrice principale' and 'responsible du logement' for réseau FRANÇOIS in Paris.

(Zerling was later recommended for an MBE.)

Zerling recruited Henri Bois, a schoolteacher, into the group in June 1943. He joined réseau FRANÇOIS as 'chef d'équipe HENRI', taking parties of evaders himself and recruiting numerous other 'convoyeurs' until the Liberation. The evaders' files never gave any names of those who helped them. The phrase 'people from an organisation which arranged the rest of my journey' is used to describe their guides to Brittany.

Paul Campinchi organised réseau FRANÇOIS into specialist 'équipes' (groups). Henri Bois (HENRI) organised the guides, Marie-Rose Zerling (CLAUDETTE) organised the safe houses, and there were others responsible for security, making false papers (Dr Peiffert) and providing food and clothing for the evaders. Not mentioned, or known by any of the SHELBURNE evaders, were Mme Olga L'Hoir-Sivry, the 'femme du monde' who provided Campinchi with his headquarters at her home at 6 rue Nicolet, nor any of the various addresses that Ray Labrosse used to send his radio messages to London, including 1 rue

Dante where Marguerite Larue, who had worked with Campinchi at the Préfecture de Police, regularly allowed Labrosse to use her fifth-floor apartment.

The story of réseau FRANÇOIS in Paris, as even this short description shows, is far from simple. Many of the people who worked with FRANÇOIS were also associated with other organisations. Evaders were collected from several different organisations and areas: the only thing they have in common is their being in Paris prior to being taken to Brittany for evacuation by sea. It should be remembered that Campinchi's escape line work didn't end with the BONAPARTE operations – many evaders handled later by FRANÇOIS in Paris were also taken across the Pyrenees to Spain.

Once an operation was given the green light, the meeting-point for the evaders was the Café de Biarritz on the Boulevard Saint-Michel, run by Georges Labarthe, a veteran of two wars from south-west France, and his wife. The Biarritz was frequented by young men from the nearby École Polytechnique, Saint-Cyr, École Navale and the École de l'Air. This meant that Allied military men passing through were less likely to be recognised. Marie-Rose Zerling organised accommodation for escaping airmen, who were taken in small groups by courier, boarding the night train to Brittany from the Gare Montparnasse. Arriving at the last moment in order to avoid undue attention, they often encountered hostility from passengers in crowded trains obliged to vacate seats booked for the airmen – a hostility increased due to airmen not responding, being unable to give themselves away by talking.

At first, the groups were limited to two or four men, accompanied by a guide. The crucial part was getting off the train at St Brieuc, a mile or so from the coast, where Germans were aided by French gendarmes checking special permits to the restricted coastal zone in addition to identity papers. The first two groups were arrested by the police who handed them over to the Germans because they had no residence permits and restricted zone passes. Subsequent parties had better papers. Convoyeurs on the train handed their 'parcels' over to the local réseau.

Upon arrival at the station of St Brieuc the key contact on the north coast of Brittany was Georges Jouanjan. Together with the station staff and local gendarmes, he arranged the meeting and transfer of the airmen, supported by the villagers of Plouha. Those involved gathered at the café and tobacconist shop of François Le Cornec and together they organised the ferrying of airmen from the station to safe houses.

The evaders arrived at St Brieuc at about four o'clock in the afternoon, when the inspections started to relax. Apart from the first two airmen, none of the evaders was ever questioned. They were handed over to the St. Brieuc group until the transfer for Plouha. The evaders were looked after by either Mme Boschat at her café-tabac, or others who lived nearby. At St Brieuc they were dropped off at safe houses in small groups at Ketugal, Plouha-Ville, Plouha-Embranchement and Lanloup. At each stop, a member of the Plouha group, Marie-Thérèse Le Calvez, or Jean Tréhiou, waited to take the men to their new hosts scattered among the community including Françoise Montjarret at Ville-Dé, Marie Tréhiou at Lizandré, the Couffons at Kérizag, Georges and Anne Ropers at Cambla'h and Jean and Marie Gicquel at Saint-Samson.

When the message of 'Bonjour tout le monde à la Maison d'Alphonse' was finally repeated on the BBC, signalling the start of the first BONAPARTE operation, Calvez, François Le Cornec, Louis Mainguy, Henri Le Blais, Adolphe Le Troquer, Jean Tréhiou and Lucien Dumais set off to bring the evaders to Jean and Marie Gicquel's house (la Maison d'Alphonse) before taking the whole party down to Plage BONAPARTE.

Pierre Huet and Job Mainguy were the first two down the cliff as it was their responsibility to act as guides. Job Mainguy stayed half-way down the cliff with a torch that he used to send the letter recognition signal – the recognition signal was the Morse letter 'B' flashed three times every few minutes. Marie-Thérèse Le Calvet stood at the bottom with a blue light to guide the surf-boats from the MGBs.

Before the second BONAPARTE operation took place, the German authorities took all the passenger trains to Paimpol off the line to make way for the Todt Organisation traffic (involved in building coastal fortifications). This forced a change in plan. They had to

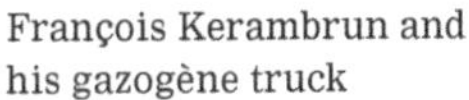

François Kerambrun and his gazogène truck

Kerambrun's garage in Guingamp

continue on the Paris train past St Brieuc to Guingamp. It also meant finding a new group to meet the men and take them to Plouha.

Yves Hugues of Loudéac commanded the Notre Dame Resistance group in Guingamp. He put them in touch with a group of people who could move the airmen. Mathurin Branchoux, a potato wholesaler, was the local leader of the group. He met Dumais and advised him to see François Kerambrun about transport. Kerambrun agreed to move them in his employer's gazogène Citroën as did George Le Cun. They were taken to Pomment-le-Vicomte (north east of Guingamp) where they were first interrogated by Jacques du Pac de Marsoulies to ensure they were genuine, before they entered the final part of the network.

In Guingamp, the usual first stop for evaders was M. and Mme Laurent at rue de l'Étang.

Others went to the flour mill of M. Lanoë on rue Châteaubriand. Once the evaders got to Plouha the local team, under the leadership of François Le Cornec who owned the local café and butchers, took control. The key members of the group in Plouha were:

Francis Baudet: brother-in-law of Guiguite Le Saux.
Jean and Mimi (Marie) Gicquel: who owned the Maison d'Alphonse, where the airmen were housed just prior to each evacuation.
Pierre ('Tarzan') Huet: a guide and former military pilot.
Marie-Thérèse ('Yvonne') Le Calvez: a 19-year-old guide.

Marguerite (Guiguite) Le Saux Pierre: 17 years old; Baudet's young sister-in-law and good friend of Marie-Thérèse Le Calvez; could not participate in SHELBURNE until her 18th birthday.
Joseph ('Job') Mainguy: former merchant marine officer until the outbreak of the war.
Jean Tréhiou: French naval officer.

In addition, the réseau was supported by people allowing their houses to be used as safe houses:

Léonie Le Calvez: widowed mother of Marie-Thérèse and five sons (four of whom were killed during the war).
Madame Le Saux: mother of Guiguite; housed Labrosse and Dumais from time to time.
Anne Ropers: she and her family housed Lt Guy Hamilton and others (see Chapter 11). Marie Tréhiou: sister of Jean Tréhiou.[41]

Most escape line couriers only travelled with one or two evaders. On SHELBURNE, however, up to twenty evaders at times were placed in the back of Le Cun's truck with shovels and picks; they were required to remember a sentence in Polish and told that their cover story was that they were workmen working on coastal defences for the Germans. Le Cun was philosophical about the risk: 'They will shoot me with one evader, and they will shoot me with twenty evaders. What is the difference?'

The general routine was for evaders to be taken from their safe-houses to the coastal cliffs where they would lie low while their courier checked the route and the beach for mines. If mines were located the courier would place a white handkerchief carefully on top of them. On the approach of the surf-boat(s) the courier signalled the evaders to descend along the cliff path, avoiding the 'white handkerchiefs' on the way. Once the evaders were safely boarded the courier returned back up the cliffs, collecting in the handkerchiefs.

The SHELBURNE Line was well organised, well prepared and had a good plan. It was time to begin operations.

41 The detailed structure, location and functioning of the network is covered extremely comprehensively in *L'Incroyable histoire du Réseau Shelburn* by Claude Bénech.

CHAPTER 11 – BONJOUR TOUT LE MONDE À LA MAISON D'ALPHONSE

'Now good or bad, 'tis but the chance of war'

William Shakespeare, *Troilus and Cressida*

The sound left a sinking feeling in the stomach. The men in the surf-boat – Guy Hamilton, Leading Seaman Albert 'Lofty' Dellow and Able Seaman 'Rocky' Rockwood, an eighteen-year-old Newfoundlander – could all hear the familiar thrum of the engines of MGB 718. What led to the sinking in the stomach wasn't the noise of the MGB's engines themselves. It was the fact that the MGB's engines were getting quieter.

It was just before dawn on 16 June 1944. A few minutes before, the surf-boat had successfully landed Jean Tréhiou at the BONAPARTE pinpoint, together with a large amount of kit. 718 had been late arriving and there was no reception committee to meet, hence Hamilton and his men transferring Tréhiou to the Anse-Cochat gully by surf-boat. The landing had been smooth: the goodbyes and good lucks heartily meant.

But success had turned to disaster in a matter of seconds. 718 had lost contact with the surf-boat and sight of it against land. At the same time the anchor was dragging. Ronnie Seddon decided to go in closer to the pinpoint. Still no sign. He had tried using an Aldis lamp to flash intermittent light signals. Nothing. No one was quite sure how it happened, but somehow the MGB and surf-boat had completely missed each other. At 0350, just as dawn was breaking, a decision needed to be made. It wasn't an easy one, but Seddon knew it was the right one – to return to Dartmouth, leaving his First Lieutenant and two sailors to their fate.

Back on the surf-boat, Hamilton was desperate. Chasing an MGB in a rowing boat wasn't a fair fight. Dellow and Rockwood gave their all: Hamilton was flashing his Aldis lamp for all he was worth, in the hope that someone on board might spot them. But in the darkness, neither boat could see the other: and while the surf-boat could hear the MGB, the splash of their oars was nothing against the noise of the engine and the sound of the sea. Hamilton continued to flash in the direction of the engines. Dellow and Rockwood rowed on, but they all knew their efforts were for nothing. They sat there, the surf-boat rippling on the waves, as the sounds of the MGB began to fade away.

'They had missed us,' Hamilton later recalled. 'Dellow knew it – Rocky knew it – I knew it: we'd had it. I made the painfully obvious remark that I had failed to rejoin the parent ship, apologised, and quickly changed the subject with a loud "Give way together". The boat did not glide. My two anything-but-jolly Jacks were physically whacked, with every right after two hours' solid rowing. I goaded them on verbally and took spells at relieving them as we struggled against the tide and freshening wind.'

The surf-boat headed for the nearest rocks, which were reached, as Hamilton noted, 'after a grim display of tired rowing and frayed tempers'. Hamilton threw the walkie-talkie overboard with much satisfaction. His next action, jumping overboard, produced somewhat less satisfaction: 'On reaching the surface I tried to swear but the water was so cold I could only gasp.' While Dellow unloaded and hid their gear and Rockwood filled the boat with rocks, Hamilton dug holes in the bottom with a jack-knife. To round off a miserable night, he broke a finger in the process. Pushing the boat in front of him, Hamilton swam out into deeper water. He stayed, treading water as he watched the boat slowly sink. Then he started to swim back to the others, trying to figure out what they were going to do next.

*

Although the SHELBURNE team maintained they had been ready in December, the first operation didn't take place until the night of 28/29 January 1944. Code-named BONAPARTE I, it was carried out by 503. The pinpoint was fairly straightforward to find, particularly in comparison to the previous year's operations. The gunboat had to leave Start Point, head south east until landfall was made at a group of rocks called Le Grand-Léjon, which had a tower on top, in the middle of the Baie de Saint-Brieuc. Then the course was changed 90 degrees towards the Pointe de Plouha. The surf-boats were now lowered by hand, and the gunboat steamed slowly forward towing the surf-boats, until they sighted the Le Taureau rock, with another tower on it. As soon as they saw the light signal from the beach – blue letter 'B' – anchor was dropped. The anchor point was about 1,600 metres from the German radar and artillery position on Pointe de Guilben. The surf-boats were manned by two oarsmen and a Coxswain armed with a sub-machine gun who would be in the bow of the leading boat.

Those on the beach felt as though they had been waiting for ever. But eventually, the surf-boats were spotted. Dumais, Le Cornec and Huet waded out with pistols at the ready. Dumais gave the challenge 'DINAN'. Patrick Wyndham-Wright, the MI9 conducting Officer, replied 'SAINT-BRIEUC'. Dumais and Wyndham-Wright had a brief discussion while stores were unloaded. Then those waiting embarked – three RAF, fourteen US Air Force, Val Williams, the former OAKTREE organiser, Ivan the Russian and two Frenchmen. The process was like clockwork: the whole operation on the beach had taken just twelve minutes.

One of those taken out on BONAPARTE I was Flying Officer Vaughan Moffet, a fighter pilot. The following is an extract from his debrief notes:

'BRANCHAUX got in touch with a man in BREST (no name) who was to come for me between 14 and 16 Jan. On 14 Jan I was taken to GUINCAMP to meet this man, but he did not turn up. I remained at GUINCAMP however, staying till 24 Jan with Mme LE CUN, Place du Centre, whose son is a member of BRANCHAUX's organisation.

'On 23 Jan a British Intelligence Officer, Captain HAMILTON, having heard of me by chance, came to GUINCAMP to look for me. I was away for the day, and BRANCHAUX could not get in touch with me in time for me to go on an operation which Captain HAMILTON had planned for that night from PLOUHA (S1323). This operation, however, was delayed by storm.

'On 22 Jan news had been received from the man in BREST that he was coming for me on 23 Jan, having been in PARIS on business. After Captain HAMILTON's arrival on 23 Jan, BRANCHAUX thought it advisable to take advantage of his offer.

'On 24 Jan Captain HAMILTON telephoned BRANCHAUX and asked him to "bring the sack of potatoes". That day M. LE CUN took me by car to PLOUHA. M. LE CUN is very reliable. He owns a wireless dealer's business in the centre of GUINCAMP. He gave me half a French ten-franc note and asked that anyone wishing to get in touch with him should produce this as a means of identification. (Note: this note has been passed to Major LANGLEY, I.S.9 [X].)

'In PLOUHA I met Captain HAMILTON who cross-examined me on my general knowledge of ENGLAND and RAF matters. I learnt from him that the man from BREST was working on similar lines and was told later that the BREST operation did not come off because the Germans had fortified an island, possibly the one from which the party was leaving.

'The PLOUHA operation was delayed till the night of 28–29 Jan. Meanwhile I stayed with nine other British and American Airmen at a house at PLOUHA rented by the organisation from a doctor, who visited us occasionally. The other British members of the party were Sgt CUFLEY (S/P.G.(-)1728) and Sgt HARVEY (S/P.G.(-)1729).

'Captain HAMILTON who was in charge of the operation, received a message by wireless on the night of 28 Jan that the operation was on. We left the house in small parties about 2200 hrs and were taken to the coast to a point near Sheet 7, S1525. We waited on the beach from about midnight till 0230 hrs (29 Jan) when four small rowing boats appeared and took us out to an MGB. Captain HAMILTON entrusted me with secret papers which I handed to Captain WYNDHAM-WRIGHT on arrival in the UK.

'The MGB arrived at DARTMOUTH about 0900 hrs on 29 Jan. The "passengers" on board consisted of Sgt CUFLEY, Sgt HARVEY, myself, thirteen Americans, one Russian, one Frenchman, and a British Intelligence Officer.'

Back in London at MI9, Airey Neave, who had taken over from Jimmy Langley, had had a long night. He kept phoning the duty officer at

Dartmouth for news. It wasn't until 0900 on the 29th that he heard that Operation BONAPARTE I was a complete success. The MGB had not been picked up on radar, there was no difficulty in seeing the recognition signals and the beach transfer had gone well – although Dumais thought it had been too slow.

On Bonaparte beach, meanwhile, the reception committee had struggled back up the cliff with the cases of equipment. At the Maison d'Alphonse, Dumais opened the cases. They contained brand-new .45 Colt pistols for the Plouha group; a new radio for Labrosse; cigarettes, gin and whisky as presents or bribes; and a suitcase containing four million francs to fund the SHELBURNE operation. They waited until dawn when the curfew was lifted then returned home.

Dumais and Labrosse headed back to Paris, with Dumais having a close call when he arrived back in the French capital with the suitcase full of money. At the Lamarck-Caulaincourt Metro station he walked into a police check looking for black marketeers. Dumais knew he would have a difficult time explaining the money away. Outrunning the police with the suitcase was not an option. He took a risk, chose the youngest-looking policeman and told him the money was for the Resistance. The policeman had better let him through, Dumais warned, or it might not go well for the young man. The young policeman looked terrified. Dumais was let through.

Dumais's concerns about security bordered on the obsessional. He was right to be so careful, with the Gestapo desperate to penetrate the Campinchi network in Paris. It was a continual game of cat and mouse. Fortunately, Gestapo penetrating agents were often clumsy or not well briefed, and they were easily uncovered. They either fled if they were lucky or were disposed of in the Paris sewers, if not.

In St Brieuc there was an incident when one of the local team, Le Blais, got drunk and started boasting that he was a member of the British Intelligence Service. Dumais was furious and took the next train to St Brieuc. Luckily for Le Blais, Dumais calmed down en route and instead of confronting Le Blais and executing him, he first spoke to Le Cornec. They decided to tell Le Blais that London had decided that the operations were too dangerous and had called them off. He was also given a generous severance payment and told to keep his mouth shut. The meeting did produce one positive outcome: Dumais liked the look of a girl Le Blais had brought to the meeting. He followed her and asked her to work for SHELBURNE, in Paris. Her name was Lisetta Lorre and she agreed to become his key liaison officer (Lorre survived the war and joined the French Army. She was killed in Indo-China in 1951.)

*

BONAPARTE II took place on 26/27 February, again carried out by 503. David Birkin was once again the Navigating Officer. Two agents from SIS/BCRA were put ashore: Michel Bourgeois (MAXIME) and Gerard Bernard (JULIAN). Bourgeois was arrested in July and sent to Neuengamme but survived. The operation itself ran completely smoothly with the exception of one airman who caused problems and had to be evacuated with his hands tied.

In total, seventeen airmen were taken out including a fighter pilot shot down over Boulogne only five days before. There were reports from the airman of increasing controls inland. Owing to the curfew, François Kerambrun had been forced to collect the airmen in daylight. It was his plan, if questioned, to say that the twenty airmen were workmen needed for a 'rush job'.

Disaster almost struck. About thirty kilometres from the beach, on the road from Guingamp to Plouha, the Germans had begun the construction of a tank trap at a village called Gommenec. The trap was similar to a cattle grid, with steel spikes. The one godsend was that work had not yet been completed, and only wooden struts protruded above the surface of the road. Kerambrun's lorry was half over the obstacle before he found one sticking through the steering.

It was a desperate position. The time for the curfew was drawing near and the twenty-one airmen rushed to lift the lorry bodily off the spike. By great efforts, they had just succeeded when two French gendarmes appeared and started questioning what was going on. Kerambrun, a bold, shrewd Breton, made a quick decision. He told the gendarme everything. As he later said, 'if they were not patriots, we would have killed them with our bare hands.' Thankfully, the gendarmes were sympathetic to the Allies and the lorry continued on its journey to the Maison d'Alphonse. But it had been a terrifying moment.

As the operations continued, Dumais faced some internal difficulties. First, there was a temporary cooling of relations with Le Cornec over the disappearance of some money from the BONAPARTE II drop somewhere between Plouha and Paris, and the retention of a sub-machine gun against instructions. Then, with the next in the series of operations scheduled for 18/19 March, Dumais and Labrosse arrived in Guingamp to discover a lot of radio direction-finding vans operating. They did not worry unduly as Labrosse had never transmitted from there. However, when they met Le Cornec, he told them there was a general alert on the coast. Dumais was worried enough to think about cancelling the operation. But he was unable to signal before the gunboat, 502, left Dartmouth. BONAPARTE III would have to go ahead as planned.

When 502 got close to shore Dumais used a walkie-talkie to warn them about increased enemy activity and to be very careful. Suddenly there was an echoing explosion, followed by a second. Convinced they were under fire, they decided they should withdraw and try again later. After a long wait, and with no further explosions, 502 came back, four surf-boats landing under the command of Lloyd Bott and Andrew Smith. Equipment was put ashore and twenty-four airmen collected. The atmosphere was incredibly tense. It was low tide, and with no cover at all the passengers had to cross three hundred metres of shingle and sand to get to the waterline. Had they been seen, they would have been at the mercy of the German machine guns and searchlights on the Pointe de la Tour. 502, too, was also in range of the 76mm gun. At the peak of the operation there were forty or so people on the beach. That everyone emerged unscathed felt like a minor miracle. Slocum later wrote that he thought this was probably the riskiest twenty minutes in the whole cycle of operations to Brittany.

Dumais had been severely rattled by this operation. He wanted to call off BONAPARTE IV but the message failed to get through. BONAPARTE IV took place on 19 March and sixteen airmen, one soldier and two agents were taken off. Dumais was not there, having gone to check on things in Paris, but the operation went off without a hitch. This time, it was high tide. The surf-boats were able to come right to the pebble beach at the bottom of the cliff, without the nerve-wracking risk of detection from Pointe de la Tour.

Three days later, on 22/23 March, BONAPARTE V took place. 503 picked up twenty-six airmen, five RAF, twenty-one US Air Force, two agents and Jean Tréhiou from the SHELBURNE team in Plouha who wanted to join the Free French.

This was to be the last of the Plouha operations on this run. Between January and March 1944, one hundred and eleven people were embarked, seventy-four of them in the space of seven days. This was quite an achievement on behalf of the gunboats from Dartmouth, but even more so on the SHELBURNE network, somehow conducting these operations on a heavily defended coast and under the noses of the Gestapo with the attendant penalties of torture and death if they were caught.

Wyndham-Wright told Le Cornec on the beach during BONAPARTE V that operations would be temporarily suspended because the nights were getting shorter. In fact, the truth was that DDOD(I) and MI9 were under instructions not to stir up the Germans on the French coast because of the impending D-Day landings. For security reasons this was not explained to Dumais and Le Cornec.

On 6 June, D-Day, Dumais and Labrosse were in Paris. On the 7th MI9 ordered them back to Brittany. Under prevailing restrictions on travel, they went by bicycle. The journey took them three weeks. When they eventually arrived, Dumais ran into Job Mainguy who told him that the Plouha group was intact and had survived the three-month period since BONAPARTE V. They agreed operations could resume.

On 16 June DDOD(I) sent 718 to land Jean Tréhiou, who had gone out on BONAPARTE V, and two other agents, to conduct MI9 operations in western Brittany. Tréhiou knew the BONAPARTE pinpoint from his days with SHELBURNE. 718 had just returned to Dartmouth from a detachment to the Shetland Islands where she carried out two very successful operations for DDOD(I). She returned to Dartmouth on 6 June.

This operation, REFLEXION, was Ronnie Seddon and Guy Hamilton's first solo run to Brittany. But as we saw earlier, only one of them made it back to Dartmouth.

*

'Taking revolver, sten gun and binoculars with us, we reached the cliff top after a hard climb and wormed our way through the gorse and bracken 'til we were completely hidden from the morning light. Dellow and Rocky tried to doze. I was too wet and cold to do anything but lie, shiver and think. Our morale was so low it would have passed under a snake's belly.'

Guy Hamilton, Dellow and Rockwood made for their escape packs. These provided breakfast of a Horlicks tablet and a 'cup' of Benzedrine: 'I felt better so had another "cup" and felt much better. We stayed in our prickly hide-out 'til noon, Dellow and Rockwood having elected to stay under my command – chiefly, I suspect, because of my fluent French. There were no signs of enemy activity so, after a lunch of two Horlicks tablets apiece, we set off in the vague direction of farm noises inland. Nearing a farm, I hid the other two and went scouting; over hedges, along ditches, avoiding various pieces of wire strewn about the place. As I climbed through a fence on to a path, the absence of German patrols near our hide-out was explained: "ACHTUNG MINEN" – we'd been hiding in a minefield. Those odd bits of wire ...'

The trio covered seven miles overnight, hiding in the undergrowth as dawn arrived. Hamilton was freezing cold: spotting an old farmer by himself in a field, he decided to risk making contact. But no sooner had Hamilton approached him than the farmer ran for the farmhouse. Hamilton was worried at first, but it turned out he needn't have been. Instead, the farmer reappeared with a bottle of cider and some pancakes – the first food the three of them had eaten for two days.

Although the farmer was helpful in providing sustenance, he was unable to tell Hamilton where to find the Resistance. As Hamilton, Dellow and Rockwood continued their journey across the countryside, the pattern of food and no information continued. Then the three got a lucky break, though it didn't appear that way at first: 'Our first gleam of hope came when a farmer prevented us from stumbling across a main road used by the Germans, in the nick of time. He offered to give us lodgings in his barn when it was dark; meanwhile he hid us in a pit covered with brambles, in the middle of a field. There was no exit from this pit and I disliked the hiding place immediately, particularly as the farmer had been indiscreet and we started getting visitors, who stood at the edge of the pit peering down at us, as if we were animals in a zoo, though we must have looked more like animals than men by this time. Altogether we got four offers of help, to take effect from midnight, but it was difficult to judge which would be genuine. Finally, Marie-Thérèse came for us at midnight. She made us disappear from the face of the earth, and in doing so she just beat a Gestapo agent to it who also had designs on us.'

To begin with, Hamilton had his suspicions about Marie-Thérèse, and she likewise about the three of them: 'How was she to know that we were not Germans posing as British survivors, a popular trick which had caused many deaths in this area. And how was I to know that she was genuine?' But Hamilton decided to follow her, even if his compatriots were less certain: 'With some reluctance, Dellow and Rockwood came too; with Mata Hari in mind they were convinced that their First Lieutenant was off "chasing skirt" again.'

Hamilton's instinct had been correct: 'This young French girl's skill in leading us past patrols left us amazed. It took a near-disaster to convince us finally that she was genuine. We were going along by the side of a hedge when suddenly we heard Germans approaching. Automatically, we threw ourselves into the nearest cover – my choice was a ditch, but when I'd finished falling down all fourteen feet of it, I realised it was of the anti-tank variety. In the best tradition of cartoons, I saw stars and added a broken nose to my list of breakages. The patrol passed – not a murmur from Marie-Thérèse – from then on, she was our goddess.'

The farmer who found Hamilton and his men was Eugène Harscouët. Joseph Mainguy, one of the key members of the Plouha

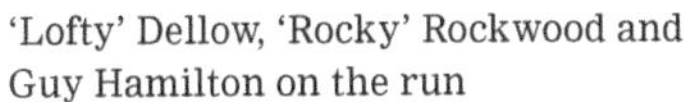

'Lofty' Dellow, 'Rocky' Rockwood and Guy Hamilton on the run

Picnic with the Ropers girls

group, heard about the three fugitives but thought it was a Gestapo 'come on' and was inclined to ignore it. It was down to the young nineteen-year-old, Marie-Thérèse Le Calvez, to volunteer to investigate. She came back with the news that they were genuine – the surf-boat crew who had landed Jean Tréhiou.

Marie-Thérèse took them to her mother's house on the 18th and did a sweep of the beach to get rid of any traces of the surf-boat. The next day, June François Le Cornec moved them to the farm of Marie Tréhiou at Lisandré, before transferring them to a house at Kervenec in Pléguien. On the night of 21/22 June, Job (son of Joseph) Mainguy moved them to the Camblach home of Georges and Marie Ropers, near to the Gicquels' Maison d'Alphonse. Marie-Thérèse had confirmed on 16 June that there was no sign of the surf-boat, and some days later Guy Hamilton went with her and Job Mainguy to show them the hiding place and recover the four oars, compass and sub-machine gun.

By now, the three sailors were wearing Breton clothes and in mortal danger of being shot as spies if caught. At Camblach the Ropers received an urgent tip-off that the Gestapo was searching for them locally. The three of them were forced to hide in a loft for ten days before being moved to a shed in the woods. After this scare died down, Hamilton, who spoke excellent French, was able to accompany Pierre Huet and Job Mainguy on expeditions, including on one occasion playing boule at the Café Le Meur alongside Germans who also frequented it. This appealed to Hamilton's sense of mischief but was

'Knackered'

Marie Thérèse Calvez with her mother Léonie

an extraordinary risk both for him but in particular for his French friends.

Hamilton later said that he owed his life to Marie-Thérèse: the relief was equal on the French side. Marie-Thérèse recalled that, 'I cycled to report to Dumais and Le Cornec. They were waiting for me with concern. Without taking the time to sit down I reassured them: I found the three English; they are in Mama's house. They are sailors from the Royal Navy. Then, for the first time since I had known Dumais, I saw appear on his face an intense emotion. In a changed voice, he explained to me: Marie-Thérèse, you've saved the SHELBURNE network. If these sailors had been picked up it was the end for all of us because, even assuming that their courage resisted interrogation, their mere presence here proved the existence of our network. At our next shipment, we would have had a German reception committee and that would be the end of us.'

*

Dumais and Labrosse had arrived back in Plouha after their lengthy and uncomfortable bicycle trip, shortly after Hamilton, Dellow and Rockwood were found. Dumais was working hard to get SHELBURNE back up to speed. He got Mainguy and Huet to find and mark the Teller mines that had been laid on the old path to the rock-fall above the beach. They located seventeen and, to make sure they could find them in the dark, they prepared to tie strips of white cloth to the stakes with which they had marked the mines' positions. By the end of June, Dumais had a new headquarters and a new safe house for Labrosse to transmit from. After a three-month interval, SHELBURNE was back in business.

The scope of Dumais's mission had been broadened to include paramilitary action: he arranged a parachute drop on 27 June to a new Maquis group at Bois-de-la-Salle, south of Pléguen, and this included two mine-detectors, which he kept for SHELBURNE operations, as well as some of the weapons. There was a second parachute drop to the same Maquis on the night of 5/6 July.

The Plouha group resumed contact with the group of Guingamp and on the night of 2/3 July Mainguy collected fifteen airmen who had been driven over from Guingamp in a van. With the three naval personnel already at Plouha, there were now eighteen for evacuation. But from 1 July and for the next ten days a strong north-easterly gale made landing impossible.

The wind wasn't the only point of concern. By now the German troops stationed near the coast were thoroughly on edge: they included members of the collaborationist Russian Liberation Army, who had defected under General Vlasov to fight with the Germans; among them, the Georgians were particularly aggressive and ill-disciplined. Like other units of this kind on the coast, they were a menace, with their extortions, thefts and attempted rapes. The area north of Plouha, where Gicquel's Maison d'Alphonse stood, suffered particularly from their habit of calling at houses and demanding drink at all hours of the day and night. The Resistance thought it prudent to evacuate some of the arms stored in the farms there since the BONAPARTE landings. In spite of this state of tension, Gicquel and Mainguy used the newly arrived mine-detectors to check the road down to Anse-Cochat. This they did in broad daylight and once completed, SHELBURNE had, at low tide, a second and far easier route to the beach.

While the gale was still raging on 5 July, the Gestapo told the Gendarmerie two days later that they knew an organisation was active in the area. The Gendarmerie passed on the warning to SHELBURNE and the fifteen candidates for evacuation were moved from the Gicquel and Ropers houses. By now they had been in the hands of the Plouha group for nearly a month.

Finally, on 11/12 July, the agreed message was broadcast by the BBC. When it was repeated on the evening programme, they knew that the gunboat must be on its way. CROZIER I was on. Hamilton, Dallow and Rockwood were going home.

After nightfall, Mainguy ventured into the minefield and tied strips of white cloth on to the sticks marking the mines. The evacuees were briefed by Dumais. He armed all the evaders, including Hamilton, and told them that if the Germans ambushed them, whatever happened, they must fight and kill as many Germans as possible. The evaders made their way very carefully to the beach. MGB 503 had been sent to carry out this operation and the landing and embarkation of the passengers went without a hitch. The sight of the MGB must have been a sweet one for Hamilton and his men. As they set off back for Dartmouth, the SHELBURNE beach party made their way back through the minefield, picking up the white cloth markers as they went.

The moonless period was now over, presaging a pause in operations. The land battle was drawing nearer, and paramilitary activity was now in full swing inland and further south. On 20 July, the Resistance group at Bois-de-la-Salle became a permanent group of 160 men under training to use the arms supplied via SHELBURNE.

No 4 SAS, a Free French unit under the indomitable one-armed Commandant Bourgoin, had parachuted an advance party into Brittany soon after midnight on D-Day-minus-one. They landed north east of Vannes on the Landes-de-Lanvaux, accompanied by the SOE French Section team under André Hué who had gone to England on EASEMENT II via 502. Their allocated task was to sever, as far as possible, all communications between Brittany and the rest of France. Within a few days a crowd of some 2,000 Maquisards had congregated round Bourgoin's Dingson base to collect small arms, uniforms, boots and food; and a similar situation had developed at Bourgoin's second concentration area, SAMWEST, near Guingamp. Inevitably, these over-large gatherings attracted German attention. SAMWEST was attacked on 12 June and scattered. Dingson's turn came on 18 June, but Bourgoin received air support and beat the Germans to a standstill, before ordering his force to disperse during the night, thereby avoiding a disaster such as was to befall the unwise defenders of the Vercors a month later.

A small team was dropped into the Morbihan on 21/22 June to find out what had happened to the Dingson base, and to bring Bourgoin orders to protect port installations at Morlaix, Saint-Malo and Vannes. This was because General Eisenhower's Supreme Headquarters Allied Expeditionary Force (SHAEF) at that time entertained the idea of a landing in Brittany, probably on the west coast at Port Navalo and the Vilaine estuary in the Morbihan, as a means of circumventing the tenacious German resistance to the enlargement of the Normandy beach-head. This mission, which revelled in the code name LOST, was led by Major Oswald Cary-Elwes. Lieutenant Fleuriot of the French 2e Régiment de Chasseurs Parachutistes was second in command.

By 17/18 July the prospects of a break-out from the Normandy beach-head were bright enough for SHAEF to lay aside all thought of a second landing in Brittany. The LOST team was ordered to return to the United Kingdom via SHELBURNE. As Cary-Elwes and Mills made their way north towards Plouha with the help of local Maquisards, they heard that Marty had been killed, together with Captain Marienne, Bourgoin's second in command. A further Maquis group at Coat-Mallouen, which had been linked with Bourgoin's SAMWEST base near Guingamp, gave them civilian identity cards and clothes: thus equipped, the party reached Plouha, where Dumais and Le Cornec escorted them to the Maison d'Alphonse. There were five in the group: Cary-Elwes and another SAS Major named Smith, Mills, Cary-Elwes's batman, Flight Sergeant Philip Farger, an RAF fighter pilot shot down near St Gildas, and Major William A. Jones, USAAF.

A few minutes after Dumais and Le Cornec had left them, everyone was seated at the table in the kitchen of the farmhouse when Mme Gicquel thought she heard a noise outside. Everyone fell silent and listened: there could be no doubt that someone was walking round the house. Gicquel, thinking that perhaps Dumais and Le Cornec had returned, opened the door and found himself face to face with two German soldiers. He shut the door in their faces and rushed to tell his Allied guests to hide in the loft as quickly as possible. It was at that moment that the first shots were fired somewhere outside. Gicquel was on his way back to the front door when he was confronted in the passage by two soldiers, who were in time to see his five guests disappearing through the trapdoor in the kitchen ceiling.

The soldiers – Vlasov Russians – called on them to surrender, firing up into the ceiling. For the second time in a matter of minutes, everything fell silent: the Russians stopped short of attempting to climb into the loft, which was just as well for them as Mills had a grenade ready to throw. Instead, they ordered Gicquel out into the yard where one of their patrol lay wounded: he had been hit in the backside by ill-directed fire from one of his compatriots positioned on a bank that overlooked the house and was in agony. They ordered Gicquel to go and fetch a horse and cart from a nearby farm. When he returned with it, they lifted their wounded comrade into it and left without posting a sentry.

The five Allied evaders in the Gicquel loft, caught in a trap, armed and in civilian clothes, had assumed the worst. When they heard the cart approaching, they imagined that reinforcements had arrived, but after cries and lamentations from the wounded man, they were surprised to hear the cart leave the yard and their host call out 'Bonne nuit'. Gicquel appeared shortly afterwards on the ladder leading to the loft and announced that all the Russians had thanked him for his help, taken the cart and left. He predicted that rather than blaming their bad shooting, they would attribute their comrade's injury to the terrorists seen disappearing into the roof. It wouldn't be long before they were back in strength. They must evacuate the house immediately.

Mme Gicquel, mother of a six-week-old baby, made off straight away with the child for her mother-in-law's house, which was no more than 400 metres away. Gicquel stayed behind. When his five guests came down from their attic, they saw with dismay that in their hasty retreat they had left a number of compromising articles, including a British Army cap, on the kitchen table. They snatched up their kit and were just about to leave when Major Jones remembered that he too had lost his cap. Cary-Elwes remarked that he now understood why a Frenchman never took his headgear off, which provoked a laugh. The cap was retrieved and Gicquel led them off to a cornfield, where they hid in a ditch, in the freezing cold, to wait until first light.

Gicquel's instinct about the house, meanwhile, proved prescient. As he had foreseen, the Germans and their Russian acolytes returned in strength to the Maison d'Alphonse. After a vain search for the fugitives, they ransacked it, blew it up and set the ruins on fire. The enemy failed to find a stock of arms hidden in the stable since the CROZIER operation earlier that month, and it blew up when the fire reached it. The Maison d'Alphonse, so important a link in six of the SHELBURNE operations, was reduced to rubble. It was never rebuilt.

When the following day began to break, Mills set off along the bank to see whether anyone was around. After going some three hundred metres, he saw two silhouettes. Unable to identify them, he crawled back to warn his fellow evaders. They were preparing to do battle when the two silhouettes revealed themselves: it was Dumais and Le Cornec, who had been told by Gicquel what had happened and had come to find them.

Dumais took charge. Arming each of them with a Colt automatic and some grenades he led them off across country at a cracking pace, walking in circles so as to confuse any tracker dogs the Germans might use. Though none of them had slept for forty-eight hours, they all felt fit and alert. After they had covered several kilometres Dumais found them a refuge where there was plenty of natural cover. A church clock could be heard striking eight when he left them, promising to return after nightfall. They had a long wait before them.

Dumais returned that evening as promised, announcing that the operation to evacuate Cary-Elwes and his companions would take place that night (Operation CROZIER II). By now, the countryside between the Pointe-de-la-Tour and the Pointe-de-Plouha was in a high state of alert and criss-crossed by trigger-happy enemy patrols. But Dumais was prepared in response. He got Le Cornec to provide half a platoon of Maquisards armed with sten sub-machine guns and a bren light machine-gun to escort and cover the column on its three-kilometre progress from Kerlerot, just north of Plouha, to the beach. He also arranged to have a horse and cart waiting, concealed, at Kerlerot to carry away any arms that might be landed.

When at last they set off, Huet and Mainguy acted as scouts and guides, keeping well away from roads where patrols might be encountered. As they crossed the fields, dogs in the farms started barking. On a normal night, that would have caused concern, but they were already so unsettled by the bursts of indiscriminate firing and the intensified patrol action that it made little difference. Equally, such was the sporadic noise that the barking failed to attract the attention of the enemy. The tide was low, so they made their way across country to the gully leading down to the Anse-Cochat, where Huet and Mainguy had noted and marked the mines.

Reaching a track much frequented by enemy patrols, the column halted. On their left, where the ruins of the Maison d'Alphonse lay smouldering, they could hear firing which seemed to be getting nearer. It was no place to hang about, so they crossed quickly into the coastal minefield. The Germans, reckoning that no one would be stupid enough to venture into such a danger zone, particularly on a dark night, did not bother to patrol it.

When the long single-file column finally reached the barbed wire that marked the landward side of the minefield and the entry to the narrow gully, a bren-gun crew were posted on a rise from which they could dominate the track. With this three-man rearguard to protect them, the column made its way down to Anse-Cochat, past the marked mine positions and on to the beach.

It was nearly low tide. A wide expanse of sand lay uncovered as they turned left and made their way along the shingle at the foot of the cliff to the usual position at the rock-fall. Mainguy climbed partway up it and the business of signalling began. After all the noise of getting there, it was suddenly strangely quiet.

At 0130, Mainguy heard the sound of oars. The three surf-boats from MGB 502 materialised out of the night. In the bows of the first boat was Major John Verney of the Special Boat Squadron. Dumais conferred with him while fifteen cases of arms were brought ashore and the departing passengers embarked: they now totalled six in number, as it had been decided that Jean Gicquel must also leave for safety's sake. Then the surf-boats were off into the night as quietly as they had come.

The large size of the shore party was a great help in handling the heavy suitcases. As their column left the mined zone, they picked up their three-man rearguard, who had seen nothing, though had heard much shooting from the patrol routes. Somehow or other, they carried their heavy cargo of arms the further two kilometres (1.2 miles), cutting across fields of wheat to get to the point where the horse and cart had been hidden. The cart set off soon after daybreak with the arms hidden under a load of hay. The next night, they were delivered to the Maquis at Bois-de-la-Salle.

*

With liberation coming to Plouha on 6 August in the shape of a troop of four US tanks, SHELBURNE had had its last clandestine sea operation. When MGB 718 came back on 8 August for CROZIER III, to collect one SIS and two French agents and any Allied evaders still in the hands of the Plouha group, the enemy forces who had manned the block-house on the Pointe-de-la-Tour had already surrendered several days previously. Rather than slipping in at night, the operation took place in daylight. It still wasn't completely safe: the party escorting the three outward-bound passengers were armed to the teeth, for there were still isolated German and Russian stragglers in the area. But when they emerged from the gully at Anse-Cochat on to the beach, they could for the first time see the gunboat riding at anchor.

Dumais, meanwhile, had already gone about other business. After helping a confused and non-French-speaking American town mayor to deal with the post-Liberation power vacuum at Saint-Brieuc, he made his way east with Louisette Lorre to contact Major Airey

Neave, MI9's new head, and find out what happened to the redoubtable Campinchi, the Paris linchpin in turn of the PAT organisation, OAKTREE and SHELBURNE.

In total, nine operations had taken place successfully (less the REFLEXION mishap), combining to deliver one of the most splendid exploits in which the Navy, MI9 and French Resisters took part. Dumais had been central to this success. His firm discipline had stopped the rot that destroyed MI9's two previous French networks, and his punctilious security arrangements allowed the SHELBURNE organisation to flourish and achieve its outstanding results. Altogether, the SHELBURNE Plouha group shipped out between 138 and 145 people by the Dartmouth gunboats – in doing so, not a single member of the SHELBURNE organisation was lost. The only casualty of the entire series of operations was the farmhouse of La Maison d'Alphonse.

La Maison d'Alphonse

CHAPTER 12 – THE NELSON SPIRIT

'Bravery never goes out of fashion'
William Makepeace Thackeray, *The Four Georges*

It was the most difficult pinpoint, according to Peter Williams, that 502 ever had to make. The pinpoint was on the east bank of the Tréguier River, taking 502 well inside the estuary and battling a formidable set of natural hazards. Not only was the approach extremely rocky, but there was a strong tide running across it. The channel was unlit: the only way to navigate along was by following a series of stakes marking the route. Fighting the strong tidal current, it took all of the crew's skill to manoeuvre the boat from stake to stake. Somehow, they made the pinpoint. There, 502 waited. But as the minutes ticked over into an hour, it became clear that for all the effort in making the pinpoint, the boat was going to have to return home, the rendezvous not met.

It wasn't until the way back to Dartmouth that 502 was to make any form of contact, and when it came, it was not the sort of contact they had been hoping for. Out in the open seas, the MGB found herself in the middle of a full-blown naval battle, between the Cruiser *Black Prince* and four destroyers on one side, and three German E-boats on the other. Clearly visible to both sides, one of the destroyers mistook her for an E-boat and opened fire. 502 desperately fired recognition signals, but with no response. Thankfully, all the shells fell harmlessly astern. They weren't the only shots to miss: a staff officer from DDOD(I) was on board as an observer. When the firing started, he drew his Colt .45 pistol, with what purpose remains unclear, and promptly accidentally discharged it, the bullet narrowly missing Williams and Signalman College.

For MGB 502, Operation SPLINT had culminated in a night of disappointments and dangerous misses, and the stories of the individuals they had meant to pick up from France would prove no more fortunate.

*

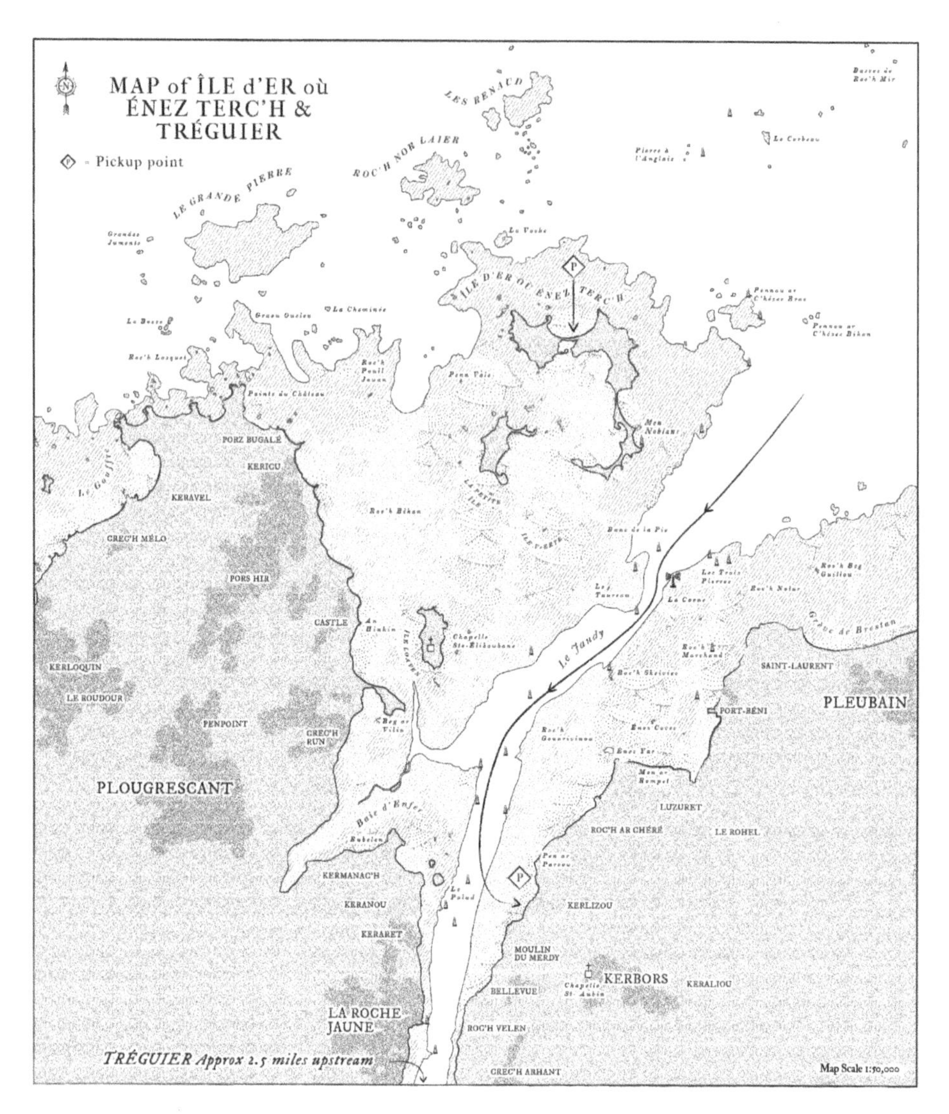

Operation SPLINT, carried out on the night of 25/26 April, was intended to pick up, among others, two of Kenneth Cohen's SIS agents: Yvon Jézéquel and Jeannie Rousseau (AMNIARIX). Yvon Jézéquel was important, but Rousseau was arguably one of the most crucial agents that SIS had in France. Jézéquel's attempts to make the crossing barely failed to make the start line: he was arrested at the Gare de Montparnasse with his young sister on the way to the

Jeannie Rousseau

pick-up. They were both deported and died in concentration camps. But Rousseau's own escape was one that came desperately close to success.

Rousseau worked for ALLIANCE, an intelligence-gathering network that Cohen had set up in conjunction with the Free French BCRA. ALLIANCE was run by Marie-Madeleine Fourcade, having initially been set up by Georges Loustaunau-Lacau (NAVARRE). After his arrest, Fourcade took it over. Its focus was strategic intelligence and, in particular, intelligence related to U-boat activity and, subsequently, V1 and V2 rockets.

Jeannie Rousseau had a job as an interpreter for the Germans in Dinard. Approached to work for ALLIANCE, she began to provide excellent information. But German counter-intelligence suspected there was an agent in place in the Dinard area and eventually she was arrested by the Gestapo in January 1941. Rousseau was tried by military court martial but was defended by officers in Dinard and was released. Her only punishment was an order to leave the coastal prohibited zone.

Rousseau moved to Paris and looked for work that would enable her to continue her intelligence gathering. She searched for a new job that would give her access to truly sensitive information, a job 'that would take me into the lion's den, which was where I wanted to go'. Soon enough, she found what she described as 'an amusing piece of work': the French industrialists syndicate needed a translator at its offices on the rue St Augustin. Rousseau took the job and became the organisation's Chief of Staff, regularly meeting with the German military commander's staff, based at the Hotel Majestic. Visiting the

Germans almost every day, she discussed commercial issues – complaints that the Nazis had commandeered inventories, while making offers to sell strategic goods such as steel and rubber to the Germans. All the while, Rousseau was accumulating a vast amount of basic intelligence.

The Hotel Majestic had certain offices which were out of bounds. These had the highest restricted access because the Germans were working on 'special weapons' plans. Fortuitously Rousseau met some of the German officers she had worked for in Dinard, who were now working on highly classified projects. By 1943 she was overhearing extremely sensitive information. The German officers were a close-knit group, and they would often gather in the evenings at a house on the Avenue Hoche. They would drink and talk in the company of their beautiful French friend who spoke such good German. Many of the men were attracted to Rousseau, and probably liked her all the more because she always refused their advances.

Rousseau played dumb, lulling the Germans into a false sense of security. She would cajole and tease them into proving some of their fantastic claims about flying bombs and rockets. They would talk openly among themselves about their work, and though they generally wouldn't talk to Rousseau directly, they didn't mind her being there. 'I had become part of the furniture,' she recalls. 'I teased them, taunted them, looked at them wide-eyed, insisted that they must be mad when they spoke of the astounding new weapon that flew over vast distances, much faster than any airplane. I kept saying: "What you are telling me cannot be true!" I must have said that 100 times. "I'll show you," one of the Germans said. "How," I asked, and he answered: "It's here on a piece of paper!" So, the German officer displayed a document explaining how to enter the test site at Peenemünde, the specific passes that were needed and what colour each one was.'

Jeannie, with her photographic memory, recorded each word in her mind. Her German 'friends' were so trusting, and so eager to impress, that they even showed her drawings of rockets. After these sessions, Rousseau would make her way to a safe house at 26 rue Fabert, on the Left Bank near Les Invalides. Here, she would sit down at the kitchen table and write out what she had heard, word for word:

'I would absorb it, like a sponge. I wasn't asked to paraphrase, or to understand.' When the Germans referred to 'Raketten', for example, she had no idea what they were talking about, as such long-range rockets had never before been built.

By September 1943 Jeannie had gathered enough information about the V2 rockets to send a detailed report to England. Her reports were seen by Reginald Jones, the Chief Scientific Officer of SIS who, in turn, sent them to Churchill. The report made such an impression that it was decided to get her out to London for a full debrief. This was the pinpoint on the Tréguier River for the night of 25/26 April 1944: Operation SPLINT.

The plan was to get Rousseau (AMNIARIX) into the prohibited zone and evacuate her with two other ALLIANCE operators: Raymond Pezet (FLYING FISH) and André Collard (CACTUS). Elie de Damipierre (SHEPHERD), their local contact, was quite confident of getting them to the pinpoint. He was to be assisted by Emile Hédin (BEAVER). When the three passengers were assembled at an inn in Tréguier, BEAVER went to fetch Yves Le Bitoux, a local veterinary surgeon, who drove them to the coast. Here, one of his friends, François Margeau, was to take over and lead them through the minefields to the pinpoint.

At this point, the plan began to unravel. In spite of the pitch darkness, Le Bitoux had easily found Margeau's house, and knocked on the door. But it opened to reveal the silhouette of a German officer against the bright light inside. AMNIARIX could speak fluent German and despite her heart thumping, calmly asked the officer where Margeau was.

'Opposite,' he snapped, slamming the door.

SHEPHERD decided there and then to get out of the village. He had the car stopped in a side road and left the mail with FLYING FISH and Dr Le Bitoux, while he himself went off to find out whether there was a road by which he, AMNIARIX and BEAVER could get away. He had scarcely gone forty yards in the thick darkness when he was surrounded by six German soldiers. They were all searched. Surprised to find their papers in order, the officer who had opened the door to them a short time before asked to see the car. He motioned to AMNIARIX to lead the way. She decided to go as slowly as possible, speaking German at the top of her voice to warn Le Bitoux and FLYING FISH in the hope that they would get away.

Her plan was partly successful. After twenty minutes of uncertainty, a scream of brakes signalled the capture of the car. AMNIARIX and Le Bitoux were captured, but warned by AMNIARIX's loud voice, FLYING FISH had fled. The stoical veterinary surgeon had decided to remain where he was. He was too well-known in the district and had no wish to escape and be responsible for bringing reprisals on his village. As the Germans took AMNIARIX and Le Bitoux to a house in the town, BEAVER felt that this was his only chance. Charging at them, he scattered his guards and dashed towards a large courtyard enclosed by a wall some eight feet high. A burst of fire followed him, but, protected by the corner of a house, he scaled the wall, jumped down into the street and ran off. Looking for somewhere to hide, BEAVER found a garden, went in through the iron gate, and there, hidden in a clump of trees, was an outdoor earth closet lavatory. He lifted the seat, crouched inside. Here, he waited for first light, listening to the shouts of the German troops who were searching the village.

As daylight broke, BEAVER could hear the owner of the house approaching the closet. 'I'm the man they're after,' he explained, stepping out. The woman suppressed her surprise, but refused to take him into her house. The Germans were continuing to search every house, she told him, and more than 100 inhabitants had been arrested. Early in the afternoon she returned to say that the Germans were no longer keeping such a strict watch. She gave him clothes and her bicycle and BEAVER was able to get away.

He was the lucky one. SHEPHERD, CACTUS, Yves Le Bitoux and AMNIARIX were taken away to Paris. Le Bitoux was deported and died in a concentration camp. AMNIARIX was sent to Ravensbrück but survived (her full report is at Annex F). The debrief demanded by SIS had never materialised: instead, they had to rely on the additional intelligence on the V1 and V2 rockets brought out to Dartmouth on Operation SCARF, as described earlier.

*

Aside from the SHELBURNE operations, the Flotilla's operations during the rest of 1944 fell into five groups: SPLINT, as described above, GLOVER, ROBESPIERRE, HAVEN and KNOCKOUT. Two administrative operations KORDA and SCRUBBY were carried out in September 1944 to photograph the French coast

The GLOVER series of operations (I–IX) was considered, along with the SHELBURNE operations, as textbook. Overall, they were all very successful. Their purpose was to support the SIS network ALIBI-MAURICE run by Georges Charaudeau. ALIBI acted as a collecting house for intelligence for four other SIS networks that did not have reliable or rapid means of communication. The pinpoint used in the Île Grande – Île Losquet – was treacherous even by Breton standards with high winds and strong tides and the ever-present rocks. Some of the early GLOVER operations were a mixed bag. Although the MGB always got to the pinpoint, some were more successful, others not, due to the reception committee not being there. On GLOVER III the reception committee warned 503 that there were enemy at the pinpoint. The surf-boats beat a hasty retreat and 503 left at best speed for Dartmouth.

The presence of enemy at the pinpoint prompted a need to change position for future operations. A new pinpoint was selected on the north side of the Île Grande. From here six further operations were carried out to it. GLOVER IV was carried out on 19 May by two newly arrived US PT boats 71 and 72 under instruction from 15th MGBF. It was unsuccessful. On 24 May they went again, with Peter Williams, David Birkin and Andrew Smith as boat officers. After some difficulty with equipment and the lack of experience of the US Navigating Officer, quickly corrected by David Birkin, they arrived at the pinpoint and successfully took on board the classified mail. There were further mechanical problems on the way back to Dartmouth. They eventually made it, but Peter Williams's report was scathing about the PT boats' crews' complacency.

Five further GLOVER operations took place: GLOVER V (17/18 June) was completed successfully; GLOVER IV (16 July) was unsuccessful – no reception committee; GLOVER VII (23/24 July)

carried out by 318 was a success; GLOVER VIII (29/30 July), also carried out by 318, was to pick up Guy Lemoire. In spite of the changeable weather and odd mechanical problem, Lemoire was picked up and they arrived in a sunny Start Bay at 0645. Lemoire was landed back on Île Grande by 318 on the night of 5/6 August (GLOVER IX).

In many ways, GLOVER IX really concluded the main operations of the 15th MGBF. Their area of operations on the French coast was liberated and their clandestine activities were at an end. There were further operations, KNOCKOUT, SCRUBBY and HAVEN, for slightly different purposes: to land stores for what had become the French Forces of the Interior, who were still fighting German pockets of resistance; to make contact with those that had made up networks and reception committees in France; and to document in daylight the pinpoints and to show both agents and themselves what the pinpoints looked like by day.

Operation KNOCKOUT needs a special mention as it involved the one and only time 15th MGBF took direct offensive action against the enemy. The objective of the operation was to land eleven tons of stores and embark six Jedburgh agents. (Jedburgh teams were mixed Allied military teams of three men, one French, one British and one American, parachuted in to train and lead Resistance groups in the run-up to D-Day.) 718 was carrying twenty-five cases of 9mm ammunition, one bren gun, eight rifles, two pistols and twenty grenades, plus 450 pairs of army boots, 900 pairs of socks, three medical packages and 2,000 pounds of flour for the FFI. Additional to her usual ship's complement, 718 was carrying Lieutenant Commander Nigel Warrington-Smyth, CO of the Helford River Flotilla, Lieutenant David Birkin as specialist Navigating Officer, Lieutenant M. H. A. McNeill, Naval Photographer, an SOE Conducting Officer, Lt Tandy, and RSM Peake of the Intelligence Corps.

The destination, Bénodet, was situated between Brest and Lorient on the west coast of France; Brest had just been liberated but the Germans were to continue to hold Lorient right up to the war's end in May 1945. Among the pockets of enemy still holding out in Brittany was one that 718 would have to pass, at Audierne. Because the major ports of Lorient, St Nazaire and La Rochelle were still enemy-occupied, Bénodet had become important as a port, once it had been cleared of obstructions left by the retreating Germans.

As 718 proceeded south in a calm sea, all seemed peaceful enough. Ronnie Seddon knew, however, from information received from the FFI at L'Aber-Wrac'h, that there was an enemy pocket of resistance at Lézongar on the western side of Audierne. It was while photographs were being taken of the coastal area westward of the Pointe de Lervily that 718 was engaged by cannon fire from the shore a mile away. Fire was returned by 718's six-pounder, the two-pounder pom-pom and the twin Oerlikon guns, the exchange lasting for ten minutes from 1103 to 1113. For good measure gun emplacements were then bombarded in the vicinity of the Pointe de Lervily by 718 at a range of half a mile. There was no reply from shore and 'cease-fire' was ordered at 1137. This was just as well: it subsequently turned out that fire directed at 718 had come from an FFI unit believing 718 to be an E-boat.

Once 718 was secured, a small stores boat came alongside, and the ammunition and stores were transferred. The local people swarmed all over the boats. All were extremely friendly. 718 left Bénodet at 0700 on 18 September, having been briefed by Ronnie Seddon that they might be engaged in action off Audierne. The crew were not aware that he had had a meeting with the FFI Colonel Commandant of Audierne who had apologised for his guns opening fire on 718. The Colonel Commandant expressed disappointment that an arranged bombardment of the German positions by HMS LONDONDERRY the day before had been cancelled, and supplied a large-scale map of the town indicating where the German and FFI troops were respectively located, plus positions and calibres of the enemy guns.

Arriving off Audierne, the harbour and enemy gun positions were photographed, and the gun positions positively identified. It was no real surprise when the order was given to close in at ten knots and open fire with all weapon systems. Hits were observed on gun emplacements and trenches in the Lézongar area. Four minutes later the Germans returned fire from 75mm, 40mm, 20mm canons as well as machine guns. This time, the enemy aim was accurate and 718 was hit. As speed was increased to maximum and a smokescreen laid,

718 zig-zagged to gain the protective cover of the Pointe de Lervily, and to enable the six-pounder aft to engage. The action lasted exactly ten minutes. The most immediate problem was to repair the centre fuel tank which was holed. The engines were stopped, the electrical circuits cut, petrol was pumped from the after-fuel compartment, and the compartment ventilated to disperse the vapour. Patches had to be fitted over the two holes in the ship's hull, engines restarted and 718 returned to Dartmouth.

The day after returning to Dartmouth, Ronnie Seddon 'cleared lower deck', as was the normal drill after an operation, in order to have a debrief as to what had happened. He started by saying how appropriate it was that this particular operation just completed was code-named KNOCKOUT. He was generous in his praise for the way the ship's company had performed during the action, and at this point even the Oerlikon gunner Jack Walker, and his loading number Stan Rodgers, could join in the merriment as he described the way they had danced while the 20mm shell ricocheted around their band-stand (the nickname for the gun positions on board). It had been a close call for the two of them.

What no one knew at the time was that Ronnie Seddon was in trouble with DDOD(I). He was subjected to a lot of close questioning about his unprecedented attack on enemy forces when the standing orders forbade offensive action in the interests of security. He was eventually exonerated, largely due to the post-operational report written by Warrington-Smythe which played on the 'Nelson Spirit'. His crew admired him for his initiative and aggressive spirit, and took pride in what he had done.

*

There was one other series of operations. ROBESPIERRE I–III, which were carried out by 502 and 318. The last of these, ROBESPIERRE III, was carried out in daylight as David Birkin describes:

'It seemed right to me that this last journey across the Channel should be in MGB 318 in which I did my first operation in 1942 – she

Approaching Clougouron beach

was beginning to show signs of age, a few dents and scars, and inevitably water-logged so that she no longer moved sprightly in a rough sea. It was also fitting that Lieutenant Jan McQuoid Mason, who had deservedly been decorated with the Distinguished Service Cross' should be in Command, the friend with whom I had taken part in that memorable operation on Christmas night 1943 and that Chief Petty Officer Mould, wearing the DSM ribbon, who had been Coxswain of 318 throughout her career, should be at the wheel.

'We slipped from Westward Ho at 05.20 as the sun was rising over a mirror blue sea, and with the Dart Buoy abeam set course S26°W at our maximum cruising speed en route for the Île de Bas and the beach of Grac'h Zu into which we had dug so many vast containers in the winter of 1942. The 100-mile cruise took five hours and apart from a look-out for floating mines we all relaxed in the sunshine, cocking an occasional eye upwards in case of the unlikely appearance of a German aeroplane.

'The small beach, which had been cleared of land mines, was buzzing with activity in anticipation of our arrival and as the MGB turned shorewards at Méan Névez, the rock which had been our seamark on so many winter nights, a cheer went up from the welcomers, and we replied with gun buzzers, fog horns and shouts.

'After anchoring we rowed ashore to meet those who up until then we had only known as whispers and shapes in the night. In the middle of the group stood a slim strikingly beautiful girl. This was Madame Le Duc and with her stood her husband, the famous doctor

David Birkin

David Birkin talking to Docteur and Madame le Duc who ran the VAR line

from Morlaix. It was these two who had played such an important role with the Resistance team of that area.

'Supplies of coffee and cigarettes were exchanged for masses of onions – and one lady invited me to her house to meet her seventeen-year-old daughter who longed to "be friends with" an English sailor. But our time ashore was limited to an hour, which was not long enough for fraternising!

'At 1300 after countless toasts of Calvados we said goodbye to our friends – and with many a "Vive La France", "Vive La Grande Bretagne" and the Churchill "V" sign, we rowed somewhat drunkenly back to 318 and weighed anchor.

'A quarter of an hour later we were speeding home at 20 knots. The sun was setting as, for the last time, MGB 318 passed the Boom Ship which guarded the entrance to Dartmouth Harbour. It had been an extremely happy excursion for all of us and a fitting end to the 15th Flotilla's clandestine operations.'

CHAPTER 13 – SOMETHING SPECIAL

'27 May 1944, Saturday morning. There is a new boat in; MGB 718. She has no torpedo tubes and is British. She was here only two days. Something special I think'

Wibby Leask, a 12-year-old schoolboy who from 1942–45 kept a secret diary of all the comings and goings from Stornaway.

The first part of the journey from Aberdeen for the Norwegian coast had proved uneventful. For the 718 crew, used to travelling in the pitch dark of a moonless phase, the lunar glow washing across the waves of the North Sea felt something of a luxury. It helped them to see and avoid the floating mines, bobbing and glinting in the moonlight. Such was the visibility that the Norwegian coast was first sighted at thirty-two miles. But before they could reach there, and the planned drop-off, someone spotted another sight to deal with first.

The objective of the operation was to extract Norwegian agents from the island of Skarvøy in the approaches to Egersund, on the south-western tip of Norway between Stavanger and Kristiansand. The agents had been operating a coastal watching station up in the mountains and reporting shipping movements by radio to London. Their location was well-chosen, their beat an area of south-western Norway close to the regular enemy convoy route and patrolled by aircraft from Stavanger and E-boats from their base at Egersund. But

MGB 718 in Norway

their role was becoming increasingly dangerous: the Germans had become extra-vigilant as a result of the raiding activities by British and Norwegian gunboats operating from Lerwick, and the continuing threat of commando raids.

It was one of these German convoys that 718 spotted now: the unmistakable silhouettes and shapes of five coasters, together with a minesweeper and armed trawlers as escort. Ronnie Seddon ordered 718 to a halt, keeping her bows to the convoy to reduce their silhouette in the hope of not being spotted. No such luck. It was a heart-in-mouth moment as the crew saw two of the trawlers altering their course and heading in their direction. This was followed by the sight of distant puffs of smoke and the sounds of low booms from the minesweeper as she started to fire star shells in their direction.

It was time for evasive action: Seddon withdrew 718 westwards and there followed a tense number of minutes as they waited to see if the trawlers would follow. But no boats followed: whatever the coasters had on board, they were more important to protect than taking 718 down. But the crew didn't relax completely, not yet. Seddon knew the convoy would have radioed an alert. The ships might not be coming for them, but the air force would. The engines were killed again: any phosphorescence from their wake would be clearly visible from above. Sure enough, it wasn't long before the distant sound of a Dornier flying boat appeared, growing louder as it got nearer. Seddon watched as it made two passes over the convoy and then directly over 718. Guns were manned. Everyone was to fire. But Seddon held his nerve and ordered everyone to wait. The Dornier buzzed over and then turned and faded from view. Silence. Had it seen them? Decided they weren't worth bothering with? Either way, they'd got away with it. Seddon knew it had been another narrow escape. The engines were fired up once more. More wary, more watchful, they pushed on for Skarvøy.

*

Although the focus of this story has been on Dartmouth and the coast of Brittany, DDOD(I)'s remit for clandestine operations extended from Norway to the Adriatic. The result was that 718 was also detached to the Norway theatre for very important and high-risk

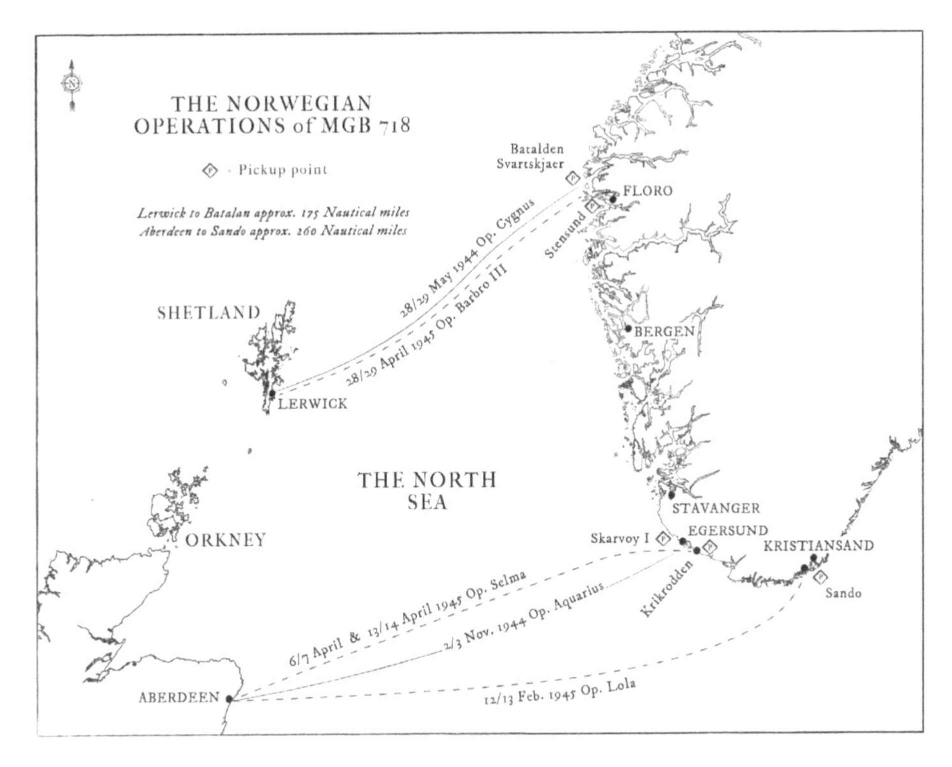

operations: one on detachment from Dartmouth and five later when the Flotilla moved north, at the end of 1944.

Throughout the war SIS had established a network of coast-watching stations along the whole Norwegian coast. These posts provided significant intelligence on the movement of shipping and contributed to the sinking of the German battleships *Bismarck*, *Scharnhorst* and *Tirpitz*, as well as the *Prinz Eugen*, *Hipper* and *Admiral Scheer*.

In May 1944 718 was sent north to support SIS and the Norwegian Resistance. This involved an 850-mile journey from Dartmouth, via Holyhead and the Caledonian Canal to Lerwick in the Shetland Islands. The seas of Brittany had been stormy enough. But the fjords and islands awaiting that laced the Atlantic coast of Norway were every bit as threatening and dangerous. And the operations would be attempted without the hardened experience and knowledge built up from multiple journeys to Brittany.

Although neutral, Norway, like Denmark, had been occupied by Nazi forces in April 1940 in a bid to keep the Skagerrak, Kategatt and all-important Atlantic approaches through the North Sea open for German naval operations. As in Vichy France, a puppet government was set up under Vidkun Quisling. While the exiled Norwegian King and Government continued to work in exile in London, a resistance movement was set up to defend the 'hjemmefronten' ('home front') run by Milorg ('military organisation') and an intelligence-collecting wing XU (short for 'unknown agent'). Their work was considered particularly vital given the importance attached to the Norsk Hydro heavy-water production that was so important to the German nuclear programme.

At a distance of 223 miles, Bergen is nearer to Lerwick, the main Shetland settlement, than many people think. But even so, this distance is considerably further than the 100 miles that separated Dartmouth and Brittany. There was also the challenge of considerable traffic across the Norwegian Sea on the famous 'Shetland Bus', whose story has been widely told elsewhere.

The mission that 718 had been sent north for, Operation CYGNUS, took place on 28/29 May 1944. The mission was to rescue two SIS agents who had been transmitting radio reports of enemy shipping movements to London: such reports had led to the find and eventual destruction of the battleship *Bismarck* in May 1941 and later on the *Tirpitz*, which was sunk off Tromsø in November 1944. As well as the agents, 718 was also to extract a family who had previously been engaged in the same business. All were in immediate danger of capture by the Gestapo.

718's destination was the island of Batalden, a strikingly tall island off the Norwegian coast, midway between Bergen and Ålesund and close to the town of Florø. In addition to its regular crew, commanded by Ronnie Seddon, the boat took along Lieutenant Salmond as Navigating Officer and some Norwegian navy specialists: Lieutenant Leif Utne would act as interpreter and Petty Officer Ole Hovden as pilot. Four ratings from the Norwegian MFC Flotilla, based at Peterhead, Aberdeenshire, were to act as surf-boat crews if required. The W/T complement was doubled by drafting in one of the base wireless station telegraphists. There was one other key difference to the Brittany operation: because of the long distance to be covered, a deck cargo of one thousand gallons of fuel would be carried in four-gallon jerrycans, making the boat unduly heavy and potentially explosive in the event of attack by air or sea.

The MGB left Lerwick at 1510 on the 28th in a moderate swell, accompanied by drizzle and low cloud. Almost immediately they started having fuel problems with the engines, further complicated by having to refuel the main tanks from jerrycans on a rolling deck. Visibility was poor and as they neared the Norwegian coast Ronnie Seddon decided to risk turning on his radar, opening up the danger of being detected. They immediately picked up a strong land echo at a range of 24,000 yards which was the high ground on Batalden Island. They reduced speed and Lieutenant Salmond guided them in.

At 0305, Batalden was sighted half a mile ahead. The Norwegian pilot, Ole Hovden, a fisherman from the nearby village of the same name, knew the waters well and with him at the wheel, 718 headed toward the pinpoint on the islet of Svartskjær, just to the north of Batalden. As they were heading there, they saw a small open motor boat and a rowing-boat leaving Batalden and heading towards the MGB. Was this who they were meant to be picking up? They didn't have long to wait as the boats were alongside by 0320. The formalities of the correct passwords were exchanged, and then the agents and family of nine were helped aboard. The motor boat was holed and left to sink. Then Ole Hovden, still at the wheel, used his local knowledge to take 718 through the treacherous waters out and between the numerous lurking rocks. Once they were far enough out, Hovden was relieved. Taking advantage of the persistent fog that now enveloped them, Seddon increased speed to twenty-five knots and they sped westward without incident. MGB 718 was back in Lerwick harbour at 1400 on 29 May, after a round trip of 450 miles.

The SIS agents 718 brought out were Lieutenant Ivar Møller and Lieutenant Dagfinn Ulriksen. Before he had been evacuated Ulriksen had sent out, on a resupply mission, a Christmas tree for the exiled King of Norway, King Haakon, to be delivered by SIS on Christmas Eve. This may have been the precedent which led to the annual delivery of a Christmas tree to London for display in Trafalgar Square as a gesture of thanks from the people of Norway for wartime support. The family the mission had rescued were the Karstensens. Saron, the father, was the post master on the island of Fannoy. The family had run a coast-watching operation until the autumn of 1941, when the SIS agents took over. Thereafter Saron supported refugee and agent extractions as well as providing food for the SIS agents.

While 718 had been north, major events in the war had been happening further south. On 31 May, the BBC broadcast a coded message to the French Resistance. It contained the opening lines of Paul Verlaine's 'Chanson d'Automne' – 'Les sanglots longs, des violins de l'automne'. This was the code the Resistance had been waiting for, signalling that invasion was imminent. 718 left Lerwick on the 31st on the day of the broadcast, arriving back in Dartmouth on 6 June, hearing the news of D-Day on the battery radio given to them by the Windmill Girls.

*

Operation CYGNUS had been a one-off mission. But in October 1944, 718 once again left Dartmouth, this time for good, arriving in Aberdeen on 31 October. She was soon to be joined by 502 and 503, but not 318, which was deemed unsuitable for the long runs across to Norway.

The second Norwegian operation that 718 was involved in was AQUARIUS III, which took place on 2/3 November. This time the crew did not include a specialist Navigating Officer but there was a Norwegian Quartermaster to assist with inshore navigation. The objective of this operation, as mentioned earlier, was to extract the Norwegian agents operating a coastal watching station from the island of Skarvøy.

Following the altercation with the convoy, Seddon knew that he couldn't approach the island on the same bearing as he had planned, in case the MGB was detected again, and the men waiting for them were put in further danger. He decided instead to approach the island from the south which had the added advantage of keeping them out of range of the radar station at Obrestad. At 0115 he set course on

Guy Hamilton at the aft six-pounder

silent engines. The convoy route was crossed at eight knots and the final approach was made to the pinpoint, a shelving beach about twenty-five yards long, which was identified by the Norwegian pilot when one mile away. In the brilliant moonlight, supplemented by the Hestnes Light three-quarters of a mile away, the four agents could be seen quite clearly. The pre-arranged code letter 'M' was flashed. They replied with 'S', which meant they required a boat to take them off. Guy Hamilton and two ratings took the SN6 surf-boat away at 0403 and with only ten yards of water to cross, they were back in twelve minutes with the four passengers.

The Norwegian agents were relieved to see the MGB. Jan Larssen, his cousin Arnold Hovland, Sverre Vinningland and Jen Johannsen had crossed from the mainland to Skarvøy in a small boat and walked over the hilly island to wait for extraction in a cave shielded from the sea by a huge boulder. The MGB was expected at midnight, but they had seen the German convoy leave Egersund and later an E-boat, which they mistook for 718 and hailed, fortunately to no avail. As the deadline of 0400 approached they had dejectedly decided that they dare not wait any longer and set out to retrace their steps over the hill back to their boat. It was only as they were heading back up the hill that one of them looked round and saw 718 close in to the beach. To which they then returned in double-quick time.

At 0415, 718 set off back slowly to the west. Four minutes later another convoy of five ships – two trawlers and three coasters – was sighted. Seddon tried a different tactic, increasing speed to twenty-five knots in the hope that this, together with a course alteration, might persuade the convoy commander that he had sighted an Egersund-based E-boat. His tactics worked: there was no attempt to engage, and course was duly set for Aberdeen. Apart from avoiding two further floating mines, there were no incidents and they were back in Aberdeen at 1830.

*

The last winter of the war saw the tide turning decisively for the Allies. In November, the German battleship *Tirpitz*, whose operations had been severely restricted by mini-submarine and aerial attacks, but still retained a significant symbolic importance, was finally sunk by the RAF, near Tromsø in the north. The Germans imposed a scorched-earth policy, destroying towns and settlements as they retreated south. In October 1944, exiled Norwegian troops had liberated Finnmark, also in the north, and preparations began for the repatriation of the royal family and government. Even so, the occupying forces remained dangerous, arguably more so as they faced the reality of defeat.

718's third venture in northern seas was Operation LOLA. It took place between 12 and 15 February 1945. SIS had an urgent requirement to instal a coast-watching station between Larvik and Stavanger. Though the war was drawing to a close, with Russian and Allied troops encroaching on German territory and beginning to surround Berlin, there remained 400,000 German troops in Norway alone: an astonishing garrison for a country that numbered just over three million souls. The two agents selected for the mission were Hans Møller and Lars Larsen; the former was the brother of Ivar Møller, who had been brought out on Operation CYGNUS.

718 was in Lerwick when Seddon received orders for Operation LOLA, which was to be mounted from Aberdeen. The journey south to the Scottish mainland was terrible. Force 8 gales caused considerable damage to the boat, most significantly the loss of the long-range

wireless, which could not be replaced in time for the mission date of 12 February. Seddon 'cleared lower deck' and, with the full crew gathered on the for'ard mess deck, he told them that it was going to be a long operation. 718 would be sailing right into the Skaggerak, the busy strait that links the North Sea with the Baltic via the Kattegat, never wider than 90 miles and potentially full of hostile and neutral shipping. As Seddon explained, they would have to be on their toes as never before. As well as this, the weather forecast was far from good. In the event of the boat not being able to make the return journey, Seddon explained how the crew would be split into escape parties under a designated leader to make their way to Sweden. 'However,' he added with a grin, 'it is not all bad news. We have it on good authority that there is a dearth of young men in this part of southern Norway, so the girls are sex-starved and that will suit some of you lot!'

There were some personnel changes before their mission. During January 1945 Sub-Lieutenant John Townend, who had been the Navigating Officer since the boat was commissioned eleven months earlier, left to become First Lieutenant of a new Camper & Nicholson boat, MGB 509, which would be commanded by 503's Mike Marshall, who was promoted to Lieutenant Commander and Senior Officer of the 15th MGB Flotilla. Townend was replaced by Sub-Lieutenant K. O'Brien but in short order he was to be replaced just before LOLA by Sub-Lieutenant C. Wale. Ronnie Seddon was not pleased with these rapid and disruptive changes of Third Officers and insisted on retaining O'Brien for the next operation; otherwise there would be insufficient time for the newcomers to understand the behaviour of the boat under different conditions, and particularly the difficult conditions they could expect in the Skagerrak. Both O'Brien and Sub-Lieutenant Wale navigated during LOLA, and both were to need all their expertise in getting 718 to the pinpoint Sandøy, a small island near Mandal.

718 left Aberdeen at 2200 on 12 February, with 2,000 gallons of petrol in jerrycans on deck, one SN6 surf-boat, and one and a half tons of stores on the upper deck and mess decks: a total additional deck weight of thirteen tons. Helping with navigation of the over-laden

boat were a Norwegian pilot, Lieutenant Hansen, and a Conducting Officer – Lieutenant Doddington. It wasn't long before the ship hit problems. Once 718 cleared the lee of the land, the pitching and rolling started. Rough weather and additional deck weight meant that 718 shipped a lot of water, damaging the main radio. The Captain instructed that the W/T watch be kept using the back-up set, and this worked surprisingly well over a range of 150 miles from Aberdeen.

The helmsman, meanwhile, had a difficult job in the unpleasant sea conditions and struggled to keep the boat on course. Accurate steering was impossible, but constant fixes on QH kept it on track. About 100 miles off Norway, an aircraft approached and began circling half a mile away; Seddon ordered the crew to action stations. Thankfully, it was a false alarm. Once the plane had been identified as a Lockheed Hudson and thus friendly, the current two-star recognition signal was fired from the signal pistol on the bridge. The aircraft replied with the correct acknowledgement, even waggling its wings before proceeding west towards Scotland.

The process of refuelling from the jerrycans, and jettisoning the holed cans once they were emptied, began at 1430. It took an arduous two and a half hours with the crew involved working in atrocious conditions. But despite the appalling weather, they were nearing the objective. Crossing the convoy route without any sightings or encounters, the weather deteriorated still further with heavy snow showers obscuring the land ahead. Seddon had two choices: to stop and wait for conditions to improve, or to abort the mission. The Norwegian pilot wanted to abort but Seddon, supported by the two SIS agents, decided to carry on.

It proved to be the right decision. Conditions gradually improved and at 0035 718 anchored fifty yards off the pinpoint, enabling the SN6 surf-boat under the command of Guy Hamilton to go with Hans Møller to investigate the possibility of landing. Guy reported back to the Captain by walkie-talkie that the south-easterly swell made landing too hazardous. The surf-boat was recalled and, after weighing anchor, 718 went back to the north of Sandøy and, with Able Seaman Ronnie Hunter laying on the snow-covered fo'c'sle calling out the readings from his lead-line, Ronnie Seddon took the MGB

LOLA pinpoint

gingerly through the channel between Sandøy and a smaller island, Maurholmen. After anchoring again, the surf-boat was despatched once more to try and find an alternative landing place. Protected this time from the swell, Guy and Hans agreed that the new place was suitable, and the former reported back accordingly.

Hayward 'Rocky' Rockwood, who had been stuck with Hamilton in France, was detailed off to stay ashore with Hans Møller to assist in the unloading of the stores. In his keenness, he jumped from the SN6 too soon. Although only four or five yards from the shore, he had to endure what Hamilton described as an 'unpleasantly cold flounder ashore'. Rockwood was a truly wonderful character: a born seaman as tough as nails, but also a non-swimmer all his long sea-faring life, and the possessor of the most extensive vocabulary of original swearwords it is possible to imagine – some of which were no doubt uttered here. He did make it ashore but lost a torch and a watch in the process. In place of Rocky, Telegraphist Les Taylor was left ashore to help Møller with the unloading of the stores. Still swearing profusely, Rocky returned to 718 to warm up.

Back on 718, the Norwegian pram had been lowered into the water where it proved to be unseaworthy. It was shipping water rapidly until it was overwhelmed. This meant the surf-boat, returning alongside, was the only means of ferrying the fifty boxes of equipment ashore: a difficult task in the frequent snow squalls that brought visibility down to zero. When 718 disappeared from view in the squalls, Hans Møller and Les Taylor were, as Hans writes in his account, 'really afraid of being left'. He recalls Les asking him if the Germans were far away, and how far it was to Oslo and Stockholm. They were all very thankful when the snow cleared enough to see 718 come back into view again. The unloading and ferrying proceeded intermittently between snow squalls over a period of two and a half hours – the whole business conducted in the dark with no lights possible as there were Germans just over a mile away on the island of Skjernoy. Once complete, the two agents finally went ashore in the surf-boat which Seddon had left with them.

Hans Møller and Lars Larsen were by now so exhausted that for the first hour or two they just lay down next to the boxes. When daylight came, they could not at first get their bearings. Then they realised that in the confused darkness and snowstorm conditions they had come ashore on the south side of Hellersøy, not as they and the officers of 718 had thought, the north side of Sandøy. As luck would have it, this was a better place because they were not so much under the eyes of the Germans.

Hans and Lars knew that the British SN6 surf-boat, which they would need to employ to get their gear on to the mainland, would attract more attention from both Norwegians and Germans than would have been the case had the pram survived. But they also knew they had no alternative. They loaded the surf-boat with the most necessary items – radio set, tent, rifle, some food and cigarettes – and rowed northwards through the series of small islands to one nearest the mainland, to which they crossed after dark. The two agents had great difficulty in getting hold of a less conspicuous Norwegian fishing boat to transport the boxes. When they eventually did and returned to Hellersøy, they discovered that some had disappeared, obviously stolen. Frustrated, they ferried the remainder across to the mainland, and transported them by horse-drawn sledge several kilometres to Mønnesland, where they were hidden in woods.

The two agents camped nearby for the first few weeks. A friendly farmer built them a shelter: he made such a good job of the camouflage that for the first few days they couldn't find it. The work involved in setting up shop took time, but the station was operational from 8 March, keeping constant watch and reporting shipping movements by radio to London. It was hard work for just the two of them and, with London constantly requesting more details, they were pleased to have Alfred Toftenes, a friend of Hans, join them on 20 April. Thereafter they operated a three-shift system until they closed down the station on VE-Day, 8 May 1945.

As for 718, their own journey back from the pinpoint was not without incident. Initially the water was deep and there was only a slight sea swell, but it was a different story once they started to cross the North Sea. By 0800 the wind was force 6, the sea very rough and the swell long and heavy. By now the crew had been at action stations for fourteen hours. They were stood down to cruising stations, which wouldn't have been much more comfortable: in the atrocious weather conditions a speed of six to eight knots was the maximum possible. By 1700, the sea had eased sufficiently for speed to be increased to eleven knots. 718 still wasn't flying but was at least now making some progress.

At 2151 the first fix by QH was obtained, showing that 718 was fifteen miles south of track. By now, the bilges were flooded. Petty Officer Motor Mechanic Bill Cartwright was disconcerted to see that despite the continual operation of the engine room pumps, water was forcing its way through the bilge covers and on to the deck. So, he and the rest of the crew were relieved when land was finally sighted at 0710 on 15 February. The only problem was that with the sea moderating no one could identify the stretch of coastline they were off. Seddon suffered the ignominy of having to ask the crew of a fishing boat for their location. They pointed out the sands of Cruden Bay some twenty miles north of Aberdeen – not such an inappropriate landfall after such a horrific night, since it was here that Bram Stoker wrote much of *Dracula*.

Seddon had always been expert in bringing 718 alongside. But on this occasion, after entering harbour at 0830, he had great difficulty in manoeuvring the boat alongside Mearns Quay because of the weight of water in the bilges. During her fifty-eight hours at sea the CO had been almost constantly on the bridge, so if fatigue also played a part in his shaky docking it was hardly surprising.

On 718, LOLA was known as 'the bad one'. Nobody – whether ship's company or agents – who took part in the operation would ever forget the experience, and the epithet stuck. On inspection, the damage caused by the constant buffeting over two and a half days was extensive. The tally of defects to be rectified included all water-tight hatches on the upper deck buckled, all wireless gear unserviceable, water-tight bulkheads strained and leaking internally, water entering through the hull at two feet per day, engine room supports strained, frames and stringers suspect, underwater exhaust valves leaking, 24-volt batteries immersed in seawater, one Morris auxiliary engine unserviceable: the list seemed endless.

In his operational report to DDOD(I) the CO concluded that, 'I must wholeheartedly commend the spirit, resourcefulness and conduct of the officers and men under my command, during these two and a half days of appalling conditions – conditions far in excess of the normal requirements of these small craft and as physically exhausting to the men as to the boat.'

In turn, Frank Slocum wrote to Ronnie Seddon a congratulatory note on 6 March which stated, 'Will you please accept for yourself and convey to your ship's company, my most sincere congratulations on a magnificent job – well done.'

*

By 29 March, 718 was ready for sea again. As well as the repairs, 718 had also changed camouflage scheme from the Mountbatten or Plymouth Pink – used for operations to Brittany – to a more suitable grey, over-washed with sodium sulphide and hydrogen peroxide solution to tone everything down in bright moonlight. By now, the noose was tightening across Europe: Russian forces had delivered a crushing defeat on the German forces in East Prussia, while the American and British forces had crossed the Rhine. Norway, however, was still occupied. SIS wanted 718 to land two of the agents recovered on Operation AQUARIUS III – Jan Larssen and Arnold Hansen.

Operation SELMA I took place on 6/7 April. 718 left Aberdeen at 0600 on 6 April with the two agents and two Norwegian pilots. She carried 500 gallons of extra fuel in jerrycans and two surf-boats, a folding canoe and one ton of stores. For once, the weather was good

SELMA I pinpoint

as they set off. At 1820 that evening they spotted some fishing boats which they avoided. By midnight, however, visibility had deteriorated to nil. Seddon decided to risk a look at the radar. It gave a confused signal as did the soundings taken. He could have been on target. But equally he could have been five miles west of it.

At 0033 Seddon ordered 'stop engines' and, again taking a chance on not being detected by the enemy shore stations, had the radar switched on a second time. The echo this time was of land 2,000 yards ahead and was interpreted as being either Eigerøy, where the pinpoint was located, or more likely the area south of Skarvøy Island. Then suddenly all was revealed, as at 0104 the Eigerøy Lighthouse was switched on. Everyone on the bridge ducked instinctively, but the beam passed well over 718. They were two hundred yards from shore, although in the fog no land was visible. Seddon took the boat towards the pinpoint but rang down to stop engines at 0119, believing that the Germans must have detected them on their radar.

SELMA II pinpoint

Seddon asked the two agents to go with him down to the wardroom to discuss the next move. They discussed three choices: to go on to the pinpoint, although 718 was almost certainly under radar surveillance; proceed around the south of Skarvøy Island and land the agents on its north coast; or to abort the operation. Either of the alternative landings would most likely have led to an enemy search come daylight, and it would have been impossible to have hidden the ton of stores in the time available. Arnold and Jan were willing to go in without the stores but finally and reluctantly agreed that the operation should not proceed, on the understanding that Ronnie Seddon would do his best to get them ashore the following week.

Seven days later they tried again – Operation SELMA II. This time no stores would be taken, and the two agents would carry only rucksacks. Again, they took two Norwegian pilots, a surf-boat, a folding canoe and 650 gallons of extra fuel in jerrycans. They left Aberdeen at 0600 on Friday 13 April – not a good day for the superstitious among the crew.

The Eigerøy Lighthouse was first sighted from around twenty miles off shore. Shortly afterwards the Lille Presteskjær Lighthouse, to the north-west of Jøssingfjord, was also seen, and 718 stopped while accurate fixes were taken on both lights. Just before midnight engines were restarted and the course was altered to make a landfall at Haadyret. By this time three more lighthouses had been identified: Vibberodden Fyr, Varnes Fyr, and Lista Fyr. Of these Vibberodden, visible from a range of thirteen miles and white, red and green sectors occulting every five seconds, was particularly helpful.

The conditions for approaching land were near-perfect: wind light to variable, sea smooth and no swell. The only problem, as was often the case off Norway, was that 718's bow wave and wake were clearly marked by phosphorescence. Speed was reduced to six knots to minimise the effect. Land was sighted at ten miles' range. When the distance had been reduced to four miles, Leading Seaman Madland confirmed that it was Haadyret as intended.

718 proceeded a quarter to half a mile off the coast. When they were three-quarters of a mile from Skarvøy Island, the two agents pointed out that they were passing the low headland of Kviksodden and asked if they could be put ashore there instead. The advantage to them would be that they would already be on the mainland instead of having to cross to it from an island. Seddon agreed and stopped engines fifty yards off the headland at Kviksodden. Because there was neither tide nor swell, there was no need to drop anchor. At 0107 the surf-boat was sent in under the command of Guy Hamilton, with orders to investigate the western and northern sides of the headland. Only if the two agents were completely satisfied that they could get inland were they to be allowed to leave.

Hamilton kept in touch with Seddon by walkie-talkie throughout the half hour the surf-boat was away. There was no place to land on the western side of Kviksodden, and he went up the fjord to the north side until a suitable landing-place was found. Jan Larssen climbed to the cliff top and reported that they could certainly get inland from where they were. The two agents went off in excellent spirits. 718 set off homewards and entered Aberdeen harbour at 1605 on 14 April 1945.

718's final Norwegian trip was Operation BARBERO III, scheduled for 28/29 April. Its mission was to drop a ton of stores to two agents operating the BARBERO coastal watch station on the island of Steinsundøy. The operation went off without a hitch, and 718 returned to Lerwick.

The war, in Europe at least, was coming to an end. On Monday 7 May 1945, Winston Churchill announced that 'Tomorrow is Victory in Europe Day.' But on VE-Day itself, 8 May, while everyone else was celebrating, 718 was 'ploughing the oggin' (an old sailors' word for

Crew of 718 in 1945

the sea), returning from Lerwick to Aberdeen in very rough weather. Everyone was sick and they were glad when they came alongside at Mearns Quay where they met up with many of their shipmates from Dartmouth.

MGB 502, now numbered 2002, was there commanded by Jan McQuoid Mason, the former commander of 318. There was also the new boat 2009, commanded by Mike Marshall, now the Flotilla Commander as Peter Williams had gone to DDOD(I). John Townend was First Lieutenant of 2009. Everyone was given 72 hours' leave to celebrate VE-Day. Most of the crew, although very proud of their achievements, were too tired to do much except remark, 'thank fuck that's over'.

*

After the liberation of France in September 1944 the demand for clandestine naval operations from DDOD(I) had fallen away rapidly. The last major operation from Dartmouth to France was Operation KNOCKOUT carried out by 718 during daylight on 16/17 September 1944. After this, the Flotilla headquarters moved to Aberdeen. 502 and 503 were earmarked for deployment to the Far East and spent the winter of 1944/45 at Falmouth and Teignmouth being fitted with copper bottoms. The plan was for the whole Flotilla to be transferred to the Far East and redesignated the 71st Motor Gun Boat Flotilla.

MASB 36 had already been detached to support the D-Day landings. On 10 October, 718 sailed to Shoreham to join MASB 36 to run a cross-Channel ferry service for SIS and SOE personnel.

When the Far East deployment didn't materialise, 502 was redesignated MGB 2002 and 503 MGB 2003. Peter Williams had gone to join DDOD(I)'s staff and Mike Marshall, promoted to Lieutenant Commander, became the Flotilla Senior Officer. Both boats moved to Aberdeen where they joined 718 who had moved from Shoreham in October 1944. Jan McQuoid Mason commanded 502/2202. 318 did not go to join with the other boats and was decommissioned in early 1945, having had a long and successful war. Two new MGBs, 507 and 509, finally emerged from the hands of their builders. Joining the other boats at Aberdeen, they were renumbered 2007 and 2009 and the Flotilla reconstituted as the 71st Motor Gun Boat Flotilla.

Orders were now received for MGB 2002 to proceed on a special mission. She was to embark Lieutenant Commander Brian Reynold RNR, two Merchant Navy masters and a Merchant Navy radio officer and take them to Gothenburg in Sweden. Reynold and one of the masters had taken part in blockade-running operations to Sweden during the winter of 1943/44, bringing back to this country much-needed war material. The visit of MGB 2002 was therefore in the nature of a courteous gesture to the Swedes for their cooperation in the enterprise. For Reynold, it was the chance to arrange for the removal to Britain of two Norwegian merchantmen in Gothenburg, which had been used as store ships.

At the last minute, Jan McQuoid Mason, whose award of the DSC had been gazetted the previous August, was required to attend an investiture at Buckingham Palace to receive his decoration. Marshall therefore volunteered to take temporary command. When he learned that the trip was to be made, Williams asked Slocum if he could be spared to join the party, but permission was denied as he was required as Duty Officer at Palace Street. This refusal was to save his life.

On the morning of 11 May, MGB 2002 left Aberdeen for Gothenburg, being expected to arrive at 2000 next day. When no signal notifying her arrival was received in the evening of the 12th no one was unduly worried. But when nothing had been heard by midday on the 13th an aircraft search was launched and found no trace of the missing gunboat. Subsequently further air searches were carried out, but without success and were finally called off. MGB 2002 had vanished.

Five days later, on 16 May, the British Naval Officer in charge in Kristiansand in southern Norway signalled to the Admiralty that two survivors from the missing gunboat had been picked up by a Norwegian merchant vessel from a Carley raft. MGB 2002 had been blown up by a mine early in the morning of 12 May at the entrance to the Skagerrak. The survivors, Petty Officer Tommy Sheehan and Able Seaman Norman Hines, had been adrift on their raft for four days and were now in hospital at Kristiansand suffering severely from the effects of exposure. Tommy Sheehan had both legs amputated due to gangrene and Norman Hines lost all his toes. A list of those killed on 502/2002 is in Annex B.

On 18 May MGB 718 and MGB 2009, assisted by three RAF aircraft, were ordered to carry out a thorough search of the area in which 2002 had been reported sunk. They found no other survivors, but floating wreckage was picked up, and other wreckage found ashore. All indications were that a violent explosion had occurred under the gunboat's bridge. According to the survivors the whole forepart of the vessel had been blown to pieces in the initial blast, leaving only the engine room and a portion of the afterpart, which sank quickly. It was a sad end to a gallant ship which had survived so many narrow escapes from the Germans.

As for the rest of the Flotilla, MGB 718 subsequently made two trips to liberated Norway on photographic assignments. In August 1945 she was sailed by her wartime crew down to Portsmouth and paid off. MGB 2003 was sold to the Irish Navy as a patrol boat.

'Looking back now at the work of the 15th Motor Gun Boat Flotilla in the clandestine operations to Brittany and Norway,' wrote a former crew member, 'one can only marvel at the organisation and its total success in bringing off well over a hundred evaders and escapers, and landing and picking up many brave agents. In pitting the various skills we had acquired and the boats themselves as much against the weather as against the enemy, it was very satisfying to outwit both.'

The extraordinary work of the 15th MGBF did not go unrecognised in Britain and France. More decorations were awarded to the 125 sea-going officers and men of this small Flotilla than to any other comparable naval force. In each case the deeds for which they were awarded were cloaked beneath the laconic citation: 'For gallantry and distinguished service on hazardous operations.' Two DSOs, eighteen DSCs and thirty DSMs were awarded. A full list of British Gallantry Awards for the Flotilla is detailed in Annex B. The French were also generous with awards, as were the Americans.

These awards were well deserved. Their significant contributions to the war effort were numerous: the recovery of highly trained, valuable and essential aircrew; allowing the essential intelligence work of SIS to continue throughout the war by the delivery and recovery of agents and classified mail, including critical strategic intelligence relating to German U-boat operations, CROSSBOW – the V1 and V2 rocket sites – and the German coastal defences in Normandy; support for SOE operations by the delivery of stores and agents and the recovery of agents, in turn enabling SOE and the Resistance to support military operations prior to and after D-Day, through the likes of Virginia Hall and André Hué; and giving a valuable morale-boosting presence to the people of Brittany.

It should also be remembered that while the officers and men of the 15th Motor Gun Boat Flotilla showed exceptional courage and fortitude, they at least could return home to Dartmouth to the relative safety and comfort of a free country. The brave men and women of Brittany lived with the constant twenty-four-hour, seven-days-a-week, threat of discovery, torture and death, from which they had no respite from 1940 to 1944. That is a special kind of bravery, which should also not be forgotten.

As General Dwight Eisenhower, Supreme Allied Commander in Europe said, 'It takes little imagination to understand the sublime quality of the courage that, during Hitler's occupation of France, dedicated French citizens displayed in undertaking to rescue Allied fliers downed over France. They undertook the work deliberately and with the certain knowledge that they were risking not only their lives but those of all they held dear. This they did far from the excitement and frenzy of the battlefield. Their inspiration was their patriotism, the determination to see their beloved country freed from the domination of the hated Nazis and by their ideals of liberty and justice.'

Maurice Buckmaster, too, recognised the role of the French: 'The spirit and courage which informed those thousands of French patriots who worked with our envoys, "specially employed" abroad, provide evidence of the fundamental depth of French patriotism. Without the help of these brave men and women, no venture of the sort could have been attempted, and its measure of success is due to the unfailing dependability of the average man and woman in occupied France.' Francis Cammaerts, who won a DSO for his work for F Section, recognised that agents were trained volunteers: 'for the French it was their homes, their families, their children that they stood to lose. They stood to lose everything.'

The men and women agents of SIS and SOE were also exceptionally brave. They lived under constant threat of capture, certainly torture and probably death, every minute of every day, pretending to be someone else and having to be meticulous in their security. One slip was all that was required to send you to the Gestapo torture chambers of St Brieuc, or the Avenue Foch, followed by the firing squad if you were lucky, if not the meat-hooks of Buchenwald. Life as an agent was described by Jacques Baumel, the head of the Combat network in Marseille, as 'an underworld of frightening insecurity, where one slip, a discarded scrap of paper, falling asleep on an overnight train, forgetting the name of a school he had never attended in a town he had never seen, could lead to arrest, torture and death'.

*

After the war the veterans of the 15th MGBF endeavoured to keep in touch with each other, through personal contact and also through the Coastal Veterans Association. There are memorials at all the pinpoint sites in France, and, at Kingswear, many memorials to the agents and networks all over France. In the 1990s there were gatherings of Flotilla veterans and the French men and women they worked with. At one of these, David Birkin, who had been Navigating Officer on the mission that put him ashore, was presented with the Légion d'Honneur by President Mitterrand (MORLAND) in person.

On 9 May 1991 the Coastal Veterans Association erected a plaque on BONAPARTE beach. It reads:

THE CLANDESTINE OPERATIONS AT BONAPARTE AND OTHER BEACHES

BETWEEN ST. CAST AND L'ABER-VRAC'H WERE CARRIED OUT
BY ROYAL NAVY

MOTOR GUN BOATS OF THE 15TH MBG FLOTILLA OPERATING
FROM DARTMOUTH DURING 1942–44.

THE MEMBERS OF THE COASTAL FORCES VETERANS ASSOCIATION
SALUTE THEIR COMRADES OF THE RESISTANCE AND ESCAPE NETWORKS
HONOURING THEIR DEAD ALONG WITH THOSE BRITISH SAILORS WHO
DIED IN HMMGB 502.

LES OPERATIONS CLANDESTINES A LA PLAGE BONAPARTE COMME
A AUTRES ENTRE ST. CAST ET L'ABER-VRAC'H FURENT EFFECTUEES EN
1942–44 PAR DES CANONNIERES A MOTEUR APPARTENANT A LA FLOTILLE
15 MGB DE LA ROYAL NAVY DE LA BASE NAVALE DE DARTMOUTH.

LES ADHERENTS DE LA COASTAL FORCES VETERANS ASSOCIATION
SALUENT LEURS CAMARADES DE LA RESISTANCE ET DES RESEAUX
D'EVASION ET RENDENT HOMMAGE AUX FRANCAIS MORTS POUR LA
PATRIE EI AUX MARINS BRITTANIQUES QUI TROUVENT LA MORT A BORD
DE LA CANONNIERE HMMGB 502.

But the final word on the achievements of the Flotilla goes to the Director of Naval Intelligence Admiralty, who on 9 January 1945 described their achievements as follows:

'THESE OFFICERS AND MEN ARE OUTSTANDING REPRESENTATIVES OF
AN IRREGULAR NAVAL FLOTILLA WHICH HAS PERFORMED HAZARDOUS
DUTIES FOR ALL SERVICES SINCE THE FALL OF FRANCE. THE VALUE OF
THE SERVICES IS FULLY CONFIRMED.'

EPILOGUE

'My name's Bond, James Bond...'

In the opening sequence of the 1964 James Bond film *Goldfinger*, 007 climbs out of the sea in a wet suit, calmly blows up a heroin factory and then, mission accomplished, strips off his wet suit to reveal a white dinner jacket complete with red carnation buttonhole. The only jarring note – apart from the decoy gull on his head – is a touch of artistic licence that only someone with diving experience might notice. It should have been a dry suit.

Most viewers of the film probably regarded the moment as just another tongue-in-cheek Bond moment. They would be astonished to learn that the episode is based on fact.

At 0430 on the morning of 23 November 1940, a figure in a dinner jacket, smelling strongly of drink, staggered past German guards in the Dutch town of Scheveningen and subsequently made successful contact with Dutch Resistance workers. The man responsible for Operation CONTACT HOLLAND, which involved putting agents ashore from a motor gunboat, was Lieutenant Colonel Cuthbert Euan Charles Rabagliati, MC, AFC. Rabagliati was a soldier, pilot, racing car driver and an officer of the Secret Intelligence Service known as 'The Rabbi'.

The 'drunk' man in the dinner jacket was Peter Tazelaar, an SIS agent. If the guards ignored him as just another sad example of a defeated people consoling itself, they would have been astonished to learn that, not an hour before, Tazelaar had come ashore in a dry suit, but dressed to party underneath. Amazingly, the stunt worked.

To ensure his credentials when he met with Resistance contacts, Tazelaar carried, stitched inside the collar of his dress shirt, a hand-written message from Queen Wilhelmina, reduced to postage-stamp size by the Rabbi. Tazelaar's mission was to set up radio contact between Holland and London and to arrange for reports, maps or photographs which could not be transmitted by radio, to be brought out of the country by the same route through which he had just entered. The boat that put him ashore was MGB 325 from the 15th Motor Gun Boat Flotilla, then based at Great Yarmouth, but soon to move to Dartmouth. It was commanded by Peter Williams, who was destined to become the Senior Officer of the Flotilla.

The James Bond films had their imprint in the Second World War, and in the role of naval intelligence in particular. As everyone knows, the original novel of *Goldfinger* was written by Ian Fleming, who, as Commander Ian Fleming RNVR was the principal staff officer to the Director of Naval Intelligence. As with much of the content of the Bond films, the episode of the wet suit and dinner jacket was not in the original book, but during the making of the film Fleming collaborated closely with its director, Guy Hamilton. The story of Peter Tazelaar was part of a shared folklore which Hamilton knew well from his own war experiences.

Guy Hamilton had been in the film business before the war, in France. The outbreak of war found him in Nice, where he had worked a clapperboard on film sets. After the war, Hamilton went back to the film industry, working initially with John Huston on *The African Queen* and with Carol Reed on *The Third Man*. He was offered the opportunity to make the first Bond film, *Dr No*, but had to turn it down due to other commitments. He went on to make *Goldfinger*, *Diamonds are Forever*, *Live and Let Die* and *The Man with the Golden*

Peter Tazelaar

Gun. After Bond, he went on to make many other excellent films, including *The Battle of Britain*.

The screenplay for *Goldfinger* was written by Paul Dehn. Dehn spent the war in the Special Operations Executive, first as an instructor at the SOE Training School at Beaulieu and later Special Training School 103, or Camp X, in Canada, where he was the Chief Instructor. He knew Fleming and while at Beaulieu worked closely with Kim Philby to produce the SOE training syllabus. The Rabbi's daring scheme for SIS had become something of a *cause célèbre*, which many in SOE had envied and sought to emulate. Paul Dehn used his knowledge of the Rabbi's ruse to inject drama into the opening scene of the film.

'In the higher ranges of Secret Service work,' Winston Churchill once suggested, 'the actual facts in many cases are in every aspect equal to the most fantastic inventions of romance and melodrama. Tangle with tangle, plot and counterplot, ruse and treachery, cross and double cross, true agent, false agent, double agent, gold and steel, the bomb and the dagger and the firing party, were interwoven in many a texture so intricate as to be incredible, and yet true.'

The exploits of the 15th Motor Gun Boat Flotilla prove Churchill's point well.

APPENDIX – DRAMATIS PERSONAE: AFTER THE WAR

Below are some final thoughts on and information about what happened to the heroes of this story.

Claude Dansey retired in 1945 and went to live in Bathampton Manor near Bath. He died in the Lansdowne Grove Nursing Home, Bath in 1947. No doubt his toughness and ruthless determination to win created a dramatic success in the creation and maintenance of many very successful intelligence networks across France and Switzerland, even reaching into Germany, during the darkest days of the war. His collection operations sequentially enabled the Allies to beat the U-boat menace, invade Europe and counter the V1 and V2 attacks on London, all of which could have changed the outcome of the war. The close cooperation that Dansey fostered with the Free French BCRA, in particular the relationship between André Dewarvin, its head, Gilbert Renault, its principal staff officer, and Dansey and his two key officers Biffy Dunderdale and Kenneth Cohen, was the key to success. His antipathy to SOE was understandable, but perhaps unnecessarily antagonistic. SOE, although full of very brave men and women agents, did not cover itself in glory in the darkest period of the war, 1941/1942. It really came into its own in late 1943 and 1944 where its contribution to pre-D-Day sabotage and its disruption of German reinforcements heading to Normandy was essential to the overall strategic plan for the liberation of France. With the benefit of hindsight, it may have been more effective to maintain intelligence gathering, offensive action and escape and evasion under one agency to enable all three activities to be orchestrated in parallel within the overall strategic plan. It says a lot for DDOD(I) that they were able to operate so successfully for SIS while also serving the needs of SOE and MI9. Victor Cavendish-Bentinck, Duke of Portland, Head of the Joint Intelligence Committee, gave him a fitting epitaph – 'Claude Dansey? He was the best of them.'

Captain Frank Slocum, whose leadership led directly to the success of Clandestine Maritime Operations from Norway to the Adriatic, returned to SIS and took over the Administrative Directorate which was created in 1945 as part of the post-war reorganisation. When Slocum moved back to SIS from DDOD(I) he wrote to all his officers:

> 'I have today relinquished the duties of DDOD(I) to Captain H. B. Taylor and I want to express my sincere appreciation and gratitude for the loyalty and support I have received from you all.
>
> 'Through your enthusiasm and devotion, we have, between us, made a vital and successful contribution to the war effort, and it is this devotion that has made me so proud to be your leader, and to feel such regret at moving on to other duties. But, my new appointment will enable me to keep in touch with the activities of DDOD(I) as long as they continue, and I want every officer and man to know that I will, at any time in the future, do my best to help him, in return for the help and inspiration he has been to me.
>
> 'I would like to think that the brotherhood we have formed together may go on, so I have suggested a way in which we may keep in touch and meet periodically.
>
> 'Details of my plan are being sent to you separately; meanwhile I send you all my best wishes for much happiness and success in the future.
>
> F. A. Slocum Captain DDOD(I)'

The Administration Directorate of SIS that Frank Slocum (designated DO/Admin) headed was responsible for SIS's administration policies, supervised the administrative machinery, and chaired the Selection Committee and the Permanent Committee for Registry and Archives. He also managed organisational development, oversaw the administrative inspection of overseas stations, and ran the W Department, which handled the production of forged papers. Slocum went on to be Head of Station in Norway.

Commander Ted Davis, responsible for management training and clandestine maritime operations, succeeded Slocum as Head of Station in Norway and then became Head of R3 Section working out of the SIS London Station. This was the Naval Liaison Section. Davis recruited Lionel 'Buster' Crabb OBE GM, a retired Naval diver, for an operation to look at the hull of the Russian cruiser *Ordzhonikidze* on a state visit to Portsmouth Harbour. Davis, using the alias 'Matthew Smith', checked in to the Sally Port Hotel in Portsmouth on 17 April 1956. Just prior to the operation, Davis had a heart attack but carried on with the planned operation. Crabb did not return from the dive. Davis cleared their rooms at the Sally Port Hotel and removed the relevant pages from the hotel register. The government of the day handled the fallout very badly. Davis retired on health grounds and went to work for Marconi.

Davis was also responsible for Operation Jungle. This was an operation to land agents on the Baltic coast of Poland and the Baltic States from gunboats. The operation ran from 1949–55, run by SIS under the cover of the Baltic Fishing Protection Service. In all, they inserted forty-five agents, most of whom were killed or captured as the operation was compromised by Kim Philby. The gunboat part of the operation was considered a success, probably based on the experience gained in Brittany. The author, aged two in 1954, and living in Kiel (Germany) with his parents who were stationed there, remembers seeing them. The boats would anchor at times at the British Kiel Yacht Club. Operation Jungle will be the subject of a follow-up book.

Pat Whinney also joined SIS. Late in 1943 he had been sent to take command of Clandestine Naval Operations in the Mediterranean. After the war he remained in the Mediterranean area, eventually becoming SIS Head of Station in Athens.

David Birkin was offered a job by SIS but declined. He had not gone to Scotland with the Flotilla at the end of 1944 as his lungs had suffered after two years on operations almost continually at sea. Judy wanted him to take a rest and he was offered another medical procedure by the eminent ENT surgeon Sir Victor Negus. He chose a quieter life, first as a dairy farmer in Berkshire, and then living in London and the Isle of Wight, spending a lot of time painting. He also worked as a probation officer and did a lot of work for the rehabilitation of offenders. For the rest of his life Birkin kept closely in touch with his friends from the Flotilla. Frank Slocum became godfather to Andrew Birkin, his son. He also kept in touch with his Resistance friends in Brittany. He died in 1991. His wife Judy and daughter Jane scattered his ashes at Plage Bonaparte, Plage St Marguerite at Aber-Benoît, and at Beg-an-Fry. David Birkin overcame significant disabilities to become essential to the success of this dangerous enterprise.

Steven Mackenzie, who had married Slocum's secretary **Angela Sykes-Wright** in 1942, wrote DDOD(I)'s post-operational report in 1945. He joined SIS the same year, serving in Germany, Holland, Hong Kong and Argentina. He was also involved in planning the successful tunnelling operation in Berlin to tap in to the Russian Military telephone lines. He retired in 1969 and worked for Canning House, the Inchcape Group and Control Risks.

Biffy Dunderdale and **Kenneth Cohen** continued their SIS careers. Dunderdale became Controller Special Liaison, retired in 1959 and died in New York in 1990. Cohen became Director Personnel and then Controller Eastern Europe. He left SIS in 1953 with a CMG and CB and died in 1984. It should not be forgotten that many of Dunderdale and Cohen's agents were French intelligence officers who remained in France ostensibly working for the Vichy government, while, in reality, remaining 'in post' undercover and working for SIS – most notable among these were the Colonels Betrand and Rivet.

Ian Fleming who had introduced Mackenzie to Slocum, went on to write the James Bond books, as everyone knows. Many have claimed to know who were the models for the Bond characters. No one really knows, but Admiral Godfrey and Frank Slocum are contenders for 'M', and Biffy Dunderdale and Fitzroy Maclean – a close friend of Dunderdale in Paris before the war, and of Fleming's during and after the war – two of the many models for Bond.

Guy Hamilton had been in the film business before the war, in France. He went back to the film industry working initially with John Huston on *The African Queen* and Carol Reed on *The Third Man*. He was offered the opportunity to make the first Bond film *Dr No* but had to turn it down due to other commitments. He went on to make *Goldfinger*, *Diamonds are Forever*, *Live and Let Die* and *The Man with the Golden Gun*. Hamilton gave David Birkin's son Andrew his first job in the film business as a 'runner', later letting him direct the second unit on *Diamonds are Forever*. After Bond, he went on to make many other excellent films including *The Battle of Britain*. He died in 2016.

Paul Dehn continued to work for SOE until the end of the war, moving from Camp X in Canada, to missions in France and Norway. After the war he returned to the arts as an author, poet, film critic and screen writer for a long list of award-winning films including *Goldfinger*, *Murder on the Orient Express* and *The Spy Who Came in from the Cold*. He died in 1976.

Dunstan Curtis who commanded 314 and then briefly 501 before he left the Flotilla, went on to join Ian Fleming's 'Red Indians', 30 Assault Unit, whose job was to go ashore in France after D-Day and recover intelligence and technical material and equipment. He was another contender for the James Bond character, along with Biffy Dunderdale and Fitzroy Maclean. After the war he was adopted as a Liberal candidate. He then joined the European movement and helped draft the European Convention on Human Rights. He died in 1983.

Peter Williams left the Navy in 1945, became a successful solicitor and dairy farmer. He died in 2019.

Ronnie Seddon went back to and ran his father-in-law's toy-making firm – Middlesex Toy Industries Ltd, which held the Walt Disney characters franchise for the UK. He also became a very keen golfer. He died in 1998.

Jan McQuoid Mason left the Navy in January 1946. He wanted to return to South Africa and play a role in the building of the Union of South Africa Navy. However, he was disappointed that his wartime rank would not be recognised by the South African Navy, and as an English-speaking South African his timing was wrong, due to the newly elected National Government in South Africa purging the government services of English speakers in their desire to 'Afrikaner' the state. After a few years in the Johannesburg area (where he unsuccessfully ran as a candidate for parliament representing the United Party) he settled in Bulawayo, Rhodesia.

Charles Martin went on to command another gunboat – No 8, 'Grey Wolf' – and took part in the D-Day landings at Omaha Beach. After the war he didn't return to motor racing but spent his time sailing with his wife in the Bay of Biscay and Mediterranean. He died in 1993.

Lloyd Bott returned to Australia and joined the Department of Supply. He became the Deputy Secretary in 1967. He brokered the deal between France and Australia for the procurement of Mirage fighter jets. He made many trips to France and was able to keep closely in touch with many members of the VAR and SHELBURNE networks. He was responsible for the administration of US space projects in Australia including during the Apollo II moon landing. He retired in 1975 and died in 2004.

Michael Pollard left the Flotilla in April 1944 and joined the cruiser HMS DESPATCH in time for the D-Day landings, subsequently serving in HMS BULOLO in the Far East. He left the Navy at the end of the war and returned to the family printing firm in Exeter. Being a keen sailor, he would regularly sail to the Aber-Wrac'h and re-establish contact with his Resistance friends.

Mathilde Carré was held in prison in Britain, first in Holloway and then in Aylesbury, and then deported to France. She was put on trial on 3 January 1949, and sentenced to death on 7 January. Three months later her sentence was commuted to twenty years in prison; however, she was released in 1957 and became a recluse. She died in Paris in 2004.

Pierre de Vomécourt returned to France, was captured by Bleicher, but at his trial persuaded the judge to treat him as a POW. He avoided a concentration camp and spent the rest of the war in Colditz. He returned to France after the war. He died in 1996.

Ben Cowburn was awarded the MC and Bar, the Croix de Guerre and Legion of Honour. He settled in France and went back to working as a consultant, behind the scenes, in the oil industry. He died in 1994.

Peter Harratt, the SOE Conducting Officer and close friend of David Birkin, went into France in 1944 on an SOE mission to support the Maquis. He had already been awarded an MC for his work with the Flotilla, and was awarded a bar to the MC and a DSO. His mission, code-named PEDLAR, involved him being infiltrated through Spain, walking across the Pyrenees, then making his way on foot, bicycle and car across the length of France, before finally swimming the Marne river to join the PEDLAR team. After the war he left the British Army, and became briefly attached to the Dutch Army. He then joined the British Frontier Service in north-west Germany, based at Oldenburg. He died of a brain haemorrhage in hospital at RAF Rostrup on 11 March 1956. Sadly, David Birkin lost touch with him after the war. When he subsequently heard that he had died, he wrote, 'Peter was a mystery man, so I suppose it was fitting that he disappeared from my life as secretly as he had entered it.' Buckmaster noted on his file 'one of the most courageous men I have ever known. Determined and cunning. Took the greatest pains to brief himself with the fullest possible information before attempting a job, then carried it out with dash.'

Erwin Denman was awarded an MC in 1944. He served briefly in the Control Commission in Germany, before working as Secretary to the Arts Committee for the London Olympic Games in 1948. He then became an entrepreneur in the Belgian Congo, returning to London in the early 1960s. When Peter Harratt died in 1956, Denman changed his name to Peter as a mark of respect for his old friend. Denman died in Essex in 1998.

Jimmy Langley left the Army in 1946 but remained in the reserve until 1966. After the war he worked for Fison's until 1967, then ran a bookshop in Suffolk with his wife Peggy Van Lier, a member of the Belgian COMET Line whom he met in 1944. He died in 1983.

Airey Neave went on to be a prominent Conservative politician and close confidant of Margaret Thatcher. On 30 March 1979 he was killed by a car bomb planted by the Irish National Liberation Army terrorist group.

Patrick Wyndham-Wright joined SIS after the war. He worked in Africa, then retired to a farm in Kenya where he died in 1975.

Suzanne Warengham changed her surname to Charisie, and married her husband André who had worked with OSS. They settled in England, Suzanne suffering from ill health following her war time experiences. Valentine Blanche Charlet, her fellow escaper, died in London in 1985. She had been the oldest female agent in SOE. On her return to Britain in 1944 she was 'retired' from SOE on 30 June 1944, her file marked 'free to find other employment'. She never fully recovered from her war time experiences and died a recluse.

André Hué was parachuted back into France just before D-Day, in order to organise the Resistance to support Four SAS who had parachuted into Brittany to cause havoc behind enemy lines. On 18 June he took part in a very large battle between the SAS and Resistance and a large German force with tanks. After the liberation of Brittany, Hué moved on to Nevers in Burgundy to coordinate Maquis activities, followed by Dijon, where his teams attacked Germans withdrawing from the South of France. Hué was awarded the DSO for his work in France. He finished the war with Force 136 in Burma, after which he held the rank of Major in the British Army, serving in Palestine, Cyprus and Cambodia. He later joined SIS and worked in the Far East, before going on to have a successful business career in Paraguay, Senegal, Malawi and France. In 1980 he retired to Sussex, and died in 2005.

Virginia Hall, after her return to France as a wireless operator, became a network organiser and leader in the Haute Loire, where she organised the harassment of retreating Germans and eventually forced them to withdraw, liberating the area. She went on to Paris in September, and then back to Lyon to find all the people who had worked with her; many had survived but not her three nephews, who had been executed at Buchenwald. The priest and German agent, Robert Alesch, who had betrayed her network in Lyon, was captured and executed. Hall was given the MBE by Britain, the Croix de Guerre by France and the Distinguished Service Cross by the Americans. After the war she married an OSS officer and joined the CIA. She retired in 1966 and died in 1982. In 2016, a CIA training facility was named after her. The in-house CIA museum gives five individuals sections in its catalogue, one of whom is Virginia Hall, the other four being CIA directors. There is also a painting of her working her radio in France in 1944 in the CIA art collection.

Maurice Buckmaster was rather shabbily treated, only receiving an OBE in spite of General Eisenhower crediting F Section as like having 'an extra 15 Divisions. They shortened the war by six months.' MRD Foot described him as a 'colourful and, in many ways, a controversial figure. He was not universally popular, but no better Head of the Section was ever in sight.' After the war he rejoined the Ford Motor Company and died in 1992.

Joel Le Tac returned to France from the concentration camps, where he joined the French Army and served in the Korean War. After this he went to work for the fashion house Molyneaux, before joining the French Secret Service. Later, he became a war correspondent for *Paris Match* and eventually entered politics. For his war time work in SOE he was given the Military Medal as well as French and American decorations.

Pierre Hentic ('MAHO') was sent to Dachau after his arrest and imprisonment in France, from where he was liberated in 1945. After the war, in a letter to the head of MI9 dated 1 September 1945, Tom Green – an SIS officer who worked with Biffy Dunderdale – wrote, 'Of all the agents I have come into contact with during this war, none took more risks, had more successes, was more honest, and certainly less assuming, than Hentic.' Michael Pollard thought Hentic had died in Dachau until, on 9 January 1996, he received a letter from Hentic. He joined the French Army Parachute troops and went to Indo-China with the 1er Bataillon de Choc, conducting commando operations. In his second tour he became a captain, leading a team of indigenous troops in the Groupement de Commandos Mixtes Aeroportes, a parachute unit working on the Plateux Hrés. After Indo-China he went to Algeria with the action service of the French foreign intelligence service, SDECE, forerunner of the DGSE, on Operation 'Oiseau Bleu'. This was designed to train up a force of locals, the Clan Kabyle, to fight against the FLN, but having already been penetrated, they turned against the French after being armed and trained.

Hentic was sent to sort out the mess, which ended with 11e Regiment Parachutist de Choc and the 3e Regiment Parachutist Coloniaux attacking them between 9–12 October 1956. One hundred and twenty-two rebels were killed and nineteen French. Hentic was promoted to Colonel in 1960 and returned to France in 1961. He was a fanatical skier and set up a combination of parachuting, skiing and shooting competitions. He left the army in 1966, and died on 9 March 2004. Among many decorations he was awarded the Commander of the Legion of Honour, a British MBE (many believe an MBE did not reflect his bravery and contribution, and that a DSO would have been more appropriate), the US Medal of Freedom, the Resistance Medal and Croix de Guerre (with thirteen bars).

With regard to the other key members of the JADE FITZROY network, **Phillip Keun** and **SAROL** died in Buchenwald, **Joseph Mouden** in Neuengamme. Jean-François Derrien went on the run in 1944, joining the local Maquis. After the war he did not return to the Gendarmerie, but became Head of Security at the Nuclear Power Station on the Cherbourg Peninsula. He later retired to St Pol de Leon near Roscoff.

Louis Bodiger had a very close escape when the Germans came to arrest him, jumping out the window and managing to disappear. He too joined the local Maquis fighting the Germans until the liberation of Lannilis, after which he went back to running his transport business.

Amédée Rolland continued his Resistance work after the Aber-Wrac'h saga, 'going active' and arranging weapon drops, and subsequently taking part in offensive action against the Germans. He had a very close shave when, after a weapon drop, he used the billiard table in his café as a transit hide. The Germans burst into the café and went straight for the billiard table, but were puzzled and angry to find nothing – the weapons had been moved thirty minutes before. This event, and the circumstances of Job Moudan's arrest, point to a traitor within the group, but he was never caught. Rolland was highly decorated by the British, American and French Governments. Sadly, however, the stress of his heroic Resistance work took its toll, and he died a young man in June 1948.

Claude Tanguy returned to his business and built it into a huge enterprise, still based in Lannilis. His son Edouard is the last living member of the JADE FITZROY network.

Jean Tréhiou, the SHELBURNE volunteer who went to England, returned to Brittany to conduct more offensive operations. After the war he joined the First French Colonial Parachute Battalion in Indo-China. While commanding the company that made the last night parachute jump to reinforce Dien Bien Phu, he was wounded and captured. After returning to France he was posted to Algeria to the Ninth Régiment de Chasseurs Parachutistes and returned in 1961 with the rank of Lieutenant Colonel. His decorations included the Cross of Military Valour, the British King's Medal, the American Medal of Freedom and the Grand Officier of the Légion d'Honneur. He returned home to Plouha and died in 2013.

The other key members of the SHELBURNE team largely resumed their everyday lives. **Mathurin Branchoux** went back to his vegetable business. **George Le Cun** continued in his radio and electrical business, before moving to North Africa, where he is believed to have lived until he died. **François Le Cornec** found it difficult to settle, moving to Paris in 1946 to set up a café and grocery business, and afterwards to Chantenay and Dinard, finally joining the Ministry of Finance in 1959 (d. 1976). **Job Mainguy** rejoined the Merchant Marines (d. 1996). **Pierre Huet** also went back to his pre-war work as a military pilot until he retired (d. 1991). **Marie Thérèse Le Calvez** married, moved to Canada and had two children. She was quickly divorced and returned to France in the 1980s, where she died in 1990 following a long stretch of ill health.

Lucien Dumais and **Raymond Labrosse** stayed in France and helped the Resistance carry out offensive action against the retreating Germans. Thereafter Dumais helped hunt down collaborators and Gestapo men in hiding. Labrosse joined the SIS office in Paris. He retired as Captain in 1946 (d. 1993). Labrosse went back to the Canadian Army and fought in the Korean War. He reached the rank of Lieutenant Colonel, before retiring in 1971.

François Mitterrand ('MORLAND') became President of France.

ANNEX A

15 MGBF OPERATIONS

OPERATIONS	DATE	BOAT	PINPOINT	NOTES
PILLAR	1/12/41 27/12/41 5/1/42	MASB36	Île Rohen	Unable to find dead-letter box unsuitable boat
OVERCLOUD I	31/12/41	MGB 314	Île Guénnoc	
OVERCLOUD II	6/1/42	MGB 314	Île Guénnoc	
PICKAXE	10/1/42	MGB 314	Moulin-de-la Rive	
OVERCLOUD III (TURQUOISE)	1/2/42	MGB 314	Île Guénnoc	Le Tac brothers
WATERWORKS	12/2/42	MGB 314	Moulin-de-la Rive	'La Chatte'
ROWAN	19/20/21/ 26/27/2/42	MGB 314	Moulin-de-la Rive	Attempts to pick up La Chatte
CARPENTER I–VII	October/ November 1942	MGB 318	Île de Batz operations	Useless LARDERING
TENDERLEY	24/1/43	MGB 318	Île Losquet Triagoz plateau	To lay sonar buoys as an aid to navigation
TENTATIVE	13/2/43	MGB 318	Île de Batz Méan Nevez	As above
DRAPER	10/3/43	MGB 318	Île Stagadon	
COOK	28/3/43 3/4/43	MGB 318	Île Guénnoc	
HAPPEN	27/9/43	MGB 318	Clogouren	
ENVIOUS I	3/11/43	MGB 318	Île Rosservor	Beginning of L'Aber-Wrac'h saga
ENVIOUS II	26/11/43	MGB 318	Île Guénnoc	MAHO
JEALOUS II	26/11/43	MGB 502	Pointe-de-Saint Cast	VAR
ENVIOUS II b	2/12/43	MGB 318	Île Guénnoc	Polland left ashore

JEALOUS III	23/12/43	MGB 502	Pointe-de-Saint Cast	VAR Line Harratt/ Denman
FELICITATE	23/12/43 25/12/43	MGB 318	Île Guénnoc	Successful evacuation end of L'Aber-Wrac'h saga
EASEMENT	28/29/1/44	MGB 502	Beg-an-Fry	
BONAPARTE	28/1/44	MGB 503	Anse-Cochat	SHELBURNE
FLANNEL FOOT	29/1/44	MGB 318	Île d'Er	
GLOVER	23/2/44	MGB 503	Île à Canton	
EASEMENT II	26/2/44	MGB 502	Beg-an-Fry	Mitterrand
BONAPARTE II	26/2/44	MGB 503	Anse-Cochat	SHELBURNE
EASEMENT III	29/2/44	MGB 502	Beg-an-Fry	VAR
BONAPARTE III	16/3/44	MGB 502	Anse-Cochat	SHELBURNE
SEPTIMUS I	17/3/44	MGB 503	Beg-an-Fry	VAR
BONAPARTE IV	19/3/44	MGB 503	Anse-Cochat	SHELBURNE
GLOVER II	21/3/44	MGB 503	Île à Canton	
SEPTIMUS II	21/3/44	MGB 502	Beg-an-Fry	VAR Virginia Hall
BONAPARTE V	23/3/44	MGB 503	Anse-Cochat	SHELBURNE
FLANNEL FOOT II	23/25/ 3/44	MGB 318	Île d'Er	
SEPTIMUS III	26/3/44	MGB 503	Beg-an-Fry	VAR
SCARF	15/4/44	MGB 502 MGB 718	Beg-an-Fry	VAR Warengham
GLOVER III	22/4/44	MGB 503	Île à Canton	
SPLINT	25/4/44	MGB 502	Trégurier River	Rousseau
GLOVER IV	19/5/44 24/5/44	PT 71,72	Île Grande	
CYGNUS	28/29/5/44	MGB 718	Batalden	NORWAY
REFLEXION	15/6/44	MGB 718	Anse-Cochat	SHELBURNE Hamilton left ashore
GLOVER V	17/6/44	MGB 314	Île Grande	
GIRAFFE	24/6/44	PT 79	PT199	Beg-an-Fry
CROZIER	12/7/44	MGB 503	Anse-Cochat	SHELBURNE

ROBESPIERRE	14/7/44	MGB 502	Île de Batz	
GLOVER VI	16/7/44	MGB 318	Île Grande	
GLOVER VII	23/7/44	MGB 318	Île Grande	
CROZIER II	23/7/44	MGB 502	Anse-Cochat	SHELBURNE
GLOVER VIII	29/7/44	MGB 318	Île Grande	
GLOVER IX	5/8/44	MGB 318	Île Grande	
CROZIER III	9/8/44	MGB 718	Anse-Cochat	SHELBURNE
HAVEN	25/8/44	MGB 718	Lannion Bay	
ROBESPIERRE III	25/8/44	MGB 318	Clogouren	Robespierre II cancelled
ROBESPIERRE IV	27/8/44	MGB 318	Clogouren	
KORDA I	1/9/44	MGB 318	L'Aber-Wrac'h	Daylight photo recce mission
KORDA II	6/9/44	MGB 718	L'Aber-Wrac'h	
KNOCKOUT	16-19/9/44	MGB 718	Ushant	
AQUARIOUS III	2/3/11/44	MGB 718	Skarvøy	NORWAY
LOLA	12/15/2/45	MGB 718	Sandøy	NORWAY
SELMA I	6/4/45	MGB 718	Skarvøy	NORWAY
SELMA II	13/4/45	MGB 718	Skarvøy	NORWAY
BARBERO III	28/29/4/45	MGB 718	Skarvøy	NORWAY

ANNEX B

DECORATIONS

The 15th MGBF were the most highly decorated unit during World War II. Below is the list of British awards. Many of the recipients also received French, American and other Allied awards.

DDOD(I) STAFF

Captain F Slocum	CMG OBE (OBE awarded before the war, CMG after)
Lieutenant Commander S M Mackenzie	DSO and Bar
Lieutenant Commander P F Whinney	DSC
Lieutenant Commander W B Luard	OBE

15th MGBF HEADQUARTERS STAFF

Commander E A G Davis	DSO and Bar
Lieutenant D L Birkin	DSC
Lieutenant M P Salmond	DSC

GUNBOATS OFFICERS

Lieutenant Commander D Curtis	DSC and Bar
Lieutenant J T McQuoid Mason	DSC
Lieutenant Commander P A Williams	DSC
Sub-Lieutenant D N Millar	DSC
Lieutenant K M Uhr-Henry	DSC
Lieutenant Commander R M Marshall	DSC and Bar
Lieutenant A Smith	DSC
Lieutenant A F Bott	DSC
Lieutenant R F Seddon	DSC
Lieutenant M I G Hamilton	DSC
Lieutenant C Martin	DSC

SHIPS CREW

Petty Officer H E Mould	DSM and Bar
Petty Officer C F Heam	DSM
Petty Officer F S Smith	DSM
Petty Officer W Webb	DSM
Petty Officer G Cummins	DSM
Petty Officer W Cartwright	DSM
Able Seaman R Bartley	DSM
Able Seaman H Pickles	DSM
Able Seaman P Lumsley	DSM
Able Seaman J Gordon	DSM
Able Seaman J Markham	DSM
Able Seaman R Bracey	DSM
Able Seaman J Matheau	DSM
Able Seaman J Hayden	DSM
Telegraphist C Milner	DSM
Telegraphist H Banks	DSM

Telegraphist C Gadd	DSM
Stoker K Peel	DSM
Stoker S Newton	DSM
Stoker A Andrews	DSM
Leading Seaman A Hibbert	DSM
Leading Seaman C Stanley	DSM
Leading Seaman A Dellow	DSM
Leading Seaman R Rive	DSM
Able Seaman G G Hill	DSM
Able Seaman O Beasdale	DSM
Able Seaman J Daglish	DSM
Able Seaman C Wren	DSM
Able Seaman A Tomer	DSM
Able Seaman N Hué	DSM
Able Seaman J Prayle	DSM
Able Seaman H Rockwood	DSM
Able Seaman A Walker	DSM
Able Seaman P Brannon	DSM

Officers and men of the 15th Motor Gunboat Flotilla. From left to right: John Markham DSM, Kenneth Peel DSM or Ronald Bracey DSM (hidden), James Gordon DSM, Lieut. M P (Tich) Salmond DSC, Lieut. David Birkin DSC, Lieut.-Cdr Peter Williams DSC, Roger Bartley DSM, P.O. Fred Smith DSM (hidden), Alfred Hibbert DSM, P.O. William Webb DSM, Commander Edward Davis DSO & Bar, P.O. H E Mould DSM & Bar, Charles Gadd DSM, John Hayden DSM, Harold Pickles DSM (partly hidden), Henry Banks DSM, Paul Lumsley DSM, Altfred Andrews DSM.

L–R Steven Mackenzie, Ted Davis, Bill Luard
receiving the Croix de Guerre from General Koenig 1943

ANNEX C

DAVID BIRKIN'S CITATION

Lieutenant D. L. Birkin, RNVR

a Next to his Commanding Officer, Lieutenant Birkin is perhaps the most outstanding officer in the Flotilla. He joined DDOD(I) in January 1942 on being commissioned from the rating of Telegraphist, and after a course in navigation and pilotage was appointed to the 15th MGB Flotilla.

b From an enthusiastic amateur he has developed into an able navigator and pilot far in excess of his two years' experience; has 28 operations into enemy waters as Navigating Officer of the Expedition to his credit and has on 9 occasions been specially mentioned by the Commanding Officer of the Expedition.

c Since precise navigation and pilotage are essential features of these clandestine operations, and Lieutenant Birkin is handicapped by a tendency to seasickness and a chronic sinus disability which frequently gives him considerable pain, his performance is the more noteworthy.

d He has experienced in full measure the dangers and discomforts already described in this history, which in the worst weather conditions under which the Flotilla operates approach the limit of endurance of the physically fit, as DDOD(I) can testify from personal experience.

e He has in addition been in charge of surf-boats between the mother ship and the enemy shore, and on one occasion in the month of January he with another officer stood for 1½ hours in surf holding the boat in position since it could be beached or withdrawn to seaward, whilst the negotiations were proceeding onshore practically under the noses of the enemy coast patrols.

Although Birkin's citation says he concluded 28 operations, the total was in fact 33 of the 57 operations carried out by the Flotilla from 1942–44.

Of those 33 missions, 24 resulted in successful arrival at the pinpoint, the other missions were not successful due either to poor visibility or extreme weather, not as a result of faulty navigation.

ANNEX D

ROLL OF HONOUR OF THOSE WHO DIED IN MGB 502 12 MAY 1945

OFFICERS

Robert Michael Marshall	DSC	Lt Commander RNVR
Leslie Hubert Hughes-Coppins		
Gordon Hamilton Bell	Lt RNVR	
John R Boissier	Sub Lt RNVR	
J Meakes	Sub Lt RNVR	

RATINGS

Alfred A Andrews	DSM	Leading Stoker
Roger Bartley	DSM	Able Seaman
Oliver Bleasdale	DSM	Leading Seaman
Frederick J Bristow		Leading Stoker
Desmond Charlesworth		Wireman (L)
Charles K Gadd	DSM	Leading Telegraphist
James G Gordon	DSM	Able Seaman
Daniel Gourley		Leading Telegraphist
Bernard Hawksby		Leading Seaman (radar)
John Hayden	DSM	Able Seaman
Eric G Hearn		Able Seaman
Charles F Hearn	DSM	Chief Motor Mechanic
George I Hill	DSM	Able Seaman
Leslie I McLanaghan		Able Seaman
Anthony A McNulty		Ordinary Seaman (radar)
John S Markham	DSM	Able Seaman
John M Pender		Leading Motor Mechanic
Frederick S Smith	DSM	Petty Officer Coxswain
Cyril W Wren	DSM	Able Seaman

PASSENGERS

Sylvanus Brian John Reynolds		
Served as Brian Bingham	MBE, DSC	Lt Commander RNR
Herbert W Jackson		First Mate
C Newton		First Mate
G V Morgan		W/T Operator

ANNEX E

David Birkin's navigating notebook

ANNEX F

JEANNIE ROUSSEAU (AMNIARIX) REPORT

Information communicated by a captain (active list) attached to the experimental centre in question.

Concentrated on the island of Usedon (north of Stettin) are the laboratories and scientific research services for the improvement of existing weapons and the perfecting of new weapons. The island itself is very closely guarded. To gain admittance, in addition to the military identity book, three special permits are needed:

Sondergenehmigung	watermarked paper.
Zusatz	orange card.
Vorläufigergenehmigung	white paper.

The administrative services are at Peenemünde and ... (an illegible name).

Research is centred on:

(a) bombs and shells guided independently of the laws of ballistics.

(b) a stratospheric shell.

(c) bacteria employed as a weapon.

Kampfgruppe KG 100 is reported to be experimenting at present with bombs guided by the bomb aimer from the aircraft. These bombs could be guided from such a distance that the plane could remain out of range of AA fire. Accuracy is said to be perfect if the plane does not have to defend itself against fighters.

The final stage in the development of a stratospheric bomb of an entirely new type is said to have been reached. This bomb is reported to be 10 cubic metres in volume and to be filled with explosive. It is said to be launched almost vertically to reach the stratosphere as rapidly as possible. The speeds of 50 mph vertically. The initial velocity is said to be maintained by successive explosions. The bomb is said to be provided with Raketten (vanes?) and guided to specific targets. The bomb is said to be fuelled with 800 litres of petrol, necessary even in the experimental stage, in which the shell is not filled with explosive, to enable it to carry. The horizontal range is 300 miles. Trials are said to have been made without explosive charge, from Usedon towards the Baltic and to have reached Königsberg. The noise is said to be as deafening as a Flying Fortress. The trials are reported to have given at first excellent results as regards accuracy. Hitler is understood to have alluded to the success of these trials when he spoke of 'new weapons that will change the face of the war when the Germans use them'.

Difficulties are said to have developed quite recently, only half the bombs hitting the selected targets accurately. It is reported that this recent fault is expected to be remedied towards the end of the month.

Colonel Wachtel and the officer that he has collected are reported to from the cadres of an anti-aircraft regiment (16 batteries of 220 men, the 155 W, that is going to be stationed in France, end of October or beginning of November, HQ in the vicinity of Amiens, the batteries between Amiens, Abbeville and Dunkirk).

The regiment is said to dispose of 108 (one hundred and eight) catapults able to fire a bomb every twenty minutes. The army artillery is said to have more than 400 catapults sited from Brittany to Holland.

The artillery regiments would be supplied with these devices as and when there is a sufficient production of ammunition.

The expert Sommerfeld is said to estimate that 50–100 of these bombs would suffice to destroy London. (Major Sommerfeld is Colonel Wachtel's technical adviser.)

The batteries are said to be so sited that they would methodically destroy most of Britain's large cities during the winter.

Reinforced concrete platforms are reported to be already under construction. It is thought they will be fully operational in November.

The German experts are said to be aware that British experts are working on the same problem. They think they are sure of a three to four months lead.'

She also reported on the air defence regiment charged with defending the rocket launch sites in France:

Following numerous air reconnaissance flights and bombing, the H.Q. of the A.A. 'WACHTEL' regiment was transferred from DOULLENS to a chateau in CREIL region, exactly 55 km. from PARIS, and in the immediate vicinity of a small town indicated in German by the initials: 'M.b.B.' that is to say: 'Ms.B.' or 'M.e.B.' MARCQ-en-BAROEIL?). the transfer was made under conditions of the utmost secrecy; the H.Q. Staff believe that the emplacement is still unknown as there has not yet been any reconnaissance from the air.

However, the unit keeps at DOULLENS an important relay-ration called 'Dohle' in telephone conversations; the 'WACHTEL' regiment is called 'Flakgruppe Creil' in the army telephone organisation. The totem of the regiment is:

which is made from the C.O.'s name.

The full Staff is expected at H.Q. for the beginning of January which comprises 20 officers. Colonel WACHTEL himself will be in continual residence at his H.Q., for he goes on inspection missions in BELGIUM and also makes frequent journeys to PARIS, BERLIN, and ZEMPIN, to supervise the finishing touches to the stratospheric rocket. It is reported that the platforms are ready and the personnel standing by, but the guns will only be set up on their emplacement in March.

The officers of this unit expect a Commando raid or even a landing having for mission to prevent the use of this weapon. The CREIL H.Q. is said to be very strongly defended (electric network, ? patrolling, A.A. Defences always at the ready).

It might be possible for an interpreter in charge of the purchasing for the account of the unit, and acting as liaison with the French authorities, to gain access into the H.Q..

ANNEX G

MAJOLLICA

As well as being an excellent mathematician and artist, David Birkin could turn his hand to the odd ditty. He composed one called 'Majollica' (Majollica was the codeword to begin Operations for D-Day):

'MAJOLLICA'

D-Day came and D-Day went
without a codeword being sent
and thousands waited near and far
for the magic word 'Majollica'.

Majollica A-1 Stat C
plus XYZ and MFE
D4 + 10 divide by 2
many an agent wait their cue
each pinning hopes upon that star
that magic word 'Majollica'.

In London hopes were running high,
the staff of DDOD(I)
demanded when the ship would sail
and from Dartmouth came a dismal wail:
'We cannot leave the bloody bar
without the word "Majollica".'

For once at least each MGB
was fit enough to put to sea;
on each bridge, each bold CO
was raring for the word to go
but the only snag there'd be so far:
no mention of Majollica.

A coded signal came daily through
on scrambled wires to base HQ
Dartmouth then replied in kind
exactly what they had in mind
which wasn't much for no one knew
what everyone was meant to do.

Each morning sharp at half-past nine
what'r the weather wet or fine
a signal flashed from Westward Ho
presumably designed to show
the state the MGB's was in
could she be sent the word to go.

The sombre house in Palace Street
is where the cloak and dagger meet
behind whose ever guarded doors
disguised men with clench-ed jaws
sit hashing complicated schemes
involving fairy books and dreams
their veil of secrecy, these men
who with a stroke of fountain pen
or pencil as the case may be
can send an MGB to sea.

Your orders are, you must not fail
proceed at once, forget the gale
and bury this enormous box
of chewing gum behind the rocks.
A Wren arrives each night by car
each package stamped 'Majollica'.

In secret codes these chosen few
talk cautiously of D+2
and muffled voices spoke in awe
of landing on a foreign shore;
to all in vain through door ajar
one word leaked out – 'Majollica'.

It happened that a German spy
Fritz Hoffman Schloss was passing by
'Mein Gott!' he cried and rushed to get
tapping on his wireless set:
'Mein Führer das ist wunderbar
I've heard the magic word "Majollica".'

The news electrified Berlin
whose hopes had worn a little thin
experts rushed from far or near
with special trains of bulky gear.
With feverish haste they worked all night
to try and get its meaning right;
in vain by dawn they'd not got far
in breaking down Majollica.

They tried and tried for days and days
with secret inks and violet rays
and cypher experts soon became
compelled to bow their heads in shame.

SOURCES

1. PRIVATE PAPERS

The primary sources for this book are previously unpublished private papers. I am indebted to Andrew and Jane Birkin, Rodney Seddon and David Lingard, the curator of the Dartmouth Museum.

- The private papers of David Birkin. These contain audio recordings, film, photographs and letters, original documents and David Birkin's first-hand accounts of the operations.
- Documents held by the Dartmouth Museum.
  - The papers of Michael Pollard including his original hand-written account of his time ashore in Brittany and Paris, and post-war correspondence with Pierre Hentic.
  - Personal account of Able Seaman Harold Pickles DSM.
  - Letters between Michael Pollard and members of the JADE FITZROY network.
  - Personal account of JADE FITZROY operations 'La Manche et La Belle' by Louis Coum.
  - Wartime memoirs of Lloyd Bott CBE DSC.
- The papers of Ronnie Seddon held by his son Rodney Seddon, collated in the book *HM MTB 718 'Something Special'* and the associated website: www.mtb718.co.uk.
- Papers and photographs from the Slocum family archive.
- Papers and photographs from Colette Pronost and Sylvie Carette – Amédée Rolland.
- Steven Mackenzie Papers IWM.
- Photographs from Hentic collection.
- Photographs and notes courtesy of Aurélien Coquil, Musée Mémoires 39-45 de Plougonvelin.

2. INTERVIEWS AND CORRESPONDENCE

I have had help from many people either by interview or correspondence:

- Andrew Birkin
- Jane Birkin
- Edouard Tanguy – JADE FITZROY
- Geoffrey Pidgeon – SIS
- Noreen Riols – SOE
- Slocum family
- Anne Alexandre – Daughter of Pierre Hentic

- Claude Bénech
- Charles Cassells
- Donal McQuoid Mason – Son of Lt Cdr Jan McQuoid Mason
- John Andrews – Secretary Special Forces Club
- David Anderson – Secretary White's
- Jill Millard Shapiro – Windmill Theatre history and photo archive
- Sabine Stein – Buchenwald Archive
- Sylvie Carette – Granddaughter of Amédée Rolland JADE FITZROY
- Colette Pronost – Granddaughter of Amédée Rolland JADE FITZROY
- Cécile le Roux – Mayor of Lannilis
- Daniel Dagorn – Le Télégramme
- Paul McCue – SOE Archive
- Kevin Costello – Coastal Forces Veterans Association
- James Luard
- Anthony Agar
- Peter Hore
- Andrew Pollard

3. FILES

Admiralty files (ADM series)

NID(c) – institution of	**ADM 1/12835**
Lt Martin DSC award	**ADM 1/14598**
Lt Lomenech award of Croix de Guerre	**ADM 1/29690**
Shelburn Medal recommendations 1	**ADM 1/18977**
Shelburn Medal recommendations 2	**ADM 1/6951**
MGB 501 Sinking of	**ADM 234/498**
MGB 501 Court of Enquiry	**ADM 267/131**
MGB 501 Technical reports	**ADM 226/48**
Letter & Number codes for Channel Flotillas	**ADM 334/25**
Plymouth Command: War Diaries 1941	**ADM 199/655**
Plymouth Command: War Diaries 1942	**ADM 199/422**
1st Westward Ho arrives @ Dartmouth 07/12/43	**ADM 199/633**

SOE files (HS series)

Operation reports:

Operation Pickaxe report	**HS 4/340**
Operations Felicitate, Marie-Louise & Robespierre	**HS 7/25**
Operations Tenderly, Cook & Happen	**HS 7/26**
Operations Carpenter & Mirfield	**HS 7/24**

Headquarters reports:

Dartmouth & Helston flotillas Ops post D-Day	**HS8/777**
Helford & Dartmouth establishments	**HS8/777**

SOE agent files

SOE agent Cann (SOE file)	**HS9/263/5**
SOE agent Sicot (Aristide)	**HS9/1357/7**
SOE agent Bodington SOE file (extract)	**HS9/171/1**
SOE agent Racheline	**HS 9/1223/5**
SOE agent Dufour	**HS 9/455/3**
SOE agent Charlet	**HS 9/298/6**
SOE agent Schwatschko	**HS 9/1331/1**
SOE agent De Courson	**HS 9/1534/8**
SOE agent Mederic	**HS 9/1523/4**
SOE agent Laussucq	**HS 9/894/1**
SOE agent Defendini	**HS 9/412/2**
SOE agent Frager	**HS 9/536/1**
SOE agent Oronte	**HS 9/1208/5**
SOE agent Deman	**HS 9/409/7**
Shelburn Ops Summaries	**HS 8/828**

MI9 reports (interviews with escapees)

Escapee Le Droff, MI9 report	**WO 208/3729**
Escapee Le Droff, supplemental report (MI9)	**WO 208/3729**
Escapee Tréhiou MI9 report	**WO 208/3729**
Escapee Cann (SOE agent) MI9 report	**WO 208/3729**
Escapee Gerard MI9 report	**WO 208/3728**
Escapee Bourhis MI9 report I have noted this man as an agent, presumably SIS rather than SOE	**WO 208/3278**
Escapee Cann MI9 report	**WO 208/3727**
Escapee Dehan MI9 report	**WO 208/3726**
Possible OVERCLOUD escapees	**WO 208/3671**
Operation OVERCLOUD report (MI5 investigation into security)	**KV 6/12**
RAF escapees 26/10/43 + MGB crew	**WO 208/3317**
Felicitate escapees 1 (1944)	**WO 208/3319** initial reports **WO 208/5583** escape reports

4. WEBSITES

- www.bythedart.co.uk
- www.cfv.org.uk
- www.christopherlong.co.uk
- www.clydeships.co.uk
- www.dianamarahenry.com
- www.francaislibres.net
- www.libreresistance.com
- www.maho-hentic.com
- www.messages-personnels-bbc-39-45.fr
- www.mtb718.co.uk
- www.paulmccuebooks.com
- www.plan-sussex-1944.net
- www.secret-ww2.net
- www.soe_french.tripod.com
- www.wikipedia.org

5. BOOKS

Agar, Augustus (1963). *Baltic Episode.* Hodder & Stoughton.
Andrew, Christopher (1985). *Secret Service: The Making of the British Intelligence Community.* William Heinemann.
Baumel, Jacques (1999). *Resister: histoire secrète des années d'occupation.* Paris-Albin Michel.
Bénech, Claude (2019). *L' Incroyable histoire du Réseau Shelburn: Plouha-Guingamp 1943–1944.* Coop Breizh.
Bodiger, Louis (1998). *Mémoires d'un resistant.* Dominique Editions.
Bott, Lloyd (1997). *The Secret War from the River Dart.* Dartmouth History Research Group.
Bramoullé, Yves (2006). *Lannilis, l'Album du Siècle.* Editions le Telegramme.
Brown, Anthony Cave (1988). C: *The Secret Life of Sir Stewart Graham Menzies, Spymaster to Winston Churchill.* Macmillan.
Cowburn, Ben (2009 reprint). *No Cloak, No Dagger: Allied Spycraft in Occupied France.* Pen & Sword Books.
Dumais, Lucien. (1975). *The Man Who Went Back.* Leo Cooper.
Foot, M.R.D. (1966). *SOE in France.* Taylor & Francis Ltd.
Foot, M.R.D.; Langley, J.M. (1979). *MI9: Escape and Evasion: 1939–1945. The Bodley Head.*
Fourcade, Marie-Madeleine (1973). *Noah's Ark: A Memoir of Struggle and Resistance.* George Allen & Unwin.
Gleeson, James (1976). *They Feared No Evil: The Women Agents of Britain's Secret Armies, 1939–45.* James Gleeson.
Hamon, Kristian (2011). *Agents du Reich en Bretagne.* Skol Vreizh.
Hampshire, Cecil A. (1978). *The Secret Navies.* William Kimber.
Hentic, Pierre (2012). *Agent de l'ombre: Mémoires.* Editions de la Martinière.
Heslop, Richard (2014) [first published 1970]. *Xavier: A British Secret Agent with the French Resistance.* Biteback Publishing.
Hill, George (1932). *Go Spy the Land: Being the Adventures of I.K.8 of the British Secret Service.* Cassell and Co.
Huguen, Roger (1976). *Par les nuits les plus longues. Les Presses Bretonnes.*
Insall, Tony (2019). *Secret Alliances: Special Operations and Intelligence in Norway 1940–1945.* Biteback Publishing.
Jeffery, Keith (2010). *MI6: The History of the Secret Intelligence Service 1909–1949.* Bloomsbury.
Jones, R.V. (1978). *The Wizard War: British Scientific Intelligence 1939–1945.* Coward, McCann & Geoghegan.
Langelaan, George (1959). *Knights of the Floating Silk.* The Quality Book Club.
Le Tac, Joël (1994). *Le Breton de Montmartre.* Editions Ouest-France.
Macintyre, Ben (2012). *Double Cross: The True Story of the D-Day Spies.* Bloomsbury.
Marnham, Patrick (2020). *War in the Shadows: Resistance, Deception and Betrayal in Occupied France.* Oneworld Publications.

Martelli, George (1960). *Agent Extraordinary: The Story of Michel Hollard*. Collins.
Milner, Charles; Hamilton, Guy; Seddon, Ronald (2014). *HM MTB 718 'Something Special'*. Milner-Seddon.
Neave, Airey (1969). *Saturday at MI9*. Hodder and Stoughton.
Olson, Lynne (2019). *Madame Fourcade's Secret War*. Random House.
Peel, Andrée (1999). *Miracles Do Happen!* Loebertas.
Pickles, Harold (1996). *Untold Stories of Small Boats at War: Coastal Forces Veterans Remember*. Consort Print.
Purnell, Sonia (2019). *A Woman of No Importance*. Virago.
Read, Anthony; Fisher, David (1984). *Colonel Z.: The Life and Times of a Master of Spies*. Hodder & Stoughton.
Richards, Francis Brooks (2012). *Secret Flotillas: Clandestine Sea Operations to Brittany 1940–1944*, Volume 1. Pen & Sword Books.
Riols, Noreen (2014). *The Secret Ministry of Ag. and Fish*. Pan Books.
Short, Philip (2013). *Mitterrand: A Study in Ambiguity*. The Bodley Head.
Smith, Edward Abel (2020). *Ian Fleming's Inspiration: The Truth Behind the Books*. Pen & Sword Books.
Stanké, Alain; Morgan, Jean-Louis (2017). *Le Réseau Shelburne*. Editions de l'Archipel.
Stroud, Rick (2017). *Lonely Courage: The true story of the SOE heroines who fought to free Nazi-occupied France*. Simon & Schuster.
Townend, John (2000). *Broad Oceans and Narrow Seas*. The Larks Press.
Tremain, David (2018). *Double Agent Victoire: Mathilde Carré and the Interallié Network*. The History Press.
Tzu, Sun (2018 edition). *The Art of War*. Everyman's Library.
Young, Gordon (1957). *The Cat with Two Faces: The Most Amazing Spy Story of the Second World War*. Putnam.
Young, Gordon (1959). *In Trust and Treason: The Strange Story of Suzanne Warren*. Studio Vista.

INDEX

Page numbers in italic refer to pictures or maps; 'n' indicates a footnote

Flotilla: Command/Personnel

Networks and Escape Lines

Operations

Events

Miscellaneous

ILLUSTRATION CREDITS

Andrew and Jane Birkin
Front cover: painting by David Birkin; back cover: still from David Birkin's 16mm film of the MGB 502, shot in 1944 (Andrew Birkin). 40, 41, 52, 55, 56, 71, 72 (left and right), 75, 76, 79 (right), 80 (left), 82, 83, 86 (top and bottom-right), 87 (top and bottom), 89 (left), 91, 120, 125, 129, 132, 138, 251, 252

Anne Alexandre / Association MAHO
142 (left and right), 144 (left), 146 (middle), 147, 153, 171, 173

Anne Alexandre / Jamie Combot
149 (left and right)

Buchenwald Archive
188

Charles Cassels / Aurelian Coquil
144 (right), 145

Claude Bénech, from his book L'Incroyable histoire du Réseau Shelburne: Plouha-Guingamp 1943–1944, *Coop Breizh (2019)*
202, 210, 211, 212 (left and right), 219 (left and right), 240

Colette Pronost / Sylvie Carette
139, 140 (left and right)

Dartmouth Museum
68, 70, 123

Edouard Tanguy
146 (left)

Imperial War Museum
24, 26 (left and right), 114

James Luard
43

Jill Millard Shapiro – The Windmill Theatre Collection
73

Kevin Costello Coastal Forces Association / Geoffrey Hudson
89 (right)

McQuoid Mason Family
86 (bottom-left)

National Portrait Gallery
31

Paul McCue
189 (left)

Paul McCue / Alice de Charent
187 (left and right)

Paul McCue / Jean Defendini
187 (middle)

Peter Hore
44, 46 (right), 161 (bottom), 295 (bottom)

Rodney Seddon / Philip Milner
90, 231 (left and right), 232 (left and right), 253, 259, 263, 267, 270

Royal Naval College Archive
53

Sarah Desalaux
Back inside flap: photograph of Tim Spicer

Slocum Family Archive
18, 46 (left), 47, 49

SOE Archive, Paul McCue
35, 61 (left and right), 178

Tim Spicer (author)
185, 163

Westminster City Archive
38 (left and right)

Although every effort has been made to trace and contact copyright holders, in a few instances this has not been possible. If notified, the publishers will be pleased to rectify any omission in future editions.